19 95

D1607275

OPTION PRICING AND STRATEGIES IN INVESTING

OPTION PRICING AND STRATEGIES IN INVESTING

Richard M. Bookstaber
Brigham Young University

ADDISON-WESLEY Reading, Massachusetts • Menlo Park, California
PUBLISHING Don Mills, Ontario • Wokingham, England • Amsterdam • Sydney
COMPANY Singapore • Toyko • Mexico City • Bogotá • Santiago • San Juan

Library of Congress Cataloging in Publication Data

Bookstaber, Richard M   1950–
  Option pricing and strategies in investing.

  Bibliography: p.
  1. Put and call transactions. I. Title.
HG6041.B67   332.64′52   80-15013
ISBN 0-201-00123-3

Fourth Printing, January 1985

ISBN 0-201-00123-3
  DEFGHIJ-AL-898765

To my sons David and Joseph

CONTENTS

Preface

This book applies what is known about options in the academic community to option trading in the investment community. The book presents the practical implications of recent research on option pricing and shows how these results can be used to formulate the most effective option trading techniques. The book is oriented toward the investment professional and has been written with no compromise in the accuracy of the treatment. I have tried to include all that is of practical importance while eliminating the academic "windowdressing" that is meant more to impress than to inform. Since the contents rely on the literature in the field of options, the book is also well suited to college and graduate level courses on options and related finance topics. The annotated references at the end of the chapters will refer the reader to a more detailed treatment of many of the topics.

Since I began this book three years ago, I have benefited from discussions with many of my colleagues, and from classes and seminars on options during my stays at the Massachusetts Institute of Technology, Boston University, Brigham Young University, and the University of Utah. I have drawn on the comments of numerous colleagues throughout the country. Special acknowledgment should go to Charles D'Ambrosio, Gary Gastineau, Robert Klemkosky, and Victor Harper, who have read through the manuscript at various stages of its development. The ideas presented in Chapter 10 on the use of options in portfolio management are the result of research I am doing jointly with Roger Clarke. He shares credit for the work in this area, and for developing the computer programs used in preparing this chapter. Computer programs for the book have been developed with the research assistance of Leon Christensen, Richard Guthrie, and Kyle Love. The calculator program in Appendix A was written with the assistance of David Hendrickson.

The ideas presented in the book rely on the work of many in the finance area who have contributed to our understanding of options. My debt to previous research in the area is evident from the references at the end of the chapters. I owe an intellectual debt to Robert C. Merton, whose exemplary teaching first interested me in the area of finance and who first introduced me to the theory of option pricing.

Finally, I would like to thank Richard Staron of Addison-Wesley who has persisted with me in this endeavor through many drafts and revisions, and who has contributed to the development of the book in its current form.

Provo, Utah   R.M.B
October 1980

Chapter 1 BACKGROUND AND REVIEW

Since the opening of the Chicago Board Option Exchange (CBOE) in 1973, the option market has reached an unprecedented level of popularity. In the year the CBOE was organized, only eighteen stocks had options listed. Today there are three other option exchanges in addition to the CBOE, and over two hundred stocks with listed options. Option trading has increased fivefold in the past five years, and the trading activity of some options exceeds the activity in the stocks themselves. Overall, the trading volume on the option exchanges exceeds the volume on the American Stock Exchange.

The increasing popularity of the option market has been fostered by the great variety of strategies that are possible with options. For the small investor, options are popular because they are highly levered, giving the investor control over thousands of dollars of stock for an investment of just a few hundred dollars. They also provide built-in insurance—the possible loss is limited to the price of the option. For the institutional investor, options give protection against the possibility of large losses, and provide a means of receiving certain, immediate income. And for the sophisticated investor, the option market presents an almost endless number of strategies that have the potential for great profit.

The rising popularity of option trading in the investment community has closely coincided with great breakthroughs in option theory in the academic community. In the same year that the CBOE opened, researchers at the University of Chicago and at the Massachusetts Institute of Technology developed an option pricing formula. This formula gives the fair or correct option price,

1

and options that do not conform with the formula price present the knowl-edgeable investor an opportunity to make great profits with little or no risk. Since the development of the formula, option pricing has been a central point of interest in finance, and the specification and use of this option pricing technique has continually been refined and extended.

The investment opportunities in the option market keep the investment community busy, and the breakthroughs in understanding the nature of option pricing keep the academicians busy. But with the exception of academically-oriented investors and investment-oriented academicians, the two worlds of options are separated by the veil of mathematical complexity that marks these option pricing advances.

There are some investment professionals who can profit from the option pricing techniques. For example, Fisher Black, one of the developers of the option pricing formula, has an option pricing service that is used by many of the option exchange market-makers. Several investment and brokerage firms, including Goldman-Sachs, use option pricing techniques to evaluate the best option strategies for their clients. But most investors, even some of those who use these services, do not know how to turn the advances in option pricing techniques into profitable strategies.

The purpose of this book is to translate the results of the work on options into terms that the serious investor will find profitable. I use the term *serious investor* advisedly, because while the book is written on an elementary level, there is no way around the fact that options are complex, and understanding the techniques of option trading involves time and perseverance. But I also use the word *profitable* advisedly, because the pricing techniques and strategies presented in the book are sound, and will be valuable for the serious option trader.

The central objective of the book is to provide the answers to two questions:

1. How can I tell if an option is mispriced?

2. How can I best profit from an option that is mispriced?

After presenting the characteristics of options in Chapters 2 and 3, we discuss the first question in Chapters 4 and 5. In Chapter 4 we explain the intuition behind the option pricing formula, and then present the formula and show how to use it. An appendix to that chapter provides a deeper look at the derivation of the formula. In Chapter 5 we give a practitioner's guide to the use of the formula. We show how to estimate the inputs to the formula, and how to adjust the formula to get the best estimate of the correct option price.

In Chapter 6 we extend the option analysis to other securities. Stocks, bonds, convertibles, and even investment projects can be analyzed as a type of option. By using the insights of option theory, we can explain the pricing of these other securities and gain a greater understanding of their behavior.

The second question is discussed in Chapters 7, 8, and 9. In Chapter 7 we review the traditional approach to option strategies. This approach includes the familiar strategies such as the spread and the straddle. These strategies provide a good starting point for a fuller treatment of profitable trading techniques. Chapters 8 and 9 are the heart of the book, in that they provide the basis for successful option trading. Using the techniques discussed in Chapters 4 and 5 to find the mispriced option, these two chapters show how best to exploit the mispricing in a way that will give the maximum profit for the lowest risk.

While the bulk of the book deals with investment strategies for mispriced options, another topic of considerable value is the use of options in stock portfolios. Options positions can be used to mold the return distribution of a portfolio, reducing or eliminating the possibility of receiving a low return on the portfolio, or increasing the probability of receiving a return within a given range. In Chapter 10 we explain the strategy for combining options with the stock portfolio to achieve the desired characteristics in the return distribution.

Chapter 2 A REVIEW OF OPTIONS AND THE OPTION MARKET

Every security and financial market has its share of definitions and concepts. Because of its unique characteristics, the option market probably has more than its share. This chapter will cover the basic concepts that are important to understanding the operation of the option market. Call and put options are explained, the institutional framework of option trading is discussed, and the role of options in investment strategies is introduced.

Call Option

A *call option* is the right to buy a given number of shares of stock at a given price on or before a specific date.

As is evident by this definition, a particular call option will be characterized by four things: (1) the stock that the option refers to, (2) the number of shares of the stock that the option holder has the right to buy, (3) the price at which the shares of stock can be bought, and (4) the time at which the option expires.

The stock involved in the option contract is called the *underlying stock.* The price at which the stock may be bought is called the *exercise price* or the *striking price.* The last date on which the option may be exercised is called the *expiration date* or the *maturity date.* The number of shares of stock involved in the option contract is standardized on the various option exchanges to be 100 shares per contract.

For example, a Polaroid July 40 option gives the holder of the option the right to purchase 100 shares of Polaroid stock at the price of $40 per share on or before the expiration date in July. If the option is exercised, the option holder will pay $4,000 in exchange for 100 shares of Polaroid stock.

The word *right* in the definition of the call option deserves some emphasis. It is the use of *right* rather than *obligation* that makes the option market so interesting. Since a buyer has the right but not the obligation to exercise an option, the buyer will only exercise when it is profitable to do so. If the stock never rises above $40 a share the buyer will obviously not exercise the option, because the stock can be purchased at a lower price in the market. The cost of the option contract will be lost. On the other hand, if the stock price rises above $40, then the buyer will profit from exercising the option. The $40 per share stock can be sold at the higher market price. If the market price goes to $45, the buyer can sell it for $4,500, making $500 less the cost of the option. Thus the option gives the buyer great potential for gain, while limiting losses to the cost of the option contract itself.

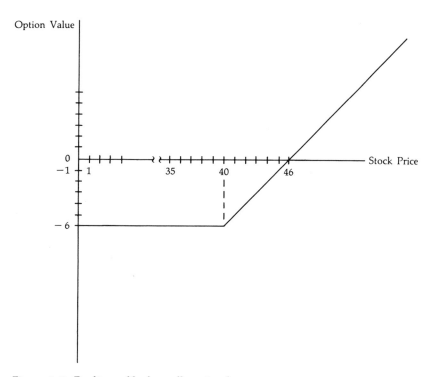

Figure 2-1 Profit profile for call option buyer

The profit profile for the option buyer is illustrated in Figure 2-1. The option giving the holder the right to buy 100 shares of stock is assumed to cost $600. The profit is expressed in per-share terms. If the stock price is below the exercise price of $40 on the expiration date, then the option expires worthless. The investor loses the initial investment in the option, which comes out to $6 per share of stock. If the stock price is above $40 per share, then the investor gains the difference between the cost of buying the stock and the higher market price at which the stock can be sold. The buyer's profit is equal to the final stock price minus the $40 exercise price less the initial cost of the option. Thus, if the stock rises to $50, the investor's net profit is $50 − 40 − 6 = $4 per share of stock, for a total profit of $400.

Call Option Writing

An option agreement is initiated between two parties. When an investor buys an option contract, there is someone on the other side of the contract who is agreeing to sell the buyer the stock at the exercise price. This person is called the *option writer.*

If the stock rises above the exercise price, the option will be exercised, and the writer will not make any gain above that price. If the writer owns the Polaroid stock and writes the Polaroid July 40, he or she will need to part with the stock at $40 per share, even though the stock is going for more than that in the market. On the other hand, if the stock drops in price, the option writer is left holding the bag—the option buyer will walk away without exercising, and the writer absorbs all of the loss. The writer thus has all of the potential loss from the stock, but has given all of the gain above the exercise price to the option buyer.

The writer may want to issue the option contract without holding the underlying stock. In this case the writer is said to *write a naked option,* which means the writer does not have the stock that he or she has agreed to sell to the buyer. Unlike the covered option writer who holds the stock on the option written, the writer of a naked option will not lose if the stock drops in price. However, there is considerable risk if the stock increases in value. For example, if Polaroid goes up to $45, the writer will have to buy the stock at $45 a share and then sell it to the option buyer at the exercise price of $40 a share, and thus realize a loss of $5 a share, for a total loss on the 100-share contract of $500.

The writer receives the option premium at the time the option is issued. If the going price for the Polaroid July 40 is $600 for an option contract of 100 shares, then the writer gets $600 at the time that the contract is issued.

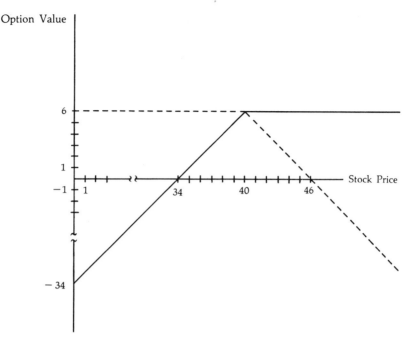

Figure 2–2 Profit profile for option writer for a covered (solid line) and a naked (dotted line) position

The profit profile for the writer of the Polaroid July 40 is shown in Figure 2–2. This figure shows the return for both the covered (solid line) and naked (dotted line) writer.

Put Option

A *put option* is the right to sell a given number of shares of stock at a given price on or before a specific date.

The put option differs from the call option only by replacing the word *buy* with *sell.* If the investor buys a Polaroid July 40 put option, and the stock drops to $35, the investor can buy 100 shares of the stock in the market for $3,500 and then turn around and sell it to the writer at $40 per share, for a net gain of $500. But if the stock is above $40 per share, the investor will not exercise the option since the stock can be sold in the market for a higher price than it can through the option contract. While the call option will increase in value as the stock increases in price, the put option will increase in value as the stock decreases in price.

Once again, the use of the word *right* is important. If the contract involved the obligation rather than the right to sell the stock, then it would be the same as selling the stock short at $40. (A *short sale* involves selling stock the investor does not currently own, with the anticipation of covering the sale by buying the stock later at a lower price.) If the stock dropped in value, the short sale will yield a profit, but if the stock went above $40, then the short sale will involve a loss, since the investor would have to buy the stock at the higher price and sell at the lower price. But with the option, the investor does not face the risk from the stock rising in price. The stock does not have to be sold at the exercise price. The investor will only do so if it is profitable. The maximum loss is the cost of buying the option.

The profit profile for the put option buyer is shown in Figure 2–3. If the stock price is above $40, then the option will not be exercised, and the buyer will lose the initial cost of the option. If the stock is below the exercise price, then the investor's profit will be $40 minus the stock price minus the option price. Assuming the Polaroid July 40 put option was bought for $500, if the stock price drops to $35 a share, the investor will break even, with the proceeds of the option equaling the $5 per-share cost of the option contract.

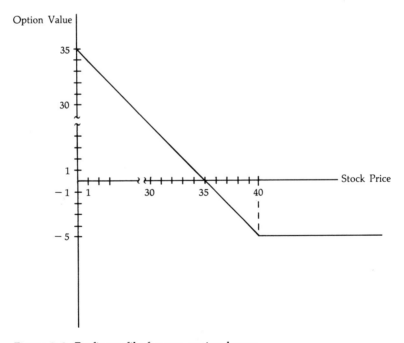

Figure 2–3 Profit profile for put option buyer

Put Option Writing

Just as with the call option, for every put option bought there is an investor on the other side of the transaction who has written the contract. If the put option is exercised, the option writer will have to buy the stock at the $40 exercise price, even though the going market price is lower. In return for this unfavorable possibility, the writer will receive a premium from the buyer for issuing the option.

THE INSTITUTIONAL FRAMEWORK

Since option contracts are arranged between investors, one might anticipate considerable difficulty in coming to terms on the contract. The investors must not only negotiate the option price, but must also decide on the exercise price, the expiration date, and the number of shares of stock that the option will cover. There is the potential for an unlimited number of types of contracts. Without some restriction on the specification of the contracts, it would be impossible for an option exchange to list or trade them all. These difficulties limited interest in option trading before the opening of the CBOE in 1973.

The formation of the option exchanges has overcome this problem. The primary contribution of the option exchanges has been to standardize the option contracts, so only a limited number of types of contracts trade. Option contracts now have a limited number of exercise prices and expiration dates, and the number of shares traded represented by each option contract is standardized at 100 shares. The restrictions on exercise price and expiration follow.

Exercise Price

For prices below $50, the exercise price is at increments of $5 with the lowest possible exercise price being $10. For prices between $50 and $200, the exercise price is at increments of $10. For prices above $200, the exercise price is at increments of $20.

The exercise prices listed for a stock are determined by the stock's current price. If Polaroid is trading at $41, it will have an option with an exercise price of $40. If Polaroid increases in price, a $45 option will be added. Generally the next higher or lower exercise price is added after the stock price moves halfway between the existing exercise price and the new exercise price. Occasionally, an option will begin trade with two exercise prices listed, one on either side of the stock price. Since exercise prices are added as the stock price changes, the more volatile stocks will have a wider range of listed exercise prices.

Expiration Date

The expiration months for options are placed three months apart, with the furthest expiration month being no more than nine months away. Thus there will be three options trading at any exercise price: one with an expiration date that is three months or less away, the next three to six months away, and the next six to nine months away.

The expiration date for an option is the Saturday after the third Friday of the expiration month. Options are listed with expiration months of January, April, July, and October; with months of February, May, August, and November; or with months of March, June, September, and December. Since the furthest maturity date is a maximum of nine months, only three of the four possible expiration months will be listed at any one time.

In addition to the standardization of option contracts, a second and related feature of the option exchanges is the interchangeability of option contracts. Contracts are not matched between individuals. All options are bought or written by the exchange through the Option Clearing Corporation. No one option buyer is connected directly with another option writer.

It is this anonymity of the option participants that permits the secondary market to operate. Rather than needing to contact a particular option writer to terminate an option position, a buyer can simply sell it back to the exchange at the current market clearing price. That price is determined by the supply and demand of option contracts at the particular maturity and exercise price.

An option buyer may sell the option contract back to the exchange before the expiration date, since there will be other investors who will want to purchase the contract at the going market price. The ability to sell a contract before maturity and without exercising it saves transaction costs. And as we will see later, the option will be worth more if it is traded than if it is exercised, so the option holder will receive more by trading in the secondary market than by exercising the option.

READING OPTION QUOTATIONS

A portion of the listed option quotations is reproduced in Figure 2–4 to illustrate the range of option contracts that are available on the option exchanges. This quotation was taken from July 10, therefore the last expiration date listed is nine months away in March.

On the left column of the quotation is the name of the underlying stock. The first stock listed on the Chicago Board Option Exchange is Alcoa. It has options with expiration dates in July, October, and January. Listed to the

Listed Options Quotations

Tuesday, July 10, 1979

Closing prices of all options. Sales unit usually is 100 shares. Security description includes exercise price. Stock close is New York or American exchange final price. p-Put option. o-Old shares.

Chicago Board

Option & price			Vol.	Last	Vol.	Last	Vol.	Last	Close
			– Jul –		– Oct –		– Jan –		N.Y.
Alcoa		...50	31	2⅝	13	4	18	5	52⅛
Alcoa		...60	1	1-16	90	⅜	83	1⅛	52⅛
Am Exp		30	a	a	20	4⅜	a	a	34⅛
Am Exp		35	10	3-16	15	1	a	a	34⅛
Am Tel		.55	a	a	13	3⅛	15	3¾	57⅝
Am Tel		.60	1	1-16	141	7-16	101	15-16	57⅝
Atl R		.. 50	a	a	28	18½	b	b	68⅜
Atl R		...60	133	8⅜	57	9¼	25	10⅜	68⅜
Atl R		...70	768	⅜	476	2 15-16	246	4⅛	68⅜
Avon		... 45	255	3	58	4	a	a	48
Avon	p	.. 45	706	1-16	128	⅞	49	1½	48
Avon		... 50	398	⅛	404	1 5-16	133	2⅛	48
Avon	p	.. 50	235	2	283	3⅛	7	3¾	48
Avon	p	... 60	11	12	86	12⅛	b	b	48
BankAm		20	a	a	a	a	2	8	27⅞
BankAm		25	115	2⅞	61	3¼	28	3⅜	27⅞
BankAm		30	a	a	64	½	102	1	27⅞
Beth S		..20	127	1 11-16	134	2⅛	b	b	21⅝
Beth S		. 25	3	1-16	49	¼	54	⅛	21⅝
Burl N		..35	2	24½	a	a	b	b	58⅞
Burl N		. 40	77	18¾	65	19	b	b	58⅞
Burl N		. 45	66	13⅞	62	14	17	15	58⅞
Burl N		. 50	56	8¾	56	10¼	77	11½	58⅞
Burl N		. 60	b	b	526	3⅞	150	5½	58⅞
Burrgh		. 70	12	⅞	2	4⅛	a	a	69⅞
Burrgh		..80	a	a	a	a	1	2	69⅞
Citicp		.. 20	a	a	5	5⅛	a	a	25
Citicp		.. 25	308	5-16	481	1⅛	84	1¾	25
Citicp		.. 30	a	a	135	¼	b	b	25
Delta		.. 35	15	7	4	7¼	a	a	41⅞
Delta		.. 40	197	1⅞	34	3⅛	9	4⅜	41⅞
Delta		.. 45	12	1-16	26	13-16	26	1⅞	41⅞
Dig Eq		. 45	3	10⅜	b	b	b	b	55
Dig Eq		50	68	5¼	2	6⅜	5	8⅜	55
Dig Eq		.60	10	⅛	8	1⅝	2	3¼	55
Disney		..35	5	9-16	92	2¼	a	a	35¼
Disney		..40	a	a	144	⅝	a	a	35¼
Disney		..45	a	a	70	3-16	b	b	35¼
duPnt o		43¾	358	¼	82	1 15-16	a	a	41⅝
duPnt o		46¾	85	1-16	126	⅞	a	a	41⅝
du Pnt		..40	376	1 13-16	110	3⅜	a	a	41⅝
du Pnt		..45	b	b	192	1¼	a	a	41⅝
Eas Kd		50	155	6⅞	b	b	b	b	56¾
Eas Kd	p	.50	4	1-16	b	b	b	b	56¾
Eas Kd		.60	1022	1-16	620	1½	80	2 13-16	56¾
Eas Kd	p	60	1269	3¼	508	4	64	4⅜	56¾
Eas Kd		..70	30	1-16	134	⅛	104	9-16	56¾
Eas Kd	p	.70	85	13	144	13	a	a	56¾
Exxon		..50	564	5⅞	493	6¼	171	6½	55¾
Exxon		..60	293	1-16	478	¾	968	1¼	55¾
F N M		. 15	1	3⅜	31	3¾	a	a	18½
F N M		. 20	a	a	62	⅜	27	⅜	18½
Fluor		.. 35	13	20½	6	21¼	a	a	55½
Fluor		...40	145	15⅜	1	16⅛	3	17	55½
Fluor		...45	161	10¾	87	11¾	53	12¼	55½
Fluor		.. 50	b	b	470	7⅞	229	8¾	55½
Fluor		.. 60	b	b	829	3	115	4¼	55½
GtWst o		16⅜	17	9	a	a	b	b	25⅜
GtWst o		.20	69	5½	a	a	b	b	25⅜
GtWst o		23⅜	a	a	6	3	b	b	25⅜
Gt Wst		20	63	5½	251	5⅜	163	6⅜	25⅜
Gt Wst		. 25	b	b	57	1¾	35	2½	25⅜
Halbtn		..60	110	10⅜	4	10	a	a	70
Halbtn		..70	757	1 1-16	498	3⅜	7	5	70
Halbtn		..80	5	1-16	b	b	b	b	70
Homstk		30	7	4⅞	32	5⅞	a	a	34⅞
Homstk		.35	142	⅜	73	2⅜	15	3	34⅞
Homstk		40	3	1-16	b	b	b	b	34⅞
Hou OM		. 15	177	5½	14	5⅞	5	6½	20¼
Hou OM		20	2034	⅜	1207	2 1-16	292	2 13-16	20¼
Hou OM		25	334	1-16	b	b	b	b	20¼
I N A		...40	20	7⅜	a	a	a	a	47¼
I N A		.. 45	138	2¼	85	2 15-16	21	3⅜	47¼
I B M		.. 65	393	7⅜	b	b	b	b	72⅜
I B M		..70	4448	2⅞	1633	5⅛	279	6½	72⅜
I B M	p	..70	4988	5-16	1601	1⅜	511	2⅜	72⅜
I B M		..75	6819	5-16	3100	2 7-16	1111	3¾	72⅜
I B M	p	..75	6104	2 13-16	1791	4	420	4¾	72⅜
I B M		..80	415	1-16	4419	1 1-16	648	2¼	72⅜
I B M	p	..80	1550	7¾	601	8⅛	413	8¼	72⅜
In Har		. 35	39	6	1	6¼	1	6⅞	41
In Har		. 40	364	1¼	102	2⅜	42	3	41
In Har		..45	a	a	36	½	99	1½	41
In Min		..45	55	4	a	a	3	5½	48¾
In Min		. 50	26	⅜	47	1¾	18	2⅞	48¾
In Pap		. 40	99	4⅛	30	5⅜	2	6	43¾
In Pap		. 45	488	9-16	239	2	9	2¾	43¾
In Pap		. 50	a	a	33	½	26	1⅛	43¾
John J		..70	83	1 15-16	66	4¼	a	a	72
John J		..80	32	1-16	1	⅞	a	a	72
Kerr M		45	19	13	a	a	a	a	58
Kerr M		.50	230	8¼	269	9⅜	13	10	58
Kerr M		.60	654	½	291	3	17	4⅜	58
Merck		..60	158	9¼	54	9¾	6	10¼	69
Merck		..70	519	5-16	599	2⅜	67	3¼	69
Merrill		..15	7	3⅜	3	4¼	2	4¼	18½
Merrill		..20	223	1-16	92	1	15	1 11-16	18½
M M M		50	7	5¾	14	6⅜	3	7⅜	55½
M M M		60	144	1-16	57	⅞	36	2⅛	55½
M M M		.70	a	a	4	⅛	b	b	55½
Monsan		.45	21	5⅞	5	6¾	a	a	50⅞
Monsan		.50	333	1 5-16	144	3¼	62	4½	50⅞
Monsan		.60	a	a	50	7-16	25	1 3-16	50⅞
Nw Air		25	38	4½	10	5	a	a	29½
Nw Air		.30	160	½	102	1¾	242	2⅜	29½
Nw Air		. 35	a	a	11	5-16	b	b	29½
Pennz		...30	5	12¼	a	a	b	b	42⅛
Pennz		.. 35	84	7¼	52	7⅞	17	8¼	42⅛
Pennz		.. 40	427	2⅜	377	4¼	82	5⅛	42⅛
Pepsi		.. 20	2	4¾	a	a	2	5	24½
Pepsi		...25	235	3-16	107	1	79	1⅜	24½
Pepsi		... 30	a	a	6	3-16	a	a	24½
Polar		...30	245	¼	251	1 11-16	251	2¾	28¾
Polar		...35	39	1-16	266	9-16	160	1 5-16	28¾
Polar		.. 40	a	a	34	3-16	82	9-16	28¾
Polar		.. 50	10	1-16	85	1-16	b	b	28¾
Sperry		..45	248	1¼	90	2¾	8	3¾	45⅞
Sperry		..50	94	1-16	53	¾	10	1 11-16	45⅞
Squibb		..25	1	5¾	a	a	10	7	30¾
Squibb		..30	121	1¼	31	2⅜	5	3⅜	30¾
Squibb		[illegible]	[illegible]	[illegible]	[illegible]	[illegible]	[illegible]	[illegible]	[illegible]
			– Aug –		– Nov –		– Feb –		N.Y.
U Tech		.40	212	7-16	97	1¼	188	1⅞	37¾
J Walt		..25	14	9	a	a	a	a	33⅞
J Walt		. 30	33	4	7	4¼	2	4½	33⅞
J Walt		. 35	49	11-16	58	1⅛	22	1¾	33⅞
Willms		..15	9	6⅜	5	6½	a	a	21¼
Willms		. 20	1007	1½	279	2½	73	2 15-16	21¼
			– Sep –		– Dec –		– Mar –		
Bruns		.. 10	40	4	12	4¼	7	4⅜	14⅛
Bruns		.. 15	1447	7-16	277	13-16	272	1⅛	14⅛
Dow Ch		25	85	2⅜	28	3	2	3½	26⅜
Dow Ch		30	235	5-16	29	⅞	38	1 5-16	26⅜
Ford		... 40	37	2⅛	161	2½	31	3	41⅞
Ford		... 45	109	¼	18	11-16	17	1 1-16	41⅞
Gen El		. 45	23	6⅜	a	a	a	a	50⅞
Gen El		50	579	2	155	2⅞	34	3⅜	50⅞
Gen El		55	82	5-16	131	¾	11	1⅛	50⅞
G M		... 50	40	8¼	26	8½	a	a	57¾
G M	p	... 50	13	⅛	534	⅞	123	1⅜	57¾
G M		60	1312	15-16	109	1 13-16	54	2½	57¾
G M	p	... 60	640	3½	128	5	44	5⅞	57¾
G M	p	... 70	21	12¼	a	a	a	a	57¾
Glf Wn		10	10	5⅛	3	5⅜	2	5½	15½
Glf Wn		15	2881	1⅛	1011	1⅜	886	1 15-16	15½
Glf Wn		. 20	205	1-16	50	⅛	a	a	15½
I T T		...25	27	5½	17	5½	a	a	30¼
I T T		...30	303	1 1-16	181	1⅜	21	2 1-16	30¼
I T T		...35	27	⅛	18	5-16	49	9-16	30¼
K mart		20	8	6⅞	a	a	b	b	26½
K mart		.25	19	1¾	42	2⅜	9	3⅛	26½
K mart		.30	38	⅜	1	⅝	22	1	26½
Kenn C		.20	16	3¾	16	4¾	6	5	23¼
Kenn C		.25	149	13-16	174	1 11-16	83	2¼	23¼
Mc Don		40	28	8½	12	9	b	b	48
Mc Don		45	121	4	24	4⅞	a	a	48
Mc Don		50	259	1¼	108	2⅛	16	3	48
N C R		..60	41	8¼	a	a	a	a	67⅜
N C R		..70	317	2	45	3½	21	5	67⅜
N C R		..80	4	5-16	1	1⅛	b	b	67⅜
R C A		..20	11	5⅛	a	a	a	a	24¾
R C A		..25	130	15-16	127	1½	34	2 1-16	24¾
R C A		..30	105	⅛	34	⅜	48	9-16	24¾
Sears		...15	8	4	5	4¼	101	4⅜	18⅞
Sears		...20	185	5-16	133	¾	57	1 3-16	18⅞
Sears		.. 25	a	a	26	1-16	10	3-16	18⅞
Syntex		..30	17	6⅞	6	7½	1	7¾	36⅞
Syntex		..35	106	3	24	3¾	5	4¾	36⅞
Syntex		..40	282	11-16	48	1⅜	42	2¼	36⅞

Total volume 149,957 Open interest 2,233,544

American Exchange

Option & price			Vol.	Last	Vol.	Last	Vol.	Last	Close
			– Jul –		– Oct –		– Jan –		N.Y.
Aetna o		23⅜	4	9¼	a	a	b	b	32¼
Aetna o	p	23⅜	a	a	10	1-16	b	b	32¼
Aetna o		26⅜	14	6	2	6	a	a	32¼
Aetna o	p	26⅜	10	1-16	30	⅛	a	a	32¼
Aetna o		.30	202	2⅜	46	3	6	3⅞	32¼
Aetna o	p	.30	10	1-16	2	9-16	a	a	32¼
Aetna o		33⅜	35	¼	123	1 5-16	9	1¾	32¼
Aetna o	p	33⅜	58	1¼	37	2	a	a	32¼
Aetna		.. 25	b	b	25	8	a	a	32¼
Aetna		...30	b	b	94	3⅛	22	3⅜	32¼
Aetna	p	.. 30	b	b	36	⅝	26	1	32¼
Aetna		...35	b	b	196	11-16	86	1 5-16	32¼
Aetna	p	...35	b	b	a	a	38	3⅜	32¼
Am Cya		25	31	1¼	10	1 9-16	31	2¼	26
Am Cya		30	a	a	7	¼	27	⅝	26
Am Exp		30	3	4¼	a	a	a	a	34⅛
Am Exp		35	2	¼	26	1⅛	a	a	34⅛
Am Hom		25	30	2	a	a	35	3	27⅛
Am Hom		30	a	a	110	½	191	¾	27⅛
Burrgh		60	59	9¾	2	10½	12	11¾	69⅞
Burrgh		70	377	1	85	3¾	11	5½	69⅞
Burrgh		. 80	a	a	112	¾	31	2	69⅞
C Tel		.. 15	7	1¾	a	a	a	a	16⅞
C Tel		.. 20	a	a	a	a	19	3-16	16⅞
Dig Eq		. 45	105	10⅛	b	b	b	b	55
Dig Eq		50	906	5⅛	356	6⅜	30	8½	55
Dig Eq		60	112	⅛	304	1 9-16	83	2⅞	55
Disney		. 35	176	¾	83	2½	42	3⅜	35¼
Disney		. 40	12	1-16	42	⅝	31	1 7-16	35¼
duPnt o		43¾	713	5-16	132	1⅞	58	2⅜	41⅝
duPnt o		46¾	515	1-16	97	13-16	43	1⅜	41⅝
du Pnt		. 40	839	2	73	3½	22	4⅜	41⅝
du Pnt		..45	b	b	216	1 3-16	27	2⅛	41⅝
du Pnt		..50	a	a	100	5-16	b	b	41⅝
Fst Ch		..15	5	5½	11	5¾	a	a	20⅜
Fst Ch		. 20	169	11-16	129	1¾	43	2¼	20⅜
Goodyr		15	16	⅜	40	13-16	49	1¼	15¼
Goodyr		20	5	1-16	110	1-16	4	⅛	15¼
Greyhd		10	a	a	5	5⅛	37	5⅛	15
Greyhd		15	813	5-16	399	1 1-16	222	1 7-16	15
Gulf O		..20	a	a	500	8⅛	b	b	28
Gulf O		. 25	148	3⅛	79	3⅜	690	3¾	28
Gulf O		. 30	348	1-16	197	13-16	279	1 3-16	28
H F C		..20	236	11-16	190	1¼	174	1½	20⅜
Lilly		50	38	6¾	15	7¼	17	8¼	56⅜
Lilly		... 60	a	a	32	1¼	18	2¼	56⅜
			– Sep –		– Dec –		– Mar –		N.Y.
Deere		.. 40	180	1 11-16	28	2 7-16	19	3⅜	39⅜
G Tel		...25	a	a	2	3¾	3	4	28⅜
G Tel		.. 30	204	¼	72	½	58	⅞	28⅜
Gillet		.. 25	142	11-16	8	1⅛	a	a	24⅜
Hercul		..15	5	4¼	a	a	a	a	19
Hercul		..20	358	13-16	168	1⅜	90	1¾	19
Pfizer		.. 30	13	1⅜	44	2⅛	a	a	30½
Pfizer		.. 35	10	3-16	130	7-16	a	a	30½
Ph Mor		.30	10	5	2	5¼	a	a	34⅜
Ph Mor		35	136	1 1-16	22	1 11-16	7	2½	34⅜
Ph Mor		.40	10	⅛	a	a	10	¾	34⅜
St Cal		..45	211	7¼	143	7¼	108	7¾	52
St Cal		..50	1162	2¾	292	3⅜	27	4¼	52

Total volume 68,157 Open interest 1,282,931

Pacific Exchange

Option & price			Vol.	Last	Vol.	Last	Vol.	Last	Close
			– Jul –		– Oct –		– Jan –		N.Y.
D Sham		20	77	5⅞	37	6⅛	35	6¼	25¾
D Sham		25	772	15-16	744	2 1-16	166	2 11-16	25¾
Disney		..35	5	¼	a	a	a	a	35¼
Hou OM		20	7	¾	11	2⅛	3	2⅞	20¼
Itel		10	b	b	222	2 3-16	318	2¾	11¼
Itel		15	40	1-16	488	½	300	⅞	11¼
Itel		20	a	a	12	1-16	1	¼	11¼
Itel		25	4	1-16	7	1-16	2	3-16	11¼
Levi	p	... 35	2	1-16	a	a	b	b	52½
Levi		... 40	7	12⅛	7	13	b	b	52½
Levi	p	... 40	a	a	1	⅛	b	b	52½
Levi		... 45	36	7⅜	16	8¼	a	a	52½
Levi	p	45	25	1-16	124	⅜	82	11-16	52½
Levi		... 50	372	2½	172	4¼	159	5⅜	52½
Levi	p	50	342	3-16	189	1¼	38	2	52½
Levi		... 60	a	a	115	½	108	1 3-16	52½
Levi	p	... 60	5	7½	a	a	a	a	52½
MAPCO		30	86	6⅜	31	7	a	a	36⅜
MAPCO		35	475	1½	288	3¼	90	4⅜	36⅜
Sambos		.10	3	1-16	17	¼	93	⅜	6
Sambos		.15	2	1-16	2	1-16	a	a	6
San Fe		20	150	4¼	134	4⅜	52	5½	24⅛
San Fe	p	.20	22	1-16	74	⅜	84	⅜	24⅛
San Fe		25	474	⅜	378	1⅜	350	2⅜	24⅛
San Fe	p	.25	64	1 3-16	124	2 1-16	81	2½	24⅛
San Fe		. 30	a	a	9	7-16	74	15-16	24⅛
San Fe	p	30	a	a	1	5⅞	8	6	24⅛
Teldyn		130	1	7¼	a	a	a	a	138
UnOil o		27½	a	a	4	12¼	b	b	39⅜
Un Oil		..30	21	9⅞	20	10½	a	a	39⅜
Un Oil		..35	219	4⅜	319	5⅞	80	6¾	39⅜
Un Oil		..40	b	b	754	2 11-16	428	3⅜	39⅜
Xerox		.. 60	20	2 5-16	1	4⅜	1	5⅜	61⅞
			– Aug –		– Nov –		– Feb –		
A B C		.. 30	10	12½	a	a	b	b	42
A B C	p	..30	3	1-16	a	a	b	b	42
A B C		..35	33	7⅜	12	7¾	50	9⅛	42
A B C	p	..35	25	1-16	3	5-16	108	11-16	42
A B C		..40	270	2¾	112	3⅞	b	b	42
A B C	p	..40	323	⅜	56	1½	34	2¼	42
A B C		..45	b	b	42	1½	65	2⅜	42
A B C	p	..45	b	b	a	a	50	4⅛	42
Heubln		. 25	91	3⅛	54	3⅜	a	a	27¾
Heubln	p	25	125	3-16	61	⅜	1	⅞	27¾
Heubln		. 30	76	¼	50	⅞	393	1⅜	27¾
Heubln	p	. 30	a	a	11	3	10	3½	27¾
Heubln		..35	1	1-16	a	a	b	b	27¾
Hilton		.. 20	5	10	1	10⅜	b	b	30⅛
Hilton		.. 25	134	5⅜	260	6¾	15	7¼	30⅛
Hilton		.. 30	578	2 1-16	330	3⅜	90	4½	30⅛
Hilton		.. 35	406	½	352	1 11-16	198	2 11-16	30⅛
Mc D D		20	97	5⅞	176	6¾	4	7¼	25⅜
Mc D D		25	852	1¾	215	3	104	3⅞	25⅜
Mc D D		30	608	⅜	269	1⅛	55	1⅞	25⅜
Mc D D		35	21	1 13-16	a	a	b	b	25⅜
RynMtl		. 30	15	4⅛	a	a	a	a	33¾
RynMtl		.35	15	¾	14	1½	5	2¼	33¾
RynMtl		40	a	a	5	⅜	5	13-16	33¾
Scher		...30	32	1⅛	17	2⅛	27	2¾	30¾
Scher	p	.. 30	38	½	43	1	5	1¼	30¾
Signal o		22½	5	5½	b	b	b	b	28
Signal		.. 20	14	8	5	8	b	b	28
Signal		..25	268	3⅛	10	4	2	4¼	28
Signal		..30	59	½	327	1½	46	2⅛	28
Travel		..30	1	9⅜	a	a	a	a	39⅜
Travel		..35	4	4½	4	5⅜	a	a	39⅜
Travel		..40	96	1	69	2⅛	5	2⅜	39⅜
			– Sep –		– Dec –		– Mar –		
Bakerln		.30	10	15¾	a	a	b	b	45⅞
Bakerln		.35	10	11¼	a	a	b	b	45⅞
Bakerln		40	69	6¼	21	7¼	6	8½	45⅞
Bakerln		45	241	2 13-16	15	3⅜	7	4⅜	45⅞
CombEn		40	200	13¼	9	14	10	14¼	53¼
CombEn		45	84	8½	36	9⅜	43	10½	53¼
CombEn		50	239	5	153	6½	66	7⅜	53¼
Lockhd		20	20	3⅛	29	4	1	5	22⅜
Lockhd		25	62	⅞	24	1¾	32	2⅜	22⅜
LuckyS		17½	a	a	5	5-16	a	a	16
PerkEl		..25	2	4½	a	a	a	a	28⅜
PerkEl		30	39	1¼	24	2 7-16	2	3⅛	28⅜
PerkEl		. 35	15	¼	a	a	5	1 5-16	28⅜

Total volume 19,572 Open interest 504,260

Philadelphia Exchange

Option & price			Vol.	Last	Vol.	Last	Vol.	Last	Close
			– Jul –		– Oct –		– Jan –		N.Y.
Alld C		..30	37	6	9	6½	3	7	35⅞
Alld C		..35	359	1 3-16	218	2⅜	16	3⅛	35⅞
Alld C		..40	15	1-16	144	¾	31	1¼	35⅞
AllisC	p	...25	3	1-16	a	a	a	a	36
AllisC		...30	15	6	11	6	a	a	36
AllisC	p	.. 30	a	a	15	⅜	15	15-16	36
AllisC		.. 35	197	1⅛	82	2½	38	2¾	36
AllisC	p	.. 35	54	3-16	40	1 7-16	5	2¼	36
AshlO o		30	3	9⅞	b	b	b	b	40
Ashl O		35	11	5	a	a	b	b	40

Figure 2–4 Listed options quotations

right of the name of the stock is the exercise price for the option. Alcoa has two exercise prices listed, one at $50 and one at $60.

The volume of the option contract is listed next. The volume is the number of option contracts traded. While the volume for the Alcoa options is relatively low (the Alcoa July 60 had only one contract trade), keep in mind that each contract represents the right to buy 100 shares of stock.

In the next column, entitled "Last," is the closing quote for the July options. The Alcoa July 50 closed at $2\frac{5}{8}$. To get the actual cost of the option trade, this number must be multiplied by 100, so that the Alcoa July 50 traded for $262.50. The Alcoa July 60 traded at just $\frac{1}{16}$, or $6.25. Its low price is due to its high exercise price and the short time to maturity. Alcoa would need to rise to over $60 from its current price of $52\frac{1}{8}$ in under two weeks for the Alcoa July 60 to have any value at expiration. Since that is an unlikely event, the current option price is low.

The following columns on the Alcoa options give the option volume and closing option price for the October and January Alcoa options. For example, the Alcoa January 50 closed at 5, meaning that the last trade of the day for this option occurred at $500.

The last column on the right gives the closing price for the stock. The closing price for Alcoa was $52\frac{1}{8}$.

An option such as the Alcoa January 50, which has an exercise price below the current stock price is said to be *in-the-money*. This is because it has value if it is exercised now. An option with an exercise price that is equal to the current stock price is *at-the-money*, and an option with an exercise price that is higher than the current stock price is *out-of-the-money*. All of the Alcoa 60's are *out-of-the-money* options.

The letter *p* after the stock price indicates that the option is a put option. If the *p* is absent, then it is a call option. The majority of the options are calls, but there are several stocks with put options listed. For example, Avon has puts listed with exercise prices at 45, 50, and 60. The quotes for the put option are read in the same way as for the calls. Since selling a stock at a higher price is more attractive, a higher exercise price will increase the price of the put option, whereas a higher exercise price will decrease the price of a call option.

The letter *a* under the option price quote means that the option was not traded. The letter *b* means that no option is offered at that exercise price and expiration date.

While exercise prices are set at multiples of five or ten, there are some options with exercise prices listed at unusual exercise prices. Dupont has exercise prices of $43\frac{3}{8}$ and $46\frac{5}{8}$. Such exercise prices arise because of adjustments for stock splits or for stock dividends. For example, if a stock at $41 a share has options with exercise prices of $40 and $45, a two-for-one split will change the stock price to $20.50 per share, and the exercise prices for the options will become $20 and $22.50.

Price quotes give the price of the last trade. Often another trade cannot be made at the same quoted price. Also, price quotes for different option transactions come from different times of day. Since the time of the last trade on the stock and on the various options may not coincide, it may be that trades in different options could never have been made simultaneously at the quote prices. Thus what you see is not necessarily what you can get.

COMMISSIONS

The commissions for options are done on a competitive, negotiable basis; there is no fixed schedule for the commissions involved in option contracts. Table 2-1 presents commission rates for one brokerage firm that may be representative of most full-service brokerage houses. Rates, of course, will vary from firm to firm. There are discount brokers who will charge commissions that can be as much as 50 percent lower than these rates.

For a single option contract costing more than $100, the rate is fairly standard at around $25. If the option has value at expiration, it must later be sold to close out the position. This entails another commission, so that the total roundtrip commission for one option contract will be $50. This can be as much as 50 percent of the price of the option, and generally will be 10 percent or more.

When it is realized that the option gives control over 100 shares of stock, a comparison with the alternative of buying and selling the stock itself indi-

Table 2-1
Commission Charge for Options

| Option price | Number of contracts bought | | |
	1	5	10
½	$10	$ 30	$ 50
1	25	66	90
2	25	70	105
5	25	87	145
10	25	110	190

Table 2–2
Comparison of Commission Charge for Options and Stock

Stock price	Option contract	Stock equivalent*
25	25	$ 35
50	25	66
100	25	85
200	25	120

*The number of shares of stock that give the same "action" as an at-the-money option contract. This will involve holding less than 100 shares of stock.

cates that in dollar terms the option commission is less than the alternative of buying and selling the underlying stock itself. This comparison is made in Table 2–2, where the commission on buying 100 shares of stock is compared with the commission charged in buying one option on the stock. As is evident from this table, in per-share terms, the option has a lower brokerage commission than the stock. Again, keep in mind that rates will vary from firm to firm.

TAX TREATMENT OF OPTIONS

The current tax treatment for options is the result of attempts to close techniques that made option trading a vehicle for reducing or eliminating taxes. Naturally, as more loopholes are discovered and closed, the law becomes more complex. We will not attempt to present a complete treatment of the tax law pertaining to options, but we will explain the tax treatment of the more common option trading techniques. The discussion will pertain only to the individual investor. The tax rules for the corporation, investment company, tax-exempt organization, nonresident alien, and investors who are considered to be dealers or traders for their own account may differ.

All option trades are taxed as capital gains. Presently, any trade closed in less than one year is considered a short-term capital gain. Since all listed options are under a one-year maturity, all option trades are treated as short-term capital gains.

More specifically, if a put or call is bought and is later sold or expires unexercised, the resulting gain or loss from that transaction is a short-term capital gain or loss. If a combination of options is traded, each option is treated separately for income tax purposes.

For example, say an investor buys an Avon July 50 call for $150 and an Avon October 45 call for $300. The July option expires worthless, and in August the October 45 option is sold for $400. The investor has a (short-term capital) loss of $150 on the July 50 option. On the October 45 option, the investor has a profit of $100, which will be treated as a short-term capital gain.

If the option is exercised rather than being sold or expiring worthless, the price of the stock purchased is adjusted by the price paid for the option, and the tax will be determined by the length of time that the stock is held.

If a call option is bought and later exercised, the investor receives 100 shares of the underlying stock. The price of the call is added to the cost of the stock. When the stock is sold, the profit from the sale is computed by adding the initial cost of the option to the cost of the stock.

If a put is bought and later exercised, the price of the put is subtracted from the proceeds of the sale.

Using the Avon example again, say that the investor decides to exercise the October 45 option rather than selling it in the market, thereby receiving 100 shares of Avon for $45 per share. For the investor's tax purposes, the cost of the Avon stock is the $45 per-share price plus the $300 paid for the option, for a total cost of $4,800. If the stock is sold within one year of the date that it was acquired, the transaction will be treated as a short-term capital gain or loss. If the stock is held for a year or more, then it will be a long-term capital gain or loss. For example, if the investor sells the stock for $5,300 within a year of acquisition, then the $500 profit is treated as a short-term capital gain.

In writing puts or calls, the same rules hold. If the option position is later closed by buying back the option, or if the option expires worthless, then the transaction results in a short-term capital gain or loss. If the option is exercised, then the proceeds of the stock transaction are adjusted by the proceeds of the option sale. If a call option is exercised, the writer adds the premium received when he or she wrote the option to the proceeds from the sale of the stock. If a put writer has the put exercised, then the amount received for the put is subtracted from the purchase price of the stock.

For example, say the investor had written the October 45 call option, receiving $300. Later, the option is exercised and the stock is called away at $45 a share. The investor's revenue from the transaction is $4,800. If initially the underlying stock had been bought for $4,000, then the capital gain would be $800. The gain will be long-term if the underlying stock has been held for over a year, or short-term if the stock has been held for less than a year. The tax treatment for these option positions are summarized in Table 2–3.

Two other rules, the wash sale rule and short sale rule, are quite complex and have several exceptions and several cases. Only the general treatment under these rules will be discussed. In more complex situations a professional tax advisor should be consulted.

Table 2-3
Tax Treatment of Option Positions

Buy a call option	
Sell	Short-term capital gain or loss
Let expire	Short-term capital loss
Exercise the option	Cost of option is added to purchase price of stock in computing the initial cost of stock. Tax treatment then follows usual procedure for stock purchases, with the purchase date being the date the stock was acquired through the exercise of the option.
Buy a put option	
Sell	Short-term capital gain or loss
Let expire	Short-term capital loss
Exercise the option	Cost of the option is subtracted from the proceeds of the stock sale in computing the revenue from the sale. The tax treatment then follows the usual procedure for stock transactions.
Write a call option	
Sell	Short-term capital gain or loss
Let expire	Short-term capital gain
Option is exercised	Cost of the option is added to the proceeds of the sale of the stock.
Write a put option	
Sell	Short-term capital gain or loss
Let expire	Short-term capital gain
Option is exercised	Cost of option is subtracted from price of stock. The tax treatment then follows the usual procedure for stock purchases, with the purchase date being the date the stock was acquired through the exercise of the option.

Wash Sale

A wash sale occurs if an investor sells one security and, within the sixty-one-day period beginning thirty days before the sale and ending thirty days after the sale, buys another security that is substantially identical to the security sold. Call options are regarded as substantially identical securities to the underlying stock. Any loss incurred from a wash sale is not deductible.

This means that if stock is sold at a loss and then an option is bought on that stock during the sixty-one-day wash sale period, the loss on the stock is not tax deductible. While the wash sale rule applies when a stock is sold at a loss and a call is purchased during the wash sale period, the wash sale rule does not apply in the opposite case where a call is sold at a loss and the stock is purchased within the wash sale period.

Short Sale

An option to sell property at a fixed price is treated by the IRS as a short sale. Since a put option is an option to sell the underlying stock at a fixed price, if an investor holds the underlying stock to hedge the put option, then the put is treated as a short sale on the stock.

If the stock has been held for less than twelve months, then the stock is considered as a hedge for the put, and any gain from exercise or sale of the put is treated as a short-term capital gain, while any loss from the put is treated as a long-term capital loss. However, if the stock has been held for over twelve months from the time of the purchase of the put, then the subsequent sale or exercise of the put is unaffected by the investor's position in the underlying stock.

MARGIN REQUIREMENTS

Buying securities on margin involves putting up only a fraction of the cost of the investment, and borrowing the remainder of the cost through a brokerage margin account. The Federal Reserve Board and the New York Stock Exchange both have regulations that set minimum acceptable margins for margin transactions. No margin is allowed for buying options—the cost of the contract must be fully paid. Since options already give the investor a high degree of leverage in the stock, any further leveraging through margin is considered overly speculative.

However, margin can be used to cover written options. One way to write a covered option on margin is to buy the underlying stock on margin. The margin requirement on stock is 50 percent, meaning that half of the cost of the stock purchase can be obtained through the margin account. Therefore, when desiring to write a covered call option, the investor can put up half the cost for the underlying stock, borrow the remainder, and then use that margined stock position to cover the option. In writing a naked option, the investor must deposit at least 30 percent of the price of the stock, plus or minus the amount the call is in- or out-of-the-money. For example, if the Alcoa January 50, selling at $500, is written while the stock price is at $54 per share, the investor must deposit 30 percent of the $5,400, which is $1,620 plus the in-the-money amount of $400, for a total of $2,020. The proceeds from the option sale can be applied to the required margin.

There are further complications of these rules when the investor takes a position in several options on the same stock. With more complicated option positions, there are often a number of ways to fulfill the margin requirement, and there will be one way that is the best from the standpoint of tying up the least amount of money. Since the actual margin requirement will vary across brokers, the investor's own broker must ultimately be consulted.

A Final Word About Commissions, Taxes, and Margin

As is evident from the discussion, the treatment of taxes, commissions, and margin requirements is highly variable. Taxes vary from individual to individual, and the commission charge and margin requirement will vary across brokerage houses. Also, while their calculation can be difficult, the investor's broker can usually provide margin and commission information for any particular trade. And when the tax computations are very involved, the investor will want to get more expert advice than can be given here.

For the remainder of this book, the effect of taxes and commissions on the profitability of option positions will be ignored. We will also ignore the possibility of holding positions on margin. These factors are not ignored because they are unimportant, but because their variability makes it impossible to give them a general treatment, and because they would add considerable complexity to an already complex subject with little return in added insight.

THE ROLE OF OPTIONS IN INVESTMENT STRATEGIES

There are two types of investors who are interested in options. The first speculates on the price of the underlying stock and wants to use the option as a means of increasing leverage in the stock or as a way of hedging against unfavorable price movements. The second speculates on the price of the option itself by trading options based on whether he or she feels they are mispriced relative to one another or relative to the underlying stock. This investor will take positions in a variety of options, buying some and writing others, in order to exploit the mispricing of the options. The investor will often have no opinion about the future course of the underlying stock. Indeed, part of the purpose of the position taken in the options is to insulate himself or herself from changes in the stock price.

Options As a Tool in Stock Speculation

To illustrate how an investor can use options to augment strategies in dealing with stocks, consider the following story of a friend who works as an investment manager for a mutual fund. He is responsible for managing a sizable amount of money, and his performance is closely monitored by the investment vice-president.

One day he was conversing with the vice-president, whom we will call Mr. Chartell. As they exited off the elevator, my friend was asked into the vice-president's office. Mr. Chartell led him over to some charts he had pinned onto the wall.

"I've been watching Avon very carefully the last few weeks, and I'd like your opinion on my analysis of its short-term potential."

"Now," he continued, taking a pen out of his shirt pocket, "this charts the price movement of Avon over the last seven weeks. You will notice that it has had three rises since its low of 39 seven weeks ago. The trend would seem to indicate that its support level has been established at 45, and there now appears to be some consolidation at 48½."

Oscar nodded assuringly, although he had never gone in for technical analysis.

The VP continued, "The technical index would seem to suggest that the chance for an upswing is only semistrongly moderate, although I have checked the Investor Sentiment and Vertigo Index, and it now stands at 85.3. That is only 23° short of reeling swally, so I would question the general market interpretation."

Oscar was amazed that the VP actually talked just like he wrote his investment newsletter.

Mr. Chartell continued, shaking his pen for emphasis, "But, here is one sign that I think others have missed. Now look at the peaks over the past seven weeks. There are three of them. The stock peaked at 45, 42, and then finally at 53. The first two peaks are divisible by three, while the last peak is not. In fact, it is a prime number. Since it follows two peaks that are multiples of three, and since it is the third peak and it is not itself divisible by three, it follows that the stock will break that level in the near term.

"The stock is ready to take off, and I want us to be in on it when it does. I haven't mentioned this to the other managers. I'll just let you take the rise off of this one."

After that stirring presentation, he escorted Oscar back to the door, and with his pen in one hand and the doorknob in the other, he gave a parting word of advice. "Now I realize that your portfolio is your responsibility, and you must handle it as you see fit. After all, you alone are responsible for any loss. But I must be sure that you and the others make sound judgments in investing our funds. So you just consider my analysis, and do with it what you see fit. Of course," he concluded, walking back to the desk, "if you decide not to buy, it will be hard to justify your decision when Avon is up at 60 or 65."

Oscar felt like he had been put on the spot. If the stock went up, he would share some of the glory with the vice-president. If the stock dropped, he would be left holding the bag. And the prospects for the stock did not seem that dazzling to him, despite the convincing presentation he had just received.

He felt that he needed to take a position in the stock in case it did rise, but at the same time he wanted to hedge himself against a possible decline. Options provide methods for doing this.

One strategy he can use is to simply buy call options on the stock. As is shown in Figure 2–4, he can buy an Avon October 50 call for $1\frac{5}{16}$ or $131.25. If Avon goes up to $60, he will realize the gain; while if Avon drops to $40, he will lose just the $131.25 cost of the option rather than $800. Thus the call option gives him the downside insurance he wants while still giving him the upside potential. Further, by using the option, he keeps more of his capital free. If he bought the stock outright rather than buying the call option, he would tie up $4,800 in the stock.

A second strategy that achieves the same goal is to buy the stock outright and then cover the downside risk by buying a put option. If he buys 100 shares of stock and buys Avon October 45 put for $\frac{7}{8}$, he will be protected if the stock drops below $45 a share. The put allows him to sell the stock at $45 a share. Since he can always unload his stock at $45 a share by exercising his put, the floor to the stock price is $45, no matter how low the market price goes.

This is just an illustration of some option strategies that may be useful to the investor who wishes to speculate on the stock. We will cover others in detail in later chapters.

Two points should be mentioned in closing this example. First, we have ignored the cost of commissions in the trade. As has already been mentioned, we will exclude the cost of commissions in examples throughout this book, since it will make the examples much clearer and will not have any effect on the concepts we cover. Second, while most institutions can write options, in practice there are legal limitations to many mutual funds and institutions buying calls or puts. So our example should not be extended too generally.

Speculating on the Relative Pricing (or Mispricing) of Options

A second set of option strategies has little to do with the investor's anticipation of the stock price. Rather than using options as tools to speculate on movements in the stock, this type of option trading involves options for their own sake.

An investor may have no opinion about the future stock price and still have an interest in trading the options of the stock. Indeed, as we will later show, a profit may be made from option trading regardless of the future course of the stock price. Such an investor is on the lookout for options that are mispriced relative to the stock or relative to other options on the stock. This person is not concerned about whether the stock is correctly priced in absolute terms, but whether, given the stock price, the options are priced correctly.

Options must be priced in a certain way relative to the underlying stock, or else there will be a trading strategy that will yield the investor a high return for little or no risk. The option trader is familiar with these properties of options, either by studying the nature of option pricing and behavior, or else by developing a "feel" for option prices through experience in observing and trading options.

Once a mispriced option is found, the investor can exploit the mispricing by using the appropriate trading strategy. This can be done with little or no concern about the future course of the underlying stock. The properties of options and the method for determining if an option is mispriced will be the next topic of the book.

To examine the techniques for this type of option trading, we must develop more groundwork. A clear, but rarely observed, example of option mispricing is given in the following modification of the July 10 Avon quote. Say an investor saw the following prices for the Avon options:

	July	October	January	Stock price
Avon 45	2	4	6½	48

The investor could buy the July options for $200 and turn around and exercise them, buying the stock at the $45 exercise price, and then sell it in the market for $48. The net profit, again ignoring commissions, would be the $300 received for each option exercised less the $200 cost of the option, for a net profit of $100. Even if it was thought that Avon was a bad stock to invest in, the investor would find this option strategy attractive.

It is the relative mispricing of options and stock that is the basis for the trading strategies of the option trader. As we will show later, if relative mispricing poses a profit potential, the investor can hedge any risk from the stock, and make the profit regardless of the future course of the stock price.

REFERENCES

Numerous references exist for the institutional structure of the options market. The most reliable source of information on the option terms of the option contract and the structure of the market is the Options Clearing Corporation Prospectus. The various option exchanges also have pamphlets that summarize the characteristics and features of the option contracts and the trading mechanism.

Information on commissions is available directly from the broker and will vary across the brokerage houses.

While the tax consequences of option trading is particularly complex, a good source of further information is the booklet, "Tax Planning for Listed Options," put out by the American Stock Exchange.

Black (1975) provides a highly readable and in-depth discussion of the benefits and pitfalls of option trading.

Chapter 3 PROPERTIES OF OPTION PRICING

It is clear from the structure of the option contract that the option price will depend on a number of variables. The role of the exercise price, stock price, and time to expiration on the option price is apparent from the discussion in Chapter 2. Other variables such as the volatility of the stock price and the prevailing interest rate will also affect the price of an option. This chapter presents a number of properties which describe the behavior of option prices. While these properties do not pin down the exact price that an option can take, they present important bounds on the possible price. These properties will give some insight into the behavior of options, and will be important in understanding the option strategies that will be presented in later chapters.

The properties presented in this chapter are derived under a set of very weak assumptions that will generally hold in a market of rational investors. The most important of these assumptions is that of dominance. It is assumed that if security A gives at least as great a return in all circumstances as security B, and that in at least one possible circumstance gives a greater return, then security A will have at least as high a price as security B. This assumption seems reasonable—if security A were priced lower than security B, then no investor would have an interest in buying security B.

BASIC PROPERTIES

The value of an option will be a function of the price of the stock, S, the time to expiration, T, and the exercise price of the option, E. Writing the option price explicitly as a function of these arguments, and denoting the price of the call option by C, we have at any point of time before expiration,

$$C = C(S, T, E). \tag{3.1}$$

Both S and T are variables; that is, they are subject to change during the life of the option. The exercise price is a parameter with a fixed value.

An option is a limited liability instrument, so that its value cannot be less than zero. Accordingly, as a first property of option pricing, we have

Property 1: The value of an option is greater than or equal to zero;

$$C(S, T, E) \geq 0.$$

On expiration, the option holder has the right to purchase the stock for the exercise price of E dollars. That right should be exercised if the stock price is greater than E, or the option should be allowed to expire unexercised if the stock price is below the exercise price. On the expiration date, then, the option will be worth the intrinsic value of the option or zero, whichever is greater.

Property 2: On expiration, the option is worth $S - E$ dollars or zero dollars, whichever is greater;

$$C(S, T, E) = \text{Max}(0, S - E) \text{ for } T = 0.$$

where $\text{Max}(0, S - E)$ means the maximum of 0 and $S - E$.

For example, an option with an exercise price of \$50 will have a value of $\text{Max}(0, S - 50)$: if the stock price on the expiration date is \$48, then the value of the option will be $\text{Max}(0, -2)$, which is 0. If the stock price is 54, then the option will be worth $\text{Max}(0, 4)$, which is \$4.

If an option sells for less than $S - E$ at any time prior to expiration, there is an arbitrage opportunity, since an investor could buy the options and immediately sell them for the intrinsic value, and in principle gain an unlimited profit. So we have

Property 3: An option will always sell for at least its intrinsic value;

$$C(S, T, E) \geq \text{Max}(0, S - E).$$

If the stock is selling for 54, and an option with an exercise price of 50 is selling for 3, then the investor could buy the option for \$300 and turn around and exercise it, obtaining 100 shares of stock for \$5,000, and then sell that stock in the market for \$5,400, netting a profit of \$100. Since such an operation is riskless, and can be done virtually instantaneously, an unlimited profit would be possible if this property did not hold.

An option with a longer time to expiration has all the characteristics of an option with a shorter expiration date; the longer-term option can be exercised for the same profit as the shorter-term one can. It therefore must be priced at least as high as the shorter expiration option. But the longer-term option has a characteristic that the shorter-term one does not—once the shorter-term option has expired, the longer-term option can still be exercised. Since the longer-term option can do everything the shorter-term option can and has some desirable characteristics that the shorter-term option does not, it must be worth at least as much as the shorter-term option.

Property 4: An option with a longer time to expiration will be worth at least as much as another option with the same exercise price but a shorter time to expiration:

$$C(S, T_1, E) \geq C(S, T_2, E) \text{ for } T_1 > T_2.$$

As is illustrated in Table 3–1, a similar property holds for options that differ only in their exercise price. Consider two options on the same stock, and with the same time to expiration. One has an exercise price of $50, and the other has an exercise price of $60. If the stock price is below $50 at the time of expiration, both options will be worthless. If the stock price is between 50 and 60, the lower price option will have a positive value equal to $S - 50$, while the higher option with the higher exercise price will still be worthless. And if the stock price is above 60, the option with the exercise price of 50 will be worth $10 more than the other option. Since the option with the lower exercise price will be worth at least as much as the other option on expiration date, and may be worth more, its price must be at least as great.

Table 3–1
Stock Price at the Time of Expiration

Terminal values of the options	$S \leq 50$	$50 < S < 60$	$60 \leq S$
$C(S, 0, 50)$	0	$S - 50$	$S - 50$
$C(S, 0, 60)$	0	0	$S - 60$
Relationship of terminal values of the options	$C(S,0,50) = C(S,0,60)$	$C(S,0,50) > C(S,0,60)$	$C(S,0,50) > C(S,0,60)$

Property 5: If two options differ only in their exercise price, the option with the lower exercise price will be worth at least as much as the option with the higher exercise price;

$$C(S, T, E_1) \geq C(S, T, E_2) \text{ if } E_1 < E_2.$$

Since the stock can be "converted" into itself at any time and for no cost, the stock can be thought of as an option with a zero exercise price and with an unlimited time to maturity. Since from Properties 4 and 5 a lower exercise price and a longer time to maturity both increase the value of an option, this suggests that any option with an exercise price greater than zero and a limited time to expiration will be worth less than the value of the underlying security. An option puts restrictions on the right to purchase the underlying stock—restrictions in terms of a time limit on the option and an exercise price that must be paid to acquire the stock. These restrictions assure that the option is not more valuable than owning the stock outright.

Property 6: The underlying stock will be worth at least as much as any option which has a limited time to expiration and an exercise price that is greater than zero;

$$S \geq C(S, T, E) \text{ if } T < \infty; E > 0.$$

An option is a levered security in the sense that for an investment of less than the price of the stock, the investor can profit from the complete movement in the stock price. In percentage terms then, the option price will change more than the stock price.

Property 7: In percentage terms, the option price will change by at least as much as the stock price changes.

These seven properties permit us to describe the bounds of a call option as shown in Figure 3–1, which plots the price of the option as a function of the stock price.

In the figure, the option is plotted for two different times to maturity. With T_1 implying a longer time to maturity than T_2, the option price is higher at time T_1 for all stock prices.

As the stock price increases, the option price becomes closer to its intrinsic value, as described by the $C = S - E$ line.

Since the option is always worth less than the stock, the option always lies below a line through the origin at 45° (the $C = S$ line). The option price line is curving upward due to Property 7. This curve, and the fact that it is always below the $C = S$ line, means that in absolute terms the change in an

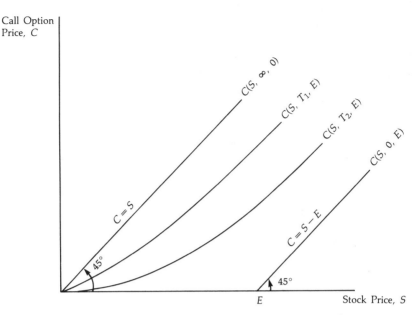

Figure 3–1 Value of a call option as a function of the stock price for various times to expiration; $\infty > T_1 > T_2 > 0$

option price will never be greater than the change in the price of the underlying stock. That is, if the stock increases in value by $3.00, the option will increase in value by an amount less than or equal to $3.00. Since the option has a smaller value than the stock, a smaller increase in absolute dollar terms can still lead to a larger percentage increase in the option's price than in the stock's price.

FURTHER RESTRICTIONS ON THE PRICE OF CALL OPTIONS

The bounds on the price of the call option can be tightened somewhat by considering the following argument. Suppose a bond that promises a payment of $1.00 six months from now currently costs $.95. Consider two portfolios, A and B:

Portfolio A: Purchase stock for $5,400.

Portfolio B: Purchase one European call with six months to expiration, and an exercise price of $50 for $c, and purchase 5,000 bonds for $5,000 \times \$.95 = \$4,750$.

A *European option* is an option that can be exercised only at the time of maturity. The option that we usually deal with, which can be exercised at or before maturity, is called an American option. The European option is used in this example to simplify the argument, since we then only need to consider the value of the option position at maturity.

Denote the stock price at the time of expiration by S^*. At the time of expiration of the option, if the stock is worth more than the exercise price of the option, then both portfolios will have the same value. The stock comprising Portfolio A will be worth S^*. The value of Portfolio B will be the value of the option, $S^* - 5,000$, plus the value of the matured bonds, which with a value of $1.00 each will be worth a total of $5,000. So the total value of Portfolio B will be $S^* - $5,000 plus $5,000, or simply S^*. If the stock price is less than the exercise price at the maturity of the option, the option will be worthless, and the value of Portfolio B will be the value of the matured bonds, $5,000. But since in this case the exercise price is greater than the stock's price, the value of the Portfolio B will be greater than the value of Portfolio A. This is illustrated in Table 3–2.

Since Portfolio B will be worth at least as much as Portfolio A, and may be worth more, it must be that the current price of Portfolio B is at least equal to that of A, so that

$$c + \$4,750 \geq \$5,400$$

or

$$c \geq \$650. \tag{3.2}$$

This minimum value for the option is greater than the minimum value suggested by Property 3. Since the exercise price is $50 while the current stock price is $54 a share, the intrinsic value of the option is $400. But by this argument, it must be worth at least $650, a full $250 more than its intrinsic value.

Table 3–2

Portfolio	Current value	Stock price at time of expiration	
		$S^* < E$	$E \leq S^*$
A	$5,400	S^*	S^*
B	$c + \$4,750$	$0 + 5000$	S^*
Relationship of terminal values of the positions		$A < B$	$A = B$

We can write the lower limit to the option price in more general terms. Let $B(T)$ be the current price of a bond that promises a payment of $1.00 T years from now. That is, $B(T)$ is the current price of a risk-free discount bond with T years to maturity. $B(T)$ is the discounting factor; if the interest rate is r, then

$$B(T) = \frac{1}{(1+r)^T}.$$

(In this example, $B(.5) = \$.95$.) Since the interest rate is positive, the longer the term to maturity on the bond, the lower the current price of the bond will be; $B(T_1) < B(T_2)$ if $T_1 > T_2$. If we denote the current stock price by S, and the exercise price of the option by E, then Equation (3.2) can be expressed as

$$c(S, T, E) \geq S - EB(T).$$

Since the option is a limited liability instrument, it cannot have a negative value, so that this condition can be further restricted to yield

$$c \geq \text{Max}(0, S - EB(T)). \tag{3.3}$$

This condition should be compared with that stated in Property 3. The intrinsic value $S - E$ of that Property is replaced here by $S - EB(T)$. This yields a stronger condition for the price range of an option, as is illustrated in Figure 3-2. Figure 3-2 is similar to Figure 3-1 except that the right-hand bound on the option price is tightened from $S - E$ to $S - EB(T)$.

This condition was derived using a European option. Since an American option has all the properties of a European option, and also gives the option holder the right to exercise before the exercise date, an American option must be at least as valuable as a European option.

Property 8: An American call option is at least as valuable as a European call option which has the same exercise price and time to maturity;

$$C(S, T, E) \geq c(S, T, E).$$

This property implies that

$$C(S, T, E) \geq \text{Max}(0, S - EB(T)). \tag{3.4}$$

If an American option is exercised, its value is simply $S - E$. But Equation (3.4) states that the value of an American option is at least $\text{Max}(0, S - EB(T))$. Prior to expiration, this will be greater than the value of the exercised option,

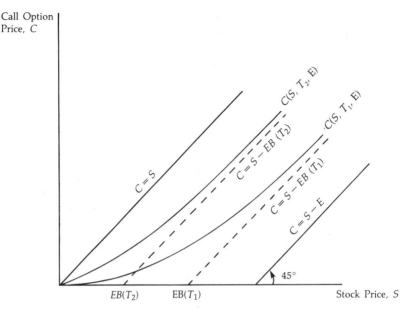

Figure 3–2 Value of a call option as a function of the stock price with the lower bound on the option price given by equation (3.4)

$S - E$, since $B(T)$ is less than one when T is greater than zero. This means that before expiration an American option will be worth more unexercised than it will be worth if exercised. That is, an American option is worth more "alive" than "dead." Thus, the holder of an American option will always be better off selling the option rather than exercising it prior to expiration.

Property 9: An American option will never be exercised before its expiration date.

If it will never be optimal for an American option to be exercised early, then the right of early exercise of an American option will have no value. This implies that an American option will have the same value as a European option.

Property 10. An American call option will have the same value as a European call option which has the same exercise price and time to maturity;

$$C(S, T, E) = c(S, T, E).$$

This property is very useful for option analysis, since a European option is a much simpler instrument than an American option. Indeed, the major option pricing results are derived for European options, and their application to the more common American option is due to this property.

Property 9 will hold for the case discussed here, where there are no dividends or other payouts on the stock. However, if there are dividends it may be best to exercise the option before the maturity date, and the American option will be more valuable than the European option. The modifications in option pricing that are necessary to take account of the possibility of early exercise will be discussed in Chapter 5.

THE EFFECT OF INTEREST RATES AND STOCK VOLATILITY ON THE PRICE OF CALL OPTIONS

Equation (3.4) suggests that the price of an option will be a function of the riskless rate of interest. The higher the interest rate is, the less $B(T)$ will be, and the higher the upper bound on the option price will be. To see the relationship between the interest rate and the value of an option more clearly, and to gain some intuition into Equation (3.4), consider the following portfolio strategy.

Suppose an investor buys 100 shares of stock worth $5,400 on margin. However, instead of securing the typical margin loan, the investor makes an initial payment K, and promises a future payment of $5,000 in six months. The future payment is promised on a no-recourse basis, with the stock used as collateral. If the investor fails to make the payment on the maturity date of the loan, the lender gains ownership of the stock, and has no further recourse or claim on the investor. If the investor makes the final payment, the stock is received free and clear.

What will be the investor's best course of action once the loan comes due? Clearly, if the stock is worth more than the promised payment of $5,000, the investor will pay off the loan to gain clear ownership to the stock. The net profit will be the value of the stock at the maturity of the loan, S^*, less the loan payment, or $S^* - 5,000$. If the stock is worth less than the promised payment, the investor will be better off just walking away from the loan and letting the lender get claim to the stock, since the payment of $5,000 to reclaim the stock will net a loss.

The position of an investor under this loan arrangement is the same as an investor who has purchased a European option on the stock with an exercise price, E, of $50 and time to expiration, T, of six months. With this loan and for an initial payment of K, the investor has obtained the right to purchase the stock for a payment of E dollars per share on the maturity date T. Looking at a European option in terms of this loan will help to illustrate some of the features and properties of options.

Since the investor promises to pay the lender E dollars at the maturity of the loan, the present value of the payment (assuming it were riskless) is $EB(T)$, which is less than E. If the loan were riskless, the initial payment would be the difference between the stock that is being delivered, S, and the present value of the promised future payment, or $S - EB(T)$. This expression is the lower bound to the value of an option which has T period to maturity, as shown in Figure 3–2.

However, the loan is obviously not riskless, since there is the possibility that the stock price will be less than E dollars at expiration, and the investor will default on the loan, leaving the lender with a loss of $E - S$ dollars. This risk requires an insurance premium or risk premium on the loan. We denote the risk premium necessary to obtain such a loan as I. The total cost of the initial levered position in the transaction to purchase the stock is thus the present value of the levered position in the stock, $S - EB(T)$, plus the cost of the insurance premium, I. Since this position is analogous to a European option, we can write the cost of a European option as

$$c(S, T, E) = S - EB(T) + I. \tag{3.5}$$

The value of a European option can then be considered as a combination of a levered position in the stock plus an insurance premium for the no-recourse loan that protects the investor against any loss if the stock drops below E dollars.

The fact that the option buyer is paying for downside insurance may not be fully appreciated. Investors are disappointed when their option expires worthless. But this is the very time that they are better off having invested in the option than if they had held a comparable position in the underlying stock. The disappointment at the loss should be tempered with the bittersweet gratitude that marks the person whose car has just been totaled, since that is the time that all the insurance premiums finally become worth it.

Expressing the value of an option in this way helps to illustrate several other properties of options. First, since a higher interest rate will decrease the value of $B(T)$, an option will be more valuable the higher the interest rate is. The reason for this is that the option buyer is essentially getting a levered position in the stock. The interest for that position is not paid explicitly, but the value of the loan received will be reflected in a higher price for the option. A higher interest rate increases the value of the loan, and therefore increases the value of the option.

Property 11: The price of an option will increase with an increase in the interest rate;

$$C(S, T, r_1, E) \geq C(S, T, r_2, E)$$

for $r_1 > r_2$, where r denotes the T period interest rate.

This property sheds some light on Property 9, and illustrates why an American option will not be exercised prior to maturity. The holder of a call option has a loan outstanding and has paid the interest cost of the loan implicitly in the cost of the option. If the option is exercised early, the value of the interest on the loan from the time of exercise to the time of maturity is lost. Because the option will continue to have the value of the carrying cost of the interest on the loan, it will always be worth more than its intrinsic value. This point can be illustrated by referring back to Equation (3.4). Equation (3.4) suggests that the minimum value for the option is $S - EB(T)$, which is greater than the intrinsic value $S - E$. The difference between these two terms is $E(1 - B(T))$, which is the interest cost of a loan of E dollars for T periods. So the option will be priced above its intrinsic value by at least this interest cost, and early exercise of the option will mean the loss of this interest cost.

A second property is apparent from the fact that the insurance premium or risk premium required on the no-recourse loan will be greater the greater the chance that there will be a loss on the loan. The chance of loss is greater the greater the volatility of the stock, so the risk premium will be higher the greater the volatility of the stock. This implies that the total value of the option will be greater the more volatile the underlying security.

Property 12: The price of an option is an increasing function of the volatility of the underlying stock.

This property may seem unusual at first, since it says that risk is "good" for options—the riskier the stock, the more the option is worth.

An interesting feature of this property is that it is total risk, not systematic risk, that is relevant in determining the value of the option. Modern finance theory has shown that the relevant measure of the risk in pricing most securities is the systematic or nondiversifiable risk. Since the diversifiable risk can be eliminated by holding a large and broadly based portfolio, the investor is not compensated for that portion of the risk of his or her portfolio. Only the risk that cannot be eliminated through diversification is rewarded with a higher expected return. However, the price of an option will be an increasing function of the total risk, not just the nondiversifiable risk. This is an important point, and one that is not fully recognized.

PUT OPTIONS

The American put option gives the owner the right to sell the underlying security for the exercise price of E dollars on or before the expiration date. On the expiration date, the put option will be worth either $E - S$ dollars or zero dollars, whichever is greater.

To gain some insights into put options, consider the following portfolio strategy. An investor buys the stock of a firm and buys a European put option on the stock. (A European put, like the European call, allows exercise only on the expiration date.) The investor then borrows $EB(T)$ dollars, promising repayment of E dollars at the maturity of the loan in T periods. At the time of expiration of the option (and the maturity of the loan), with a stock price of S^* the investor's position will be $S^* + \text{Max}(0, E - S^*) - E$ dollars. If the stock price at expiration is greater than E, the investor's position will be worth $S^* + (0 - E) = S^* - E$. If the stock is less than E dollars at expiration, the investor's position will be worth $S^* + (E - S^*) - E = 0$.

Note that the payoff structure of this strategy is identical to that of a European call option, i.e, $\text{Max}(0, S - E)$. Since the payoff structure is the same as a call option, to avoid an arbitrage profit opportunity the cost of employing this strategy must be the same as the cost of purchasing a call option.

Property 13: The value of a European call option is equal to the value of a portfolio consisting of the stock, a put option on the stock with an exercise price and time to expiration the same as that on the call, and a loan of $EB(T)$ dollars;

$$S + p(S, T, E) - EB(T) = c(S, T, E).$$

Let us rewrite the equation as

$$c(S, T, E) = S - EB(T) + p(S, T, E). \tag{3.6}$$

Equation (3.6) is called the *put-call parity equation* because it describes the relationship between puts and calls. Using this equation, the option pricing formula for call options can also be used for pricing for put options.

This equation is identical to Equation (3.5), but with the risk premium I being replaced by the value of the European put option. Thus, the European put is the equivalent of the insurance policy that is required to secure the no-recourse loan.

To see this more clearly, suppose the lender who is making the no-recourse loan buys a European put on the stock with exercise price E and time to maturity T when making the loan. If the stock is worth more than E dollars, the lender will get the promised payment of E at the maturity of the loan and the put will be worthless. So the net return will be the E dollars. If the stock price is less than E at maturity, the investor will default on the loan, and the lender will get the stock. If a put option is held, the total value of the lender's position is the S dollars of the stock plus the value of the put, $E - S$. The net position will be $S + (E - S)$, or E dollars. Thus, no matter what happens to the stock value of the stock, the lender is assured of receiving the promised payment E.

From the put-call parity equation it is evident that when the stock price is at the exercise price, a call option will be worth more than a put option. When both a put and call are at-the-money, so that $S = E$, the put-call parity equation becomes:

$$c(S, T, E) = E(1 - B(T)) + p(S, T, E).$$

Since $B(T)$ is less than one, $E(1 - B(T))$ will be positive, so the call option will be worth more than the put option.

A European put will give a maximum payment of E dollars in T years, and may give a payment of zero dollars. Thus, the current value of a European put will be worth no more than the current value of a certain payment of E dollars in T periods, or, equivalently, will be worth no more than the present discounted value of E dollars.

Property 14: A European put option with exercise price E and with T periods to expiration will be worth no more than the present value of E dollars;

$$p(S, T, E) \leq EB(T).$$

We have been considering the European put option because it is a simpler instrument than the American put. The following are some properties of the more popular American put.

Since the American put may be exercised at any time, its price must be at least equal to its intrinsic value.

Property 15: The price of an American put must at least be equal to the intrinsic value of the put;

$$P(S, T, E) \geq \text{Max}(0, E - S).$$

This property is analogous to Property 3. By the same argument that was used to demonstrate Property 8, we get Property 16.

Property 16: The price of an American put is at least as great as the price of a European put with the same exercise price and time to maturity;

$$P(S, T, E) \geq p(S, T, E).$$

Equation (3.6) shows a strong relationship between the European call and the European put options. The price of one is completely determined by the price of the other. Since the American call will be priced identically to the European call, the same relationship will hold between the American call and the European put. However, the relationship will not extend to the American put option. In Property 9 it was stated that an American call will not be exercised before maturity. That property is important for the analysis of the American call option, since it means that the analytically simpler European call option can be considered in its place. Unfortunately, the same equivalence does not hold between the American and the European put options. As we will show, it may be to the investor's advantage to exercise an American put before expiration.

To show this, consider constructing a portfolio as follows: Buy a long position in an *American* call at a price $C(S, T, E)$, a short position in the common stock, and lend $EB(T)$ dollars. If held until maturity, this portfolio gives the same payoff structure as the European put, as was demonstrated. However, since the position is now constructed with an American call rather than a European call, the time periods before maturity must also be considered. It can easily be verified using the argument similar to that used in illustrating Property 13 that this portfolio is identical in payoff structure to an American put option.

Whenever the American put option is exercised, the investor receives a payment of $E - S$. (We assume here that the put will only be exercised if it yields a payment that is greater than zero.) Will there ever be a case where the payout of the put option if exercised exceeds the value of the put if unexercised? If the value of the put option is greater when exercised, then it will not continue to be held and will be exercised before maturity. The condition for premature exercise, then, is that the value of the put is greater if it is exercised than if it remains unexercised, or, using Equation (3.6) to represent the value of the unexercised put,

$$E - S > C(S, T, E) - S + EB(T).$$

Adding and subtracting E on the right side of this inequality leads to $E - S > (E - S) + C(S, T, E) - E(1 - B(T))$. This inequality will hold if $C(S,T,E) - E(1 - B(T))$ is negative, or equivalently if $C(S,T,E) < E(1 - B(T))$. The call option price can fulfill this inequality for a small enough stock price.

And if it does, the put option will be exercised prematurely. Since there may be a circumstance where the premature exercise feature of an American put will be useful, it must be that the American put option is worth at least as much as, and possibly more than, the European put option. Property 16 cannot be strengthened to have the prices of the two types of put options be strictly equal.

This property means that the European put cannot be used to represent the more complex American put in the analysis. The treatment of the American put is thus mathematically more difficult than the treatment of the American call, and the possibility of early exercise is a major barrier in deriving an exact formula for the price of an American put option.

Figure 3–3 illustrates the price of the put option as a function of the stock price. As the stock price drops far below the exercise price E, the value of the put approaches its intrinsic value $E - S$. The higher the stock price, the lower the price of the put. As with the call option, a longer time to maturity increases the value of the put option for any stock price. If the stock price drops below the critical value $S^*(T_1)$ for the one option, or $S^*(T_2)$ for the other, the put option will be exercised, and the price of the option will accordingly be set equal to its intrinsic value of $E - S$.

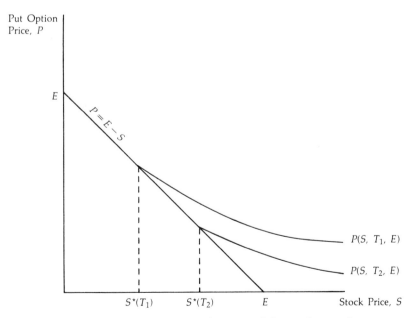

Figure 3–3 Value of a put option as a function of the stock price for various times to expiration; $T_1 > T_2$

REFERENCES

Most of the properties presented in this chapter were originally derived in Merton (1973b). This paper is one of the most important in the option pricing literature, but it requires a good mathematical background to understand. The first part of the paper includes formal proofs of some of the properties presented here. Smith also contains a number of the properties of rational options pricing. Rubinstein and Cox extend the properties of option pricing to consider dividends. Put-call parity is discussed by Stoll (1969) and by Merton (1973a, 1973b), and is tested empirically by Gould and Galai (1974), and by Klemkosky and Resnick (1979).

QUESTIONS

1. Describe the strategy that will assure a profit from the following types of mispricing:
   a. $C(S, T_1, E) < C(S, T_2, E)$ with $T_1 > T_2$
   b. $C(S,T,E_1) < C(S,T,E_2)$ with $E_1 < E_2$

2. Describe the trading strategy for taking advantage of the following mispricing:

   $$S - E < C(S, T, E) < S - EB(T)$$

3. Consider three options, $C(S,T,E_1)$, $C(S,T,E_2)$, $C(S,T,E_3)$ where the exercise price E_2 is halfway between E_1 and E_3. ($E_2 = (E_1 + E_3)/2$)

   a. Use the dominance argument to show that the value of a portfolio containing one option with exercise price E_1 and one option with exercise price E_3 is at least as great as the value of a portfolio containing two options both with an exercise price of E_2. That is, show that $C(S,T,E_1) + C(S,T,E_3) \geq 2C(S,T,E_2)$.

   b. An option strategy called a "butterfly spread" involves writing two options, one with a high exercise price and one with a low exercise price, and buying two options both with an exercise price that is halfway between the other two. (For example, a butterfly spread can be formed by writing an option with an exercise price of 50 and with an exercise price of 70, and buying two options with an exercise price of 60.) Use the result of part (a) to show that a butterfly spread will always yield a net inflow at the time the position is taken. If an investor discovers a butterfly spread that yields a net outflow at the time the position is taken, what strategy could the investor pursue that would give a certain profit?

4. Suppose a stock will pay a dividend at a time before the expiration date of an American call option on the stock. The stock price will drop when the stock goes exdividend by the amount of the dividend payment. Show how the dividend may cause the option to be exercised before expiration, thereby invalidating Property 9.

5. Describe how to profit if the pricing of a European put and call option do not follow the put-call parity equation; that is, if $c(S,T,E) \neq S - EB(T) + p(S,T,E)$. Will the same strategy always work for American put and call options?

Chapter 4 THE OPTION PRICING FORMULA

The most important breakthrough in option analysis has been the development of the option pricing formula. The formula gives the price of an option as a function of observable variables, such as the stock price, the exercise price, the time-to-maturity of the option, the riskless interest rate, and the volatility of the stock. The option formula is one of the most powerful tools in finance. The analytical method used in deriving the formula can be applied to virtually any financial security. It has thus opened up a new era in understanding and pricing corporate financial instruments.

Since the variables used in the formula are easily observable, the use of the option pricing formula has extended past the academic sphere to the investment profession at large. There are several option pricing services that provide clients with the theoretical option price. Indeed, most traders on the floor of the CBOE subscribe to option pricing services. Also, several investment firms use the option pricing formula in advising their clients.

However, the number who use the formula exceeds the number who understand it. The formula was originally derived using advanced mathematical methods that obscured the intuition behind the formula. The practical implications of the formula for profiting from mispriced options and for deriving hedges in more complex strategies has remained unexplored until recently.

In this chapter we will give an explanation of the pricing formula, and show how to exploit profit opportunities if the market price of the option differs from the option formula price.

The appendix to the chapter presents a derivation of the option pricing formula that uses only elementary algebra, progressing from the simple one-period formula to a many-period formula, and then to the more popular continuous-time formula. The next chapter will provide a practical guide to the use of the formula in option pricing. Later chapters will use the option pricing techniques of this chapter to discuss trading strategies.

A ONE-PERIOD EXAMPLE

Suppose a stock is currently priced at $100 a share, and in one period it will be worth either $95 or $110. There is a call option available on the stock with an exercise price of $100 and one period to expiration. The current price of the option is $800. (See Figure 4-1.) The riskless interest rate for both borrowing and lending is 5 percent over the one time period.

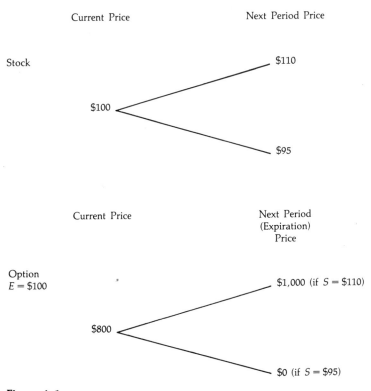

Figure 4-1

Consider the following portfolio strategy. The investor writes three call options, receiving an income of $2,400, and buys 200 shares of the stock at $100 per share. The net initial position is then $17,600. Assume the investor can then borrow at the 5-percent rate to cover the position, so that the net initial investment is zero (the stock is being purchased entirely from the proceeds of the option sale and the borrowed funds). What will the investor's return be at the end of the period?

If the stock drops to $95 by next period, the option will expire worthless. The investor will need to repay $18,480 (the $17,600 plus 5-percent interest to the bank), and will hold $19,000 worth of stock. The net position will be $19,000 − $18,480 = $520. Since the initial investment was zero, the investor will make a profit if the stock drops.

If the stock increases in value to $110, $3,000 will be needed to cover the option position, and the stock will be worth $22,000. With the cost of the borrowed funds, the investor's net position will be $22,000 − $3,000 − $18,480 = $520. Once again the strategy will net a profit. This strategy is illustrated in Table 4–1.

This transaction is remarkable because not only is a profit made in either case, but the profit is riskless—it is exactly the same no matter which way the stock moves. Also, the profit is made for no net investment. A profit that is obtained at no risk and for no initial investment is called an *arbitrage profit*. If any amount of arbitrage profit is possible, then an investor can make unlimited profits. Given a chance to make a certain profit of $520 with no investment, the investor's position needs only to increase by x times, and make x times as great a profit risklessly and with no initial investment.

There is only one price for the option that will eliminate this profit opportunity. As Table 4–2 shows, if this strategy is followed when the option is priced at $635, there will be no arbitrage profit. If the price is below $635,

Table 4–1
Trading Strategy When the Option Price Is $800

Current position		End-of-period position	
		S = 95	S = 110
Write 3 call options	2,400	0	(3,000)
Buy 200 shares	(20,000)	19,000	22,000
Borrow at 5 percent	17,600	(18,480)	(18,480)
Net profit	0	520	520

Table 4–2
Trading Strategy When the Option Price Is $635

| Current position | | End-of-period position | |
		S = 95	S = 110
Write 3 call options	1,905	0	(3,000)
Buy 200 shares	(20,000)	19,000	22,000
Borrow at 5 percent	18,095	(19,000)	(19,000)
Net profit	0	0	0

the reverse strategy of buying three options, selling short 200 shares of stock, and placing the proceeds of the transaction into the riskless asset will yield an arbitrage profit. The results of this strategy are illustrated in Table 4–3 for an option price of $500.

In this simple example the option price of $635 is the correct option price. If the option is at that price in the market, then there is no arbitrage opportunity. If it is mispriced, then there is the possibility of obtaining large profits for no risk. The option pricing formula that we will discuss in the next section gives this correct option price under far more realistic assumptions than those used in this example. There is no law that requires the market price to equal this correct option price. But if it does not, then the knowledgeable investor can make large profits for little or no risk by taking the appropriate position in the mispriced option and the underlying stock.

The existence of an arbitrage profit puts a mechanism into action that will drive the option price to the value that eliminates the profit opportunity. For example, if the option is initially priced at $800, and more and more investors follow the arbitrage strategy by selling options, the option price will need to drop in order to entice others to buy the increased supply of options. If the option price is below the correct value, the option price will be driven up as in-

Table 4–3
Trading Strategy When the Option Price Is $500

| Current position | | End-of-period position | |
		S = 95	S = 110
Buy 3 call options	(1,500)	0	3,000
Sell short 200 shares	20,000	(19,000)	(22,000)
Lend at 5 percent	(18,500)	19,425	19,425
Net profit	0	425	425

vestors try to buy more options. The pressure on the option price will continue in either case until the option is priced at $635.

Note that any of the three securities—the stock, the option, or the interest rate—can adjust to eliminate the profit opportunity. Just as the arbitrage strategy puts pressure on the option price, it also will tend to move the other securities in the direction that eliminates the arbitrage profit. As investors follow the arbitrage strategy, they will buy stock, raising the price of the stock, and they will borrow more funds, putting upward pressure on the riskless rate of interest. Thus, the option price is set by relative, and not absolute, prices.

If an arbitrage profit is possible, the option is no more mispriced than the stock or the interest rate. Given any values for two of the securities, there is a unique price for the third security that will eliminate the profit opportunity. Since the options market is usually thinner and more elastic than the other markets, it will adjust to a relative price discrepancy before the stock or the riskless asset will. So, for convenience, we generally speak of the option as being mispriced.

Making $1.5 Million at the State Fair

To see what is happening with this strategy, let us take a more down-to-earth example. Assume you are running a refreshment stand at the state fair. You find that there are three other stands there, one selling hot dogs for 50 cents each, one selling nine-ounce cups of cola for 30 cents, and another selling hot dogs with a six-ounce cup of cola for 75 cents.

It is apparent that you can package the hot dogs and six-ounce cola for less than the going price of 75 cents. You purchase hot dogs from the one stand and cola from the other in the proportions of two colas for every three hot dogs, and repackage the two to match the product of the third stand.

If the market is competitive, you can sell all the servings of hot dogs and six-ounce colas you please at 75 cents. The cost of the package is only 70 cents, so by buying the parts and packaging them as the whole, you make a sure profit. If the pricing went the other way, so that the hot dog-cola combination cost only 60 cents, you would buy the package, and resell them separately. Refer to Table 4-4.

The fact that two items can replicate the third indicates that the two must be priced in a certain proportion relative to the third. In particular, to eliminate this profit opportunity, it must be that three hot dogs and two of the nine-ounce colas must sell for the same price as it costs for three of the hot dog-cola combinations.

Table 4–4
How to Make $1.5 Million at the State Fair

1. *Buy*	*Going price*	
3 hot dogs	$.50 each =	$1.50
2 nine-ounce colas	.30 each =	.60
Total		$2.10
2. *Repackage and sell*	*Going price*	
3 hot dog-six-ounce cola combos	$.75 each =	$2.25
Total		$2.25
Profit		$.15

3. *Repeat ten million times*

The pricing of the options relative to the stock and the riskless asset is determined in the same way. The combination of the short position in the call option and the long position in the stock will replicate the riskless asset, in that the return from the position will be riskless. Since the option and stock can be packaged in a particular proportion that replicates the riskless asset, it must be that the portfolio of the two sells for the same amount as the riskless asset. If it does not, then one can construct a "home-made" riskless asset by taking the appropriate position in the option and the stock, with the home-made riskless asset costing less to produce than the going market price for the riskless asset.

Or, one can combine the stock and the riskless asset in a proportion that will yield the same payoff as the option at the time of expiration. Or, one can combine the option with the riskless asset to assure a return that will be the same as the return to the stock at the end of the period.

For example, if the investor combines a long position in three options with $18,100 in the riskless asset, the return will be the same as if 200 shares of the stock are held. If the stock drops to $95 a share, the investor will receive $18,100 (1.05) = $19,000, and if the stock goes up to $110 a share, the investor will receive $19,000 from the riskless asset and $3,000 from the option, for a return of $22,000. Since the portfolio of the options and the riskless asset exactly replicates the payoff of the stock at the end of the period, it must be that the portfolio of the two is priced so that it equals the stock price at the start of the period. Otherwise, profit opportunities will be possible by taking a long or a short position in the portfolio.

The fact that any two of the assets can be combined to produce a portfolio with the same payoff as the third is the key to the arbitrage opportunities that we demonstrated. If the relative price of the three is such that the replicating portfolio for any of the assets has a different price than the price of the asset itself, then an arbitrage opportunity will exist.

The example shown here is obviously simplified. We are dealing with one time period to expiration, and with stock price movements that are unrealistic. The extension of this example to a more realistic setting is treated in the appendix. However, this example does provide the basis for option pricing in the more realistic setting. The formation of the riskless hedge and the possibility for arbitrage profits are the motivating principles for option pricing in the more complex setting.

THE BLACK-SCHOLES OPTION PRICING FORMULA

The option example used in the previous section is unrealistic. The stock can take on any number of values, not just one of two values as assumed. Nor is trading done on a period-by-period basis. The stock market operates continuously during trading hours.

However, a more realistic approach can be developed by extending the example. If we extend the example to many periods rather than one period, and let the length of each time period become small (so that, for example, we have 180 periods of one-day duration rather than using two periods of three-month duration each), then we approach more realistic trading conditions. If we further assume that the stock price can take on any number of values in a given period of time, then we remove the objection of the two-state stock price movement of our example as well.

These assumptions are far less restrictive, and it is possible to fashion an example such as the one we used in the previous section with these assumptions. There will still be a correct option price, and it will still be the case that an arbitrage profit is possible if the option price differs from that correct price.

The extension of the illustration to the many-period case and the derivation of the option pricing formula is left to the appendix of the chapter, since it is tedious and involves the use of mathematics.

The correct option price in this more realistic case is given by the Black-Scholes formula. The formula determines the option price that is necessary to eliminate the possibility of profit opportunities. As in our one-period example, if the option price does not conform to this price, then there is the opportunity to make large profits by using the correct hedging strategy with the option and the stock. Unlike our example, the Black-Scholes formula finds the correct price under assumptions that more closely resemble the actual trading place.

The Black-Scholes formula is:

$$C = SN(d_1) - Ee^{-rT}N(d_2)$$

where

$$d_1 = (\ln(S/E) + (r + \tfrac{1}{2}\sigma^2)T)/\sigma\sqrt{T}$$

and

$$d_2 = d_1 - \sigma\sqrt{T}.$$

In this formula, ln is the natural logrithm, e is the exponential, ($e = 2.7183$), and σ^2 is the instantaneous variance of the stock price, which is the measure of stock price volatility in the formula (so σ is the standard deviation of the stock price movement). $N(\cdot)$ is the normal distribution function, which is tabulated in the back of this book and in most probability and statistics texts. The other variables are defined as before.

What Does the Formula Mean?

There is no way around the fact that this formula is complicated. Even an intuitive explanation of its derivation must be left for the appendix. Here we just present some ideas to relate the formula as more than a mass of algebra.

Consider the simple case where the underlying stock has a return that is certain. This means that the variance of the stock price, σ^2, is equal to zero. As σ^2 approaches zero, both d_1 and d_2 will become very large, and the value of the normal distribution function in both parts of the formula, $N(d_1)$ and $N(d_2)$, will equal one. The Black-Scholes formula in that case will simply be equal to

$$C = S - Ee^{-rT}.$$

This expression should look familiar. Replacing the discount factor e^{-rT} with the discount factor used in Chapter 3, $B(T)$, this expression is the same as the cost of a European call option in Equation (3.5) of Chapter 3. The only difference is that here the insurance premium I is absent, which would be expected when there is no risk to the future stock price.

In other words, in the extreme case when the stock price movement is known for certain, and hence when the stock volatility is equal to zero, the Black-Scholes formula reduces to the current stock price minus the present discounted value of the exercise price. This is the same result that we obtain by evaluating Equation (3.5) under the certainty case.

When the stock price movement is uncertain things get more difficult. If σ^2 is greater than zero, $N(d_1)$ and $N(d_2)$ will be between zero and one. The Black-Scholes formula will then involve some weighting of S and Ee^{-rT}, with the weights being between zero and one. That is, rather than having the simple case of $C = S - Ee^{-rT}$, the formula will have the form $C = pS - qEe^{-rT}$, where $p = N(d_1)$ and $q = N(d_2)$. These weights are actually probabilities drawn from the normal distribution function, but it is difficult to give an intuitive interpretation to their determination.

Computing the Correct Option Price With the Black-Scholes Formula

The use of the formula requires the input of five variables: the stock price, the exercise price, the time of maturity, the interest rate, and the volatility of the stock. To illustrate the use of the formula, we will specify particular values for these variables to calculate the value of a Honeywell October 60 option that has 88 days to expiration:

$$S = 68$$
$$E = 60$$
$$T = 88/365 = .241 \text{ years}$$
$$r = 6 \text{ percent per annum}$$
$$\sigma = .4$$

The first three variables are easily observable from the option quotation. The time-to-maturity is obtained by counting the number of calendar days until the time of maturity, and then dividing it by 365 to get the time-to-maturity in annual terms. The method for estimating the interest rate and the volatility will be discussed in Chapter 5. T, r, and σ are all expressed in annual terms. Recalling the formula and substituting the appropriate variables, we have the option price as

$$C = 68N(d_1) - 60e^{-.06(.241)} N(d_2),$$

where

$$d_1 = \frac{\ln\left(\frac{68}{60}\right) + (.06 + \frac{1}{2} .16) .241}{.4 \times .491}$$

$$= \frac{(.125 + .034)}{.196} = .808$$

and

$$d_2 = .808 - .196 = .612.$$

Using the normal distribution tables, we find:

$$N(d_1) = N(.808) = .790$$
$$N(d_2) = N(.612) = .729.$$

The values for $N(.808)$ and $N(.612)$ are tabulated in most elementary probability and statistics texts, and are also in mathematical handbooks. Using these values, we obtain the call option price

$$C = 68(.790) - 60e^{-.01446}(.729) = 10.60.$$

This option formula gives the correct option price in the sense that if the option price differs substantially from this price, there will be significant profit opportunities. The strategies to use in reaping those profits will be discussed later.

This option formula conforms with the properties of options that were discussed in the previous chapter. The correct option price as given by the formula will depend on the stock price, the exercise price, the time to expiration, the riskless interest rate, and the volatility of the stock, just as was shown in Chapter 3. In that chapter we could only determine the direction of the effects of these variables on the option price and find bounds to the possible option price. With this formula we can determine just what the option price must be to eliminate profit opportunities.

In terms of practical usefulness, what the formula *does not* depend on is almost as important as what it does depend on. In particular, the formula does not depend on any assessment of the future or expected stock price. Also, it does not depend on investors' attitudes toward risk. Since these are not observable, any formula that required them as inputs would be useless. The fact that the option formula is independent of expectations and other subjective measures bodes well for its applicability.

THE HEDGE RATIO

Going back to our initial example, the detection of the mispriced option was just the start of the arbitrage strategy. A position was not only taken in the option, a position was taken in the stock as well. This position gave the investor a hedge against unfavorable stock price movements—no matter which way the stock price moved, the value of the investor's position and the profit were unchanged.

As this suggests, a successful option strategy not only involves taking the appropriate position in a mispriced option, it also involves the second step of taking the appropriate hedge position in the underlying stock. The option position allows the investor to profit from the mispriced option, and the hedge position in the stock allows the profit to be obtained risklessly, unaffected by shifts in the stock price.

This hedge will be of critical importance later on in the book. Because the calculation of the proper hedge is related to the Black-Scholes formula, it will be introduced now.

Suppose an investor feels that a particular option currently selling at 7 is overpriced in the market. If it is overpriced, the investor will get a premium for writing it that is above the fair premium. But once the option is written, the investor will be subject to the risks of later changes in the stock price. The option may be overpriced now, but if the underlying stock increases a few points, the option will rise in price. If the investor's position in the option is not covered, a substantial amount could be lost because of the stock price changing, even if the investor was initially correct about the mispricing. Suppose the option price changes by half as much as any change in the stock price. If the stock rises by one point, the option will rise by half a point. A one-point rise in the stock will mean the value of the investor's position in the option will drop. To cover the position after the stock rise, the option that the investor originally sold for only $700 will need to be bought back for $750. The .5 point rise in the option will mean a loss of $50.

The investor can guard against this possible loss by taking a hedge position in the stock. If 50 shares of stock are bought, the investor will be hedged against a shift in the stock price—if the stock rises (or drops), the total position will be unaffected.

If the stock rises by one point, the option position will drop by $50, but the stock position will increase in value by $50—the $1 increase in the stock price multiplied by the 50 shares of stock held long.

If the stock drops a point, then the option position will increase in value by $50, since the option sold for $700 can now be bought back for $650. However, the stock position will drop by $50 from the one-point decline in the stock price. In either case, the net position is unchanged—the investor has been insulated from movements in the stock price.

If the investor had bought the option rather than writing it, the position in the option would be hedged by selling the stock short rather than by buying the stock. The hedge position in the stock is always the opposite of the position in the call option. If long in the option, the investor is short in the stock. If short in the option (that is, if the investor writes the option), then a long position should be taken in the stock to hedge. The position is always opposite because the call option moves in the same direction as the stock price, while in a hedge the option and stock position must move in opposite directions. The option may move up half a point with a one-point move in the stock, but since the investor has opposite positions in the option and the stock, one position will move up and the other will move down. And if the stock and the option are held in the right proportions, the movements will exactly counterbalance each other, so that the investor's total position will be unchanged.

The ratio of the number of shares of stock that must be held per option held in order to fully hedge against movements in the stock price is called the *hedge ratio*.

In this example, the hedge ratio was −.5. The minus sign is used to remind us that the stock and option are held in opposite positions. If the option is held long (a positive position), then the stock must be held short (a negative position). Since one position is always negative and the other positive, the ratio of the two positions will be negative. By convention, a long position in a security is denoted by a plus and a short position by a minus. A −100 share position in the stock means 100 shares are held short. Similarly, a −5 option position means the investor has written (is short) 5 options.

The ideal hedge ratio from the standpoint of eliminating the investor's exposure to the risk of the stock is denoted by h, and is given by setting the hedge ratio according to the formula

$$h = -N(d_1)$$

where $N(\cdot)$ is the cumulative normal distribution function, and where d_1 is defined as in the Black-Scholes formula. The term $N(d_1)$ is part of the first term in the Black-Scholes option formula. This term gives the change in the option price caused by a change in the stock price; that is,

$$N(d_1) = \Delta C / \Delta S,$$

where "Δ" means "change in." Thus, if the hedge ratio is set equal to $N(d_1)$, so that h times as much stock is held in a positon opposite to the position of the option (that is, with the stock held long if the option is written, and with the stock sold short if the option is bought), then the movement in the option position will exactly counteract any movement induced by shifts in the stock price, and the value of the investor's position will be unchanged on net.

Using the Honeywell 60 option from the example in the last section, we can compute the hedge ratio for that option as

$$h = -N(.808) = -.790$$

This hedge ratio means that if the Honeywell stock changes in value by one point, the value of the call option will change by just under .8 points. If the stock goes from 68 to 69, the option will go from 10.60 to 11.39. Thus, if 79 shares of stock are used to hedge each call, the change in the stock price will counterbalance any change in the option price, and the investor's position will be unaffected by the movement in the stock price. See Table 4–5.

Once a mispriced option is discovered, the investor can form a riskless hedge by buying $N(d_1)$ shares of stock for each option written (if the option is above its correct price), or by selling short $N(d_1)$ shares of stock for each option bought (if the option is below the correct price).

The hedge position for the option will change as the stock price changes. It will also change as the time-to-expiration changes. Thus, the hedging strategy involves a dynamic hedge. The ratio must be reevaluated frequently and the riskless hedge adjusted whenever the stock price changes significantly, and as the time-to-expiration declines. Also, the hedge ratio is a local measure. That is, it represents a riskless hedge only if the stock price moves by small

Table 4–5
Effect of Stock Price Change on Hedge Position

Current price

Honeywell stock	$68
Honeywell October 60 call	10.60

New price

Honeywell stock	$69
Honeywell October 60 call	$11.39

Initial position: $h = -.790$

Buy one Honeywell October 60 call
Sell short 79 shares of Honeywell stock

Effect of price change on position

Profit on option position: $1,139 - 1,060$	=	$79
Profit on stock position: $-79 \times (69 - 68)$ =		$-$79
Net change in position:		$0

amounts. If the stock price suddenly jumps five or ten points, the ratio will not assure the riskless hedge will be maintained. This means that the possibility of jumps in the stock price that cannot be covered by adjusting the hedge will affect the riskiness of the hedging strategy.

CONCLUSION

As with any mathematical construct, the option pricing formula must be carefully adapted to the realities of the market place. In the next chapter we will discuss how to estimate the formula, consider its practical limits and shortcomings, and introduce adjustments that will make it more accurate.

Once we have covered this topic, we will have the answer to the first question posed in the introduction to the book: How can I tell if an option is mispriced? We will then be prepared to tackle the next question, how to exploit that mispricing.

REFERENCES

The seminal paper in the option pricing literature is Black and Scholes (1973). This is the first paper to derive the option pricing formula by using the arbitrage argument. Other attempts to derive an option pricing formula preceded the work of Black and Scholes, and many of these formulas bear a strong similarity to the Black-Scholes formula. However, none of the previous formulas were developed in a general equilibrium framework, and none could be computed solely on the basis of observable variables. A review of these other pricing formulas, and a general survey of the option pricing literature, can be found in Smith (1976). Merton (1973b) derives the continuous-time option formula under a set of less restrictive assumptions. Both the Black-Scholes and the Merton papers are very technical. Later authors have presented less difficult derivations of the formula. Rubinstein and Cox (1981), and Rendleman and Bartter (1979) present a binomial approach to the formula that was initially suggested in Sharpe (1978). The method of derivation used in this chapter closely follows their approach, and a formal demonstration of the relationship between the discrete and the continuous-time formulas is presented in their work. Other authors, including Parkinson (1977) and Brennan and Schwartz (1977a), use a discrete-time approach to the option pricing formula based on the methods of numerical analysis.

QUESTIONS

1. Using the example presented in the first part of the chapter, show how the investor can combine the riskless asset with the stock to create an asset that will yield the same payoff as the option.

2. Referring to the first part of the chapter, how would the arbitrage argument be changed if there were two interest rates, one for lending and one for borrowing, with the borrowing rate at 5.5 percent and the lending rate at 4.5 percent?

3. An option has a market price of 4 and a Black-Scholes formula price of 3. Its hedge ratio $h = -.3$.
   a. Describe the position you would take in the option and the stock to profit risklessly from the mispricing.
   b. What position would you take if you were bearish on the stock, and wanted to receive a net increase of half a point from your position for every one point decrease in the stock price?

4. Suppose there are two call options on a stock, with hedge ratios of $-.7$ and $-.5$. How can the two options be combined together in a position that will give a riskless hedge? What would determine which option should be held long and which option should be held short?

5. Use the put-call parity equation (from Equation (3.6) of Chapter 3), $P = C - S + Ee^{-rT}$, to verify that the hedge ratio of a put option can be expressed in terms of the hedge ratio of a call option as $h_{put} = 1 + h_{call}$, where the call and put options have the same expiration date and exercise price. Why is the hedge ratio for the put option bounded by zero and one, while the call option hedge ratio is bounded by zero and negative one?

APPENDIX
THE DERIVATION OF
THE OPTION PRICING FORMULA

While Chapter 4 gives some intuition into the option formula, this appendix presents a more detailed look at the derivation of the formula. We will first derive the one-period option formula, and then extend it to a many-period formula. This formula has two unrealistic assumptions. First, trading occurs in discrete time—trading takes place period by period. Second, the stock price can take on only two possible values each period. This is called a *binomial process*. However, this formula, called the binomial formula, is easily derived with only elementary algebra, and it provides a basis for the more general continuous-time formula.

By first considering the binomial formula, we provide a basis for understanding the derivation of the continuous-time Black-Scholes formula. Indeed, as we will show, the continuous-time formula is simply an extension of the binomial formula to the case when the length of the time periods used is very small.

THE OPTION PRICING FORMULA: A SIMPLIFIED CASE

To express the option pricing formula and the hedge ratio, let us expand the example presented in the first section of Chapter 4.

Consider a stock with a current price of S which will change by either a factor of u or d by the next period. In the example of the first section of Chapter 4, $S = 100$, $u = 1.1$, and $d = .95$. By the next period, when the option reaches its expiration date, the stock will either increase to uS or decrease to dS. The option price on expiration will be uniquely related to the value of the stock at expiration, being worth $C_u = \text{Max}(0, uS - E)$ if the stock rises to the u percent, or $C_d = \text{Max}(0, dS - E)$ if the stock drops to the d percent.

The values for the stock and the related values for the option are presented in Figure A–1.

Using this specification for the behavior of the stock price, the option price with one period to expiration is given by:

$$C = (pC_u + (1 - p)C_d)/r$$

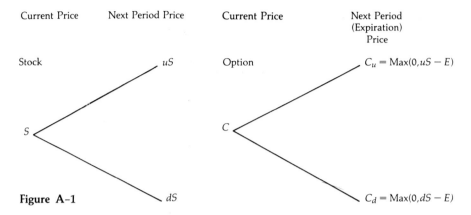

Figure A-1

where

r = one plus the riskless interest rate and

$$p = \frac{r - d}{u - d}. \qquad (A.1)$$

The derivation of this formula is presented later in this appendix. The associated hedge ratio is

$$h = \frac{C_u - C_d}{(u - d)S} \qquad (A.2)$$

This formula was used in constructing the example in the first section of Chapter 4. The hedge ratio for that example can be derived directly from Equation (A.2). The option price can be determined from Equation (A.1). Using that example to illustrate the formula, we specify:

$u = 1.1\ d = .95\ S = 100\ r = 1.05$
$C_u = \text{Max}\ (0,\ (1.1 \times 100) - 100) = 10$
$C_d = \text{Max}\ (0,\ (.95 \times 100) - 100) = 0$

The hedge ratio is computed as:

$$h = \frac{C_u - C_d}{(u - d)S} = \frac{10 - 0}{(1.1 - .95)\ 100} = \frac{2}{3}.$$

Thus, the proper hedge ratio is to write one call against ⅔ shares of stock, or write three calls against two shares of stock. (Although traded options are based on 100-share units of stock, for simplicity we will assume in the examples of this appendix that an option is based on one share of stock.)

To compute the correct option price, we use Equation (A.1), with

$$p = \frac{1.05 - .95}{1.1 - .95} = \frac{2}{3}.$$

Therefore

$$C = \left(\frac{2}{3} \times 10 + \frac{1}{3} \times 0\right)\frac{1}{1.05} = 6.35.$$

If the option is not priced according to the pricing formula (A.1), then an arbitrage profit is possible. If the option price is higher than the formula states, then the investor will make arbitrage profits by following the strategy of writing calls and buying stock in the ratio h and financing the difference between the option premium and the price of the stock through borrowing at the riskless rate. If the market price for the call is below the price given by the equation, then the reverse strategy of buying calls and selling stock short in the proportions dictated by the hedge ratio and putting the proceeds into the riskless asset will yield an arbitrage profit.

PROFITING FROM MISPRICED OPTIONS:
A TWO-PERIOD EXAMPLE

We can further illustrate how to exploit the arbitrage profit opportunities by extending our previous example to two periods. If the stock price is at $100 with two periods to go, its value with one period left will be 95 or 110, and at expiration the stock will be worth either $uuS = (1.1)(1.1)100 = 121$, $udS = (1.1)(.95)100 = 104.5$, or $ddS = (.95)(.95)100 = 90.25$. The option at maturity will be worth either zero or the final stock value at expiration minus the exercise price of $100, $C_{uu} = 21$, $C_{ud} = 4.5$, or $C_{dd} = 0$. Working back to one period before expiration, the option price can be obtained by using the one-period option formula. If the stock is at 110 with one period left, then $C_u = 21$ and $C_d = 4.5$, so that

$$C = \left(\frac{2}{3} \times 21 + \frac{1}{3} \times 4.5\right)\frac{1}{1.05} = 14.76.$$

If the stock is at 95 with one period remaining, the option price can be similarly computed

$$C = \left(\frac{2}{3} \times 4.5 + \frac{1}{3} \times 0\right)\frac{1}{1.05} = 2.86.$$

The price of the option with two periods remaining can now be obtained by again applying the one-period formula, with the values for C_u and C_d being 14.76 and 2.86 respectively. The resulting value is

$$C = \left(\frac{2}{3} \times 14.76 + \frac{1}{3} \times 2.86\right)\frac{1}{1.05} = 10.28.$$

The stock prices and the related option prices are shown in Figure A–2. The hedge ratio is placed in parentheses below the option prices in that figure. The hedge ratio is calculated using Equation (A.2).

Depending on the market price of the option, the hedge ratio will dictate either buying h shares of stock for each option written, or selling short h shares of stock for each option bought. Denoting the market price of the option C_m, trading strategies are:

Period 1

If $C_m > C$, buy 79.3 shares for each 100 call options written.
If $C_m < C$, sell 79.3 shares for each 100 call options bought.

Period 2

$S = 110$
If $C_m > C_u$, buy 100 shares for each 100 call options written.
If $C_m < C_u$, sell 100 shares for each 100 call options bought.
$S = 95$
If $C_m > C_u$, buy 31.6 shares for each 100 call options written.
If $C_m < C_u$, sell 31.6 shares for each 100 call options bought.

To illustrate the strategy, take a particular path for the stock price. Suppose the stock price goes from 100 to 110, and that the option price in the market, C_m, is at \$11.

The period-by-period steps in the strategy are:

Period 1

$S = 100,\ C = 10.28,\ h = .793$

Write 100 options at 11	1,100
Buy 79.3 shares of stock at 100	(7,930)
Borrow $(7,930 - 1,100)$ at 5 percent	6,830
Net position	0

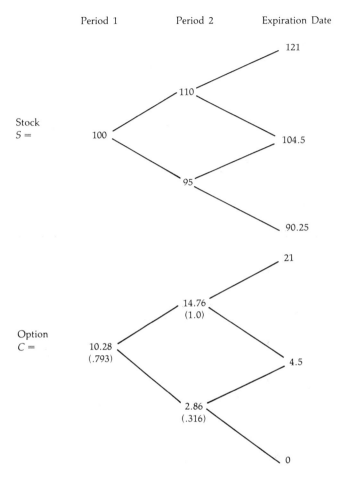

Figure A-2

By the next period, the stock is at \$110. Say that the option goes to \$16. It thus remains overpriced. The investor maintains a short position in the option, but with a hedge ratio of 1. By buying 20.7 more shares of stock in Period 2, we revise the hedge ratio to the prescribed 100 shares of stock per 100 options.

Period 2

$S = 110, \ C = 14.76, \ h = 1.0$

Buy 20.7 shares of stock at 110	(2,277)
Borrow 2,277 at 5 percent	(2,277)
Net Position	0

Following this strategy through to the expiration date, the final profit will be $79 no matter which direction the stock moves on the expiration date:

Expiration date

$S = 121$, $C = 21$

Sell 100 shares of stock at 121	12,100
Buy 100 options at 21	(2,100)
Repay loan of 6,830 $(1.05)^2$	(7,530)
Repay loan of 2,277(1.05)	(2,391)
Net profit	79

$S = 104.5$, $C = 4.5$

Sell 100 shares of stock at 104.5	10,450
Buy 100 options at 4.5	(450)
Repay loan of 6,830$(1.05)^2$	(7,530)
Repay loan of 2,277(1.05)	(2,391)
Net profit	79

The hedge ratio changes from period to period, requiring constant updating of the portfolio position. Over the two periods, h moved from .793 to 1.0. Because of the constant updating of the hedge position, this strategy is called a *dynamic hedging strategy*. In order to maintain the riskless position, the ratio of options to stock must change as the time to expiration comes closer and as the stock price changes. If the hedge ratio is not adjusted, the once riskless position will become risky, and the opportunity for an arbitrage profit will be lost.

Since the option remained overpriced in the market for both periods, the correct strategy involved keeping a short position in the option for both periods. The investor took advantage of the overpricing by selling the option and gaining the excessive premium. Suppose the option price had remained at $11 in both periods rather than increasing to $16. Then in the second period it would have become underpriced. The investor would want to buy the underpriced option, rather than holding a short position. The Period 2 strategy would then have been to liquidate the short position in the option and instead take a long position. The investor would then convert the long position in the stock to a short position, holding 100 shares of the stock short for each 100 options held long. The Period 2 strategy would have been:

Period 2

$S = 110$, $C = 14.76$, $h = 1.0$

Buy 2 options at 11	(2,200)
Sell 179.3 shares of stock at 110	19,723
Loan out (19,723 − 2,200) at 5 percent	(17,523)
Net position	0

With this strategy, the investor would have covered the short position in the option and established a long position of 1 option, and would also have a net short position in the stock of 100 shares, thus maintaining the prescribed hedge ratio.

The value of the investor's position at expiration would then have been:

Expiration date

$S = 121$, $C = 21$

Buy 100 shares of stock at 121	(12,100)
Sell 1 option at 21	2,100
Repay loan of $6,830(1.05)^2$	(7,530)
Receive loan payment of 17,523(1.05)	18,399
Net profit	869

$S = 104.5$, $C = 4.5$

Buy 1 share of stock at 104.5	(10,450)
Sell 100 options at 4.5	450
Repay loan of $6,830(1.05)^2$	(7,530)
Receive loan payment of 17,523(1.05)	18,399
Net profit	869

Once again, the strategy gives the investor a certain profit. The net profit is greater in this case because the option was further mispriced.

DERIVATION OF THE BINOMIAL FORMULA

The General One-Period Case

Referring back to the structure of the examples presented in the early part of this appendix, we can show how the option formula was derived. Again, consider a stock with a current price of S which will change by u or d by the next period. By the next period, when the option reaches its expiration date, the stock will either increase to uS or decrease to dS. The option price at expiration will be uniquely related to the value of the stock at expiration, being worth $C_u = \text{Max}(0, uS - E)$ if the stock rises to the u percent, or $C_d = \text{Max}(0, dS - E)$ if the stock drops the d percent.

The Riskless Hedge Ratio

Consider constructing a portfolio containing the option and the stock in a proportion such that we are guaranteed the same return no matter what the stock price is at the end of the period. This portfolio is formed by writing one call option against h shares of stock. With this position, the initial cost is the cost of the shares, hS, minus the income from the option, or $hS - C$. At the end of the period, the position will be worth either $huS - C_u$ or $hdS - C_d$, depending on whether the stock rises or falls in value.

We can pick any number of values for the hedge ratio h. But since we want a riskless position, we choose h so that the return to our position will be the same no matter which way the stock moves. That is, we choose an h so that

$$huS - C_u = hdS - C_d. \tag{A.3}$$

Solving for h, this implies that the hedge ratio should be

$$h = \frac{C_u - C_d}{(u - d)S}. \tag{A.4}$$

The One-Period Option Formula

With this ratio of stock held to options written we will have a return that is certain no matter which way the stock moves. This portfolio will therefore replicate the riskless asset. Since our return will be riskless, it must be that it will yield the riskless rate of interest. That is,

$$huS - C_u = r(hS - C). \tag{A.5}$$

In this equation, r equals one plus the riskless rate. Rewriting this equation, and substituting for h from Equation (A.4), we have

$$C = \left(\left(\frac{r - d}{u - d} \right) C_u + \left(\frac{u - r}{u - d} \right) C_d \right) / r. \tag{A.6}$$

Defining $p = r - d/u - d$, we can rewrite Equation (A.6) in simpler terms,

$$C = (pC_u + (1 - p)C_d)/r. \tag{A.7}$$

This is the equation for the price of a call option with one period to maturity.

Note that the call option price is a function of the price of the stock with one period to maturity, the exercise price, the riskless interest rate, and the range of the future stock price, as represented by u and d. These are the same variables that we suggested would determine the option value in Chapter 3. In this case the parameters u and d are the measure of volatility.

If the option is not priced according to the pricing formula, Equation (A.7), then an arbitrage profit is possible. If the option price is higher than the formula states, then the investor will make arbitrage profits by following the strategy of writing calls and buying stock in the ratio h, and financing the difference between the option premium and the price of the stock through borrowing at the riskless rate. If the market price for the call is below the price given by the equation, then the reverse strategy of buying calls and selling stock short in the proportions dictated by the hedge ratio, and putting the proceeds into the riskless asset, will yield an arbitrage profit.

The Two-Period Option Formula

The one-period case is unrealistic, since the stock price may move many times between a given date and the time that the option expires. However, as was previously mentioned, the same arbitrage principle can be applied in the many-period case, although the computations become more tedious. To obtain the pricing formula for many periods, let us first extend our technique to the two-period case. We go back one period from the formula we have just derived, and see what the pricing formula will be when there are two periods before the option expires.

Let the price of the stock two periods before expiration be S. With one period to expiration, the stock will be worth either uS or dS dollars. (We are assuming that the stock follows the same binomial process for price changes each period.) At the time of maturity of the option, the stock will again go up by u or down by d. At the time of maturity, then, its price will be uuS (if it goes up by u both times), udS (if it goes up one time and down one time), or ddS (if it drops by d percent both times). Note that $udS = duS$, so that the price of the stock at expiration will be the same regardless of which period it goes up and which period it goes down.

The price of the option when there are two periods to expiration can be similarly denumerated. If the price of the option with two periods to expiration is C, then by the next period it will have a price of C_u or C_d, depending on whether the stock goes up or down. Upon expiration, its price will be $C_{uu} = \text{Max}(0, u^2 S - E)$ if the stock rises both periods, $C_{ud} = \text{Max}(0, udS - E)$ if the stock goes up one period and down the other, and $C_{dd} = \text{Max}(0, d^2 S - E)$ if the stock drops both periods. The possible movement of the stock price, and the related movement of the option price, is illustrated in Figure A–3.

The value of the options with one period left can be derived by the same methods that are used in the one-period case. If the value of the option with one period left is C_u, then it will be worth either C_{uu} or C_{ud} at maturity, depending on whether the stock is worth $u^2 S$ or udS at maturity. Relating back to Equation (A.7), it is apparent that if the stock price with one period left is uS, the option price will be

$$C_u = (pC_{uu} + (1 - p)C_{ud})/r, \tag{A.8}$$

and if the stock price is dS, the call option will be worth

$$C_d = (pC_{du} + (1 - p)C_{dd})/r. \tag{A.9}$$

Moving two periods back from the time of expiration, the same reasoning is applied again. With two periods left, the stock price is S, and the stock price the next period will either be uS or dS. The related option prices will be C_u and C_d. The option will then be priced with two periods left to expiration according to Equation (A.7),

$$C = (pC_u + (1 - p)C_d)/r. \tag{A.10}$$

C_u and C_d are given by Equations (A.8) and (A.9), and substituting them into Equation (A.10), we have

$$C = (p^2 C_{uu} + 2p(1 - p)C_{ud} + (1 - p)^2 C_{dd})/r^2. \tag{A.11}$$

This equation is the two-period equivalent to the one-period option pricing formula of Equation (A.7). It is expressed in terms of known parameters, S, E, r, u, and d. Since the possible values of the option at maturity are known, the two-period value can be exactly determined.

We can illustrate the use of the two-period case by using our two-period example in this appendix.

At the time of expiration, the value of the stock will be either $uuS = (1.1)(1.1)100 = 121$, $udS = (1.1)(.95)100 = 104.5$, or $ddS = (.95)(.95)$

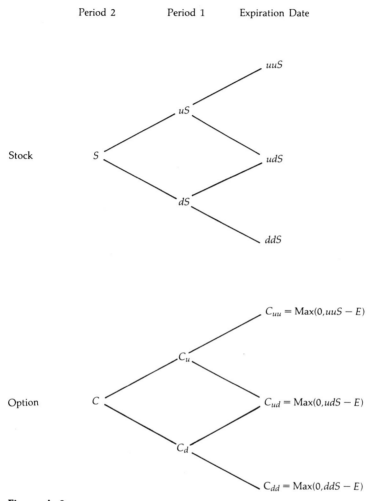

Period 2   Period 1   Expiration Date

Stock

uuS

uS

S

udS

dS

ddS

Option

$C_{uu} = \text{Max}(0, uuS - E)$

C_u

C

$C_{ud} = \text{Max}(0, udS - E)$

C_d

$C_{dd} = \text{Max}(0, ddS - E)$

Figure A-3

$100 = 90.25$. The option at expiration will be worth either zero or the value of the stock minus the exercise price, $C_{uu} = 21$, $C_{ud} = 4.5$, or $C_{dd} = 0$. Noting that $p = (r - d)/(u - d) = \frac{2}{3}$, we can use the two-period formula to compute the price of the option with two periods to expiration:

$$C = \left[\left(\frac{2}{3}\right)^2 \times 21 + 2 \times \frac{2}{3} \times \frac{1}{3} \times 4.5 + \left(\frac{1}{3}\right)^2 \times 0 \right] / (1.05)^2 = 10.28.$$

The Many-Period Case

The same procedure that is used to extend from the one-period case to the two-period case can be used to extend from the two- to the three-period case. One can continue to go back in time, step by step, to any number of periods. By continuing back, we can express the general formula for n periods to maturity. This general binomial pricing formula for n periods to maturity is

$$C = \frac{1}{r^n} \sum_{k=0}^{n} \frac{n!}{k!(n-k)!} p^k (1-p)^{n-k} \text{Max}[0, u^k d^{n-k} S - E]. \qquad (A.12)$$

While it looks complicated, it is computationally simple, and some calculators can be programmed to use it. It is important in applying this formula to remember that u, d, and r depend on the time period used. For example, if two six-month periods are used rather than one one-year period, the u, d, and r should reflect the stock price movement and the interest rate for a six-month period rather than for a year.

Consider the three-period extension of our previous example. The possible prices for the options at expiration are:

$$C_{uuu} = \text{Max}[0,(1.1)^3 \, 100 - 100] = 33.10$$
$$C_{uud} = \text{Max}[0,(1.1)^2 \, (.95)100 - 100] = 14.95$$
$$C_{udd} = \text{Max}[0,(1.1)(.95)^2 100 - 100] = 0$$
$$C_{ddd} = \text{Max}[0,(.95)^3 \, 100 - 100] = 0.$$

Using these in the pricing formula, we have:

$$C = \frac{1}{(1.05)^3} \left[\frac{3!}{0!3!} \left(\frac{2}{3}\right)^0 \left(\frac{1}{3}\right)^3 \times 0 + \frac{3!}{1!2!} \left(\frac{2}{3}\right) \left(\frac{1}{3}\right)^2 \times 0 \right.$$
$$\left. + \frac{3!}{2!1!} \left(\frac{2}{3}\right)^2 \left(\frac{1}{3}\right) \times 14.95 + \frac{3!}{3!0!} \left(\frac{2}{3}\right)^3 \left(\frac{1}{3}\right)^0 \times 33.10 \right]$$
$$= \frac{1}{1.158} \left[\frac{6}{2} \times .1481 \times 14.95 + \frac{6}{6} \times .2963 \times 33.10 \right]$$
$$= 14.20.$$

To gain some insight into this formula, consider an individual term of the summation. The first part of this term,

$$\frac{n!}{k!(n-k)!} p^k (1-p)^{n-k},$$

is the binomial formula. If p is taken as the probability that a movement u will occur, then the binomial formula gives the probability that u will occur k times in the n time periods. The second part of the term,

$$\text{Max}[0, u^k d^{n-k} S - E],$$

is the value of the option at expiration if there are k increases in the stock price of u percent, and $n - k$ decreases in the stock price of d percent in the n time periods. That is,

$$\text{Max}[0, u^k d^{n-k} S - E] = C_{u^k d^{n-k}}.$$

This term is therefore the probability that the stock will rise by u percent k times (and thus drop by d percent $n - k$ times) multiplied by the value of the option on expiration if the pattern of stock price movements does occur. That is,

$$\frac{n!}{k!(n-k)!} p^k (1-p)^k \text{Max}[0, u^k d^{n-k} S - E] = \text{(Probability } u \text{ occurs } k \text{ times)}$$

$$\times \text{(Value of the option at expiration if } u \text{ occurs } k \text{ times)}.$$

The sum of these terms is the sum of the possible terminal option values multiplied by the probability that they will occur. Thus, the option formula of equation (A.12) is the expected value of the call option at maturity discounted by the riskless rate over the n periods. The current price of the option can be interpreted as the expected value of the option on the expiration date discounted for n periods at the riskless rate.

Several properties of this formula are noteworthy. First, notice that the formula makes no assumptions regarding the investors' assessment of the probabilities that the stock will go up or down. They need only agree on the possible values, not on the probability that either of the values will occur. Since investors will generally differ on the prospects for the stock to rise or fall, this property is an encouraging sign for the formula's applicability. The investors need only agree on the range of the possible stock price. Of course, restricting the stock movement to be binomial is unrealistic, but this restriction will be removed in the next section.

Second, the entire motivation for the pricing of the option is the possibility of arbitrage profit opportunities. This is the strongest economic condition. If it does not hold, there is a tremendous profit incentive for investors to enter the market. Since the opportunity is riskless, all investors will take the opportunity, regardless of their risk aversion. Since the opportunity involves no net investment, all investors will take the opportunity regardless of their initial wealth. As investors enter the market, their very action causes the price to adjust until the profit opportunities are removed.

THE CONTINUOUS-TIME OPTION FORMULA

We extended the option formula to the many-period case. We have shown the same arbitrage argument and pricing technique applies over two, three, or any number of periods. This extension of the pricing formula removes the unrealistic assumption of there being one period to maturity. In this section we will eliminate another assumption—that of discrete binomial changes in the stock price. This leads to the continuous-time formulation of the model; which is the well known Black-Scholes option pricing formula. While their formula was originally derived using advanced mathematical techniques of stochastic differential equations, the formula is actually the continuous-time equivalent of the binomial formula we have already derived.

The binomial formula can be used for any time period. The time period can be in terms of months, weeks, days, or even minutes. As the time period that is used becomes smaller, the number of periods to expiration, n, will increase. The continuous-time pricing formula is nothing more than the binomial formula we have derived as the time period becomes arbitrarily small, permitting instantaneous trading. As the time period becomes very small, the number of price changes that are possible per day gets larger and larger, and the number of periods to expiration approaches infinity.

In the limit, as we approach continuous-time trading, the binomial formula becomes the Black-Scholes option pricing formula. As shown in Chapter 4, the Black-Scholes formula is

$$C = SN(d_1) - Ee^{-rT}N(d_2) \tag{A.13}$$

where

$$d_1 = (\ln(S/E) + (r + \tfrac{1}{2}\sigma^2)\, T)/\sigma \sqrt{T}$$

and

$$d_2 = d_1 - \sigma\sqrt{T}\,\cdot$$

In this formula, ln is the natural logarithm, e is the exponential ($e = 2.7183$), σ^2 is the instantaneous variance of the stock price, which is the measure of volatility in the formula, and $N(\cdot)$ is the normal distribution function.

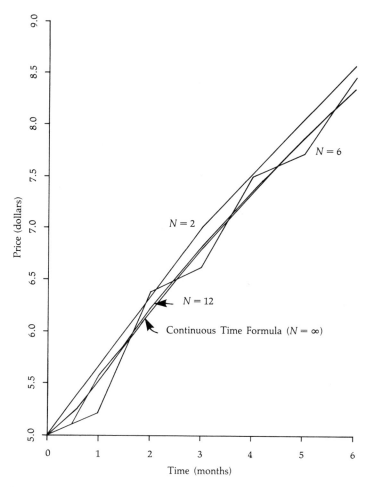

Figure A-4 The option pricing formula for various time periods (*N*) in a six-month maturity

Figure A-4 illustrates how the binomial formula converges to the continuous-time formula as the time periods used become shorter, and the number of time periods to expiration increases. Figure A-4 shows the option price derived from the formula as a function of the time-to-expiration. The time-to-maturity is taken to be six months, and the option prices depicted are for options with two periods to maturity (*n* = 2, and each period lasting three months), six periods to maturity (*n* = 6, and each period lasting one month), twenty-six periods to maturity ($n = 26$, and each period lasting one week), and the continuous-time case where essentially there are an infinite number of periods to maturity, with each period being infinitesimally small.

The error of the binomial formula is a function of n, the variance of the stock, and how close the option exercise price is to the stock price. The larger n is, the closer the binomial formula comes to the continuous-time formula.

Relating the Discrete and Continuous-Time Formulas

Comparing the two formulas, it is not at all apparent how we get from the binomial formula to the Black-Scholes formula by taking the limiting case of continuous trading. A formal mathematical derivation uses advanced concepts from probability and is quite involved. But we can gain some intuition for how this formula follows from the binomial formula by rewriting the binomial formula in a more convenient form.

The binomial formula of Equation (A.12) consists of the sum of a number of terms. Some of these terms will be zero, since they are multiplied by the maturity value of the option, $\text{Max}(0, u^k d^{n-k}S - E)$, and for a low enough stock price, the option will have a maturity value of zero. Assume that there is at least one possible value for the stock price at maturity that will be less than the exercise price, and at least one possible value that will be greater than the exercise price. The lowest stock prices range from $d^n S$, the next lowest, $u d^{n-1}S$, then $u^2 d^{n-2}S$, and so on. At some point there will be a possible value for the stock price at maturity that is lower than (or equal to) the exercise price E, and the next highest possible value will be higher than E. That is, there exists a number m, with $0 < m < n$, such that

$$u^{m-1}d^{n-(m-1)}S \le E < u^m d^{n-m}S.$$

The option will be worthless if the final price of the stock is described by the price path $u^k d^{n-k}S$ for $k \le m$. The terms in the summation of Equation (A.12) with $k < m$ will be zero. Accordingly, let us focus our attention only on these stock prices that will yield a nonzero value for the option. That is, let us consider only those price paths with a stock movement of u occurring more than m times.

Ignoring the values of k that will yield a zero in the summation, we can rewrite Equation (A.12) as

$$C = \frac{1}{r^n} \sum_{k=m}^{n} \frac{n!}{k!(n-k)!} p^k (1-p)^{n-k} [u^k d^{n-k}S - E]. \tag{A.14}$$

Here we have replaced the Max$(0, u^k d^{n-k} S - E)$ with $(u^k d^{n-k} S - E)$ because we are considering only the values of k that are large enough to assure that $u^k d^{n-k} S > E$.

Breaking up the bracketed term into two parts, we can rewrite Equation (A.14) as

$$C = S \left[\sum_{k=m}^{n} \frac{n!}{k!(n-k)!} p^k (1-p)^{n-k} \frac{u^k d^{n-k}}{r^n} \right] - \frac{E}{r^n} \left[\sum_{k=m}^{n} \frac{n!}{k!(n-k)!} p^k (1-p)^{n-k} \right]$$

This equation is an alternate version of the binomial option pricing formula.

The two terms in the brackets are the complementary binomial distribution function. The second bracketed term is the function for the probability p, while in the first term it is for the probability $p' = (u/r)p$. With the complementary binomial distribution function denoted by $B(a;n,p')$ for the first term and by $B(a;n,p)$ for the second term, we can rewrite the binomial formula in briefer form:

$$C = SB(a;n,p') - Er^{-n} B(a;n,p).$$

This form of the binomial formula bears some similarity to the Black-Scholes formula. Let us go through some of the differences in the two formulas. In place of r^{-n}, the continuous time formula uses e^{-rt}. This term is simply the discount rate when there is continuous compounding of the interest. It is the obvious extension of the discount rate compounded each of the n periods as the time period is made increasingly smaller.

The binomial distribution function $B(\cdot)$ is replaced by the normal distribution function $N(\cdot)$. This result is also a natural result of going to continuous time, since the normal distribution is nothing more than the binomial distribution as the number of trials (or in this case, as the number of time periods) goes to infinity.

On the first pass, then, the relationship of the binomial formula to its continuous-time counterpart seems reasonable. However, it is not clear how the variables inside the normal distribution come about as the limiting case of the variables inside the binomial distribution. An explanation of the relationship between these sets of variables is too involved to cover here.

One variable that deserves comment, however, is the instantaneous variance σ^2. This term is the measure of the volatility of the stock price. It replaces the values u and d as we go to the continuous-time case. The particular continuous-time stochastic process involved in the use of the instantaneous variance is a diffusion process. A diffusion process is a more general process than the binomial process. In a diffusion process, the random variable (in this case the stock price) is constantly moving, with its movement in any small time period being small. It is a "smooth" process in the sense that the stock price path is unbroken. The contrasting process is a jump process, where the random variable follows its mean path most of the time, but jumps a large amount at random times.

The attraction of the variance of the continuous-time case is that the stock is no longer limited to a fixed binomial movement. It can move to any value over a given time period so long as its path to that value is continuous—so long as the stock price takes on all the values between the two prices as it moves from the one price to the other. The variance is a measure of the probability of the stock moving away from its expected return over a given time period. The larger the variance, the more volatile the stock.

Strictly speaking, the diffusion process is the limiting case of the binomial process, but the limitations that are imposed on the stock with a binary process are eliminated by the diffusion process. The only restriction on the stock price movement is that it changes value smoothly, rather than jumping in value. Thus, by going to the limiting case where the stock price is described by a diffusion process, we have largely eliminated the second major objection to our initial binomial formulation of the problem.

QUESTIONS

1. Use the binomial formula described in the appendix to derive the one-period formula for the European put option. Verify that the formula is consistent with the put-call parity equation, Equation (3.6) of Chapter 3.

2. Modify the many-period binomial option formula to take into account:
    a. Interest rates that vary from period to period (but whose values are known).
    b. Dividend payments on the underlying stock. (Assume the dividend payment is D, implying a dividend yield $\delta = D/S$, which results in an exdividend stock price that is $(1 - \delta)$ of what the stock price would be if no dividend were paid. Assume both the time of the dividend payment and the size of the dividend yield are known.

3. Work through the one-period binomial option formula allowing for *three* possible stock price movements rather than two. Allow the stock price to either go up by u, down by d, or stay at its current price. Why does the arbitrage argument break down when there are three possible values for the stock price rather than only two possible values? What does this imply about the possibility for arbitrage profit if the future dividend yield on the stock is uncertain? (Refer to question 2.)

4. What happens to the derivation of the binomial option pricing formula if u is less than or equal to the riskless interest rate? If d is greater than or equal to the riskless interest rate? Show that such a situation results in a dominant security.

5. A "down-and-out option" is like a call option, except that if the stock ever drops below a specified value before the maturity of the option, the option contract is void and the option becomes worthless. The holder of a down-and-out option gets the maximum of 0 or $S - E$ unless the stock price drops below the critical value $\underline{S}$, in which case the holder receives nothing, no matter what the stock behavior is later. Show how the binomial pricing formula would need to be modified to price such an option.

Chapter 5 APPLYING THE OPTION PRICING FORMULA

Having derived the option pricing formula, the next task is to consider how to apply it. The journey from the derivation to the application of the formula is marked by two considerations. First, we need to be able to estimate the variables in the formula. If the variables are not easily estimated, then the formula cannot be profitably applied. Second, we need to be able to adjust the formula to meet "real world" behavior. The formula is derived under a set of restrictive assumptions. Where possible, we need to adjust the formula when these assumptions are not met. And where such adjustment is not possible, we need to weigh the effect of the assumptions on the accuracy and profit potential of the formula.

ESTIMATING THE INPUTS

The use of the formula requires the input of five variables: the stock price, the exercise price, the time-to-maturity, the interest rate, and the volatility of the stock.

The first three variables are easily observable from the option quotation. The time-to-maturity is obtained by counting the number of calendar days until the time to maturity, and then dividing it by 365 to get the time-to-maturity in annual terms. The method for estimating the interest rate and the volatility is discussed next.

Interest Rate

The interest rate should measure the risk-free borrowing and lending rate over the period of the option. Since the borrowing and lending rate typically differ, the interest rate used must serve as an average of the two. The treasury bill rate will generally underestimate the applicable rate, since it is below the borrowing rate. A better rate may be the Certificate of Deposit rate, or the rate for top quality commercial paper.

The duration of the rate is also important. The interest rate used should have a duration as close to the time of expiration of the option as possible. If the option has three months to expiration, a three-month interest rate should also be used.

As Figure 5–1 shows, the option price is not sensitive to small changes in the interest rate. This is further illustrated in Table 5–1. The interest rate will

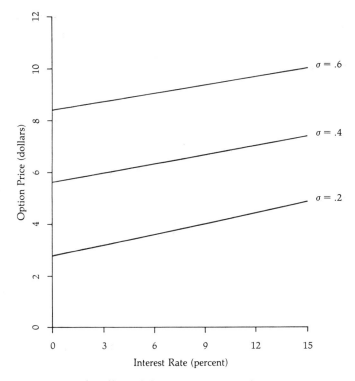

Figure 5–1 The effect of the interest rate on the option formula price for various σ

Table 5-1

The Sensitivity of the Option Formula to the Interest Rate

		$S = 50$		$\sigma = .3$		
		$T = .083$			$T = .5$	
E	$r = .060$	.065	.070	.060	.065	.070
45	5.419	5.436	5.452	7.896	7.973	8.050
50	1.846	1.857	1.867	4.941	5.004	5.077
60	1.045	1.059	1.073	1.598	1.627	1.656

generally be measured to within one percentage point of the true value, and that accuracy will give a value for the formula that will differ from the correct value by only a few cents.

Volatility

The volatility of the stock price is by far the most difficult variable to estimate. A first approximation of the volatility of the stock can be obtained by using past data. Stock price observations from the past few months should be used to obtain the estimate, since the price movements further back will be less reflective of the future volatility of the stock. Also, the estimates should be evenly spaced.

While the volatility is assumed to be stationary in the derivation of the formula, it in fact changes substantially over time. Thus, care must be taken in using past data to estimate the future volatility.

The measure of volatility used in the formula is the variance of the stock price. To calculate the variance from historical stock price data, we first must obtain the past price quotes. Say the data used in the calculation are the end-of-week quotes over the past twenty weeks. To calculate the variance, we first convert the prices into rates of return: $R_k = S_k/S_{k-1}$, where S_k is the stock price at the end of the kth week. We then take the natural log of the return in order to approximate the continuously compounded return. We then calculate the mean of the return,

$$m = \frac{1}{20} \Sigma \ln R_k,$$

where $\ln R_k$ denotes the natural log of R_k. The variance is then computed by summing $(\ln R_k - m)^2$ over all the periods, and dividing by $(N - 1)$. (We divide by $(N - 1)$ because we need to take account of the degrees of freedom in the calculation of the variance in order to get an unbiased estimate.)

If weekly intervals are used in the data, then multiply the resulting number by 52 to get an annualized variance. The final variance calculation is then

$$\sigma^2 = 52 \times \frac{1}{19} \sum_{k=1}^{20} (\ln R_k - m)^2.$$

This number is then entered into the formula for σ^2.

Of course, the interval used can be other than weekly. Monthly, bi-weekly, or even daily data entries can be used. The calculation will then use another number in the interval adjustment: 12 if monthly data, 365 if daily. Also, the number of data entries is variable. Generally more than ten entries should be used to get an adequate sample, and the more entries that are used, the more precise the sample will be.

One important consideration in selecting the period to use and the sample size is the variability of the variance. The variance of the stock changes over time, so the further into the past the data entries go, the less reflective they will be of the current or future variances. It is therefore better to use the past twenty weeks of data rather than using the past twenty months.

There is also a problem with selecting too short an interval. If daily observations are used, care must be taken to be sure that the quotes are all from the same time of day. If one quote is from 4:00 P.M. on Wednesday, the next is from 11:00 A.M. on Thursday, and the next is from 4:00 P.M. on Friday, then the variance calculation will be imprecise, since the actual time periods used in the calculation have varied from one and one-half-day intervals to a one-half-day interval. Unfortunately, it is impossible to tell from published price quotes when the last trade of the day occurred. If the stock is not heavily traded, the closing quotes may vary considerably, and give a poor estimate of the variance. If weekly quotes are used, however, a half-day variation in the time of the quotes becomes less significant. Therefore, it seems weekly quotes present the best compromise between getting timely data and assuring that a constant time interval is used in the estimation.

VARIANCE: FURTHER ESTIMATION TECHNIQUES

The variance of the stock price is the most difficult variable to measure accurately, but the profitable use of the formula demands an accurate estimate of all the variables in the formula. The investor who can overcome the difficulties in estimating the volatility and get the best estimate will most likely also get the greatest profit.

Historical Variance

A first approximation of the variance can be obtained by using past data, as was illustrated in the previous example. This technique is subject to a high degree of error, however. While the variance is assumed to be stationary in the derivation of the formula, it in fact changes significantly over time. Thus, the estimate of the variance from the past may not be reflective of what the variance of the stock will be in the future. The fluctuation of the variance is illustrated in Figure 5–2. The variance over the two-year period represented here ranges from a low value of .18 to a high value of .39, over double its lowest value. This variation is typical of the changes in the volatility of the stocks. Indeed, even the market as a whole exhibits wide swings in volatility.

The problem with the measurement of the volatility is compounded by the sensitivity of the option pricing formula to changes in the volatility. The effect of volatility on the option price is shown in Figure 5–3. Table 5–2 further demonstrates the effect on the option price for a typical stock as the volatility used in the option formula takes on different values. Even a change of a few hundredths makes a significant change in the option formula's value. As Figure 5–2 demonstrates, changes of this magnitude can occur frequently.

The direct calculation of the variance from the historical data will not capture the future shifts in the volatility of the stock. Figure 5–4 overlays the

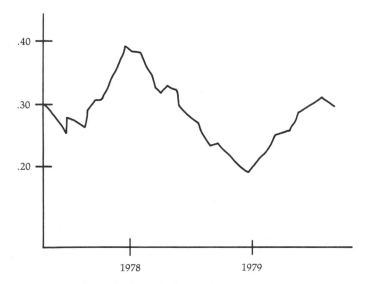

Figure 5–2 The volatility of the stock price

Table 5-2
The Sensitivity of the Option Formula to the Stock Price Volatility

S = 50   r = 6%

E	T = .0833			T = .5		
	σ = .28	.30	.32	.28	.30	.32
45	5.37	5.42	5.47	7.69	7.90	8.11
50	1.74	1.85	1.96	4.68	4.94	5.22
60	.02	.04	.05	1.35	1.60	1.83

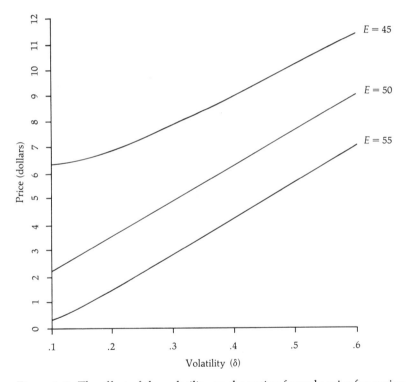

Figure 5-3 The effect of the volatility on the option formula price for various E

actual variance of the stock price pictured in Figure 5-2 with the estimate of
the variance that is obtained from the calculation method using historical data
that was previously described. The simple historical calculation misses future
shifts in the variance. However, the estimate can be refined using other estima-

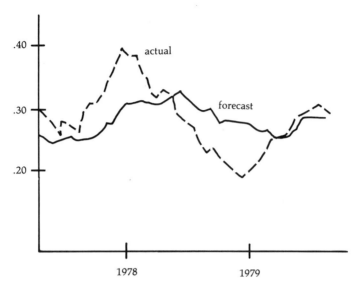

Figure 5-4 The forecast of volatility using the past average volatility

tion techniques. Statistical techniques from time series analysis, commonly referred to as Box-Jenkins analysis, and the use of other data from the firm and market can greatly increase the accuracy of the estimate.

Time Series Analysis

The use of time series analysis enters the past values of the stock price movement into an equation in a weighted form. The weights of the values reflect certain tendencies in the movement of the volatility. For example, the variance of the stock price tends to revert back to its mean level. If the variance is unusually high, a good guess is that in the future it will drop in value. Similarly, if the variance is unusually low, it will generally increase in value in the future. The timing of the movement back to its "normal" or mean value, and the measurement of what values are unusually high or low, is facilitated by the statistical techniques of time series analysis. The time series analysis also pinpoints other factors that are related to the future variance of the stock. For example, if the stock increases in price, the variance will generally drop; while if the stock price decreases, the variance will generally increase. Also, the changes in stock price volatility may be signaled by recent shifts in the trading volume of the stock.

The use of time series analysis on the accuracy of predictions is illustrated in Figure 5-5. Here the estimate of the future variance obtained

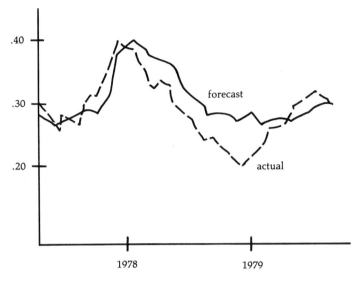

Figure 5-5 The forecast of volatility from time series analysis

through the use of Box-Jenkins analysis is compared with the actual variance that occurred. The estimate is much closer to the actual variance than the estimate using a direct application of the historical data.

The Use of Other Firm, Industry, and Market Indicators

The data can be further improved by considering other inputs in the estimation. Other variables of the firm will usually foreshadow changes in the variance of the stock. Dividend policy (especially recent changes in the dividend payout), and the debt structure of the firm are highly correlated with the behavior of the variance of the stock price.

The variance of firms in the same industry are highly correlated. The variance of a firm tends to move toward the average stock variance in the industry. For example, if the average variance of stocks in the automobile industry is .25, and Ford's variance is .12, we would expect that the variance of Ford stock will increase toward .25 in the future. By aggregating firms properly, the estimates of the variance of the individual firms are greatly enhanced.

Not only are the variances related within industry groups, but to some extent the variances of all stocks are related. That is, there is a market factor in stock variances. Macroeconomic variables such as interest rates, inflation rates, and recent political developments tend to affect the volatility of the

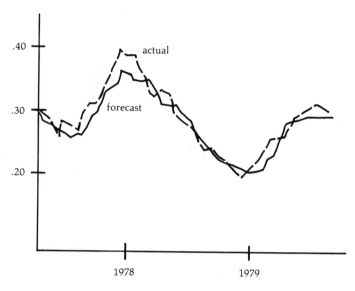

Figure 5-6 The forecast volatility using both time series analysis and other firm, industry, and market data

entire market. When these inputs are added to inputs from the firm and the industry, the estimate of the variance becomes very tight. Figure 5-6 compares the estimate of the future variance using both time series analysis and other data inputs with the actual variance of the stock. Nearly all of the error is now removed; the estimate rarely varies from the actual variance by more than .02.

Implicit Volatility

Another method for estimating the volatility is to use the market's opinion of the future variance of the stock. This opinion is contained in the market price of the option. By taking the market price of the option, an investor can work backwards through the pricing formula to obtain the volatility that is implicit within that option price. Referring back to the example of Chapter 4, upon observing that the value of an option with $S = 68$, $E = 60$, $T = .241$, and $r = .06$ was $10.60, an investor would discover that the implicit price volatility for that option is .4, since if that volatility were used in the pricing formula, the price of the option observed in the market would result. Different options on the same stock may have different implicit volatilities. There are techniques to combine the implicit volatilities from the various option prices to get the best estimate of the true volatility. A little accuracy will be lost (and much time gained) by deriving the implicit volatility from the option that is closest to the money and that has the time-to-expiration the investor is interested in.

One difficulty with the use of the implicit volatility is that it must be determined by an iterative, trial and error process. Unless suitable computer capability is available, the calculation of the implicit volatility will be time-consuming. Another difficulty is that the use of the implicit volatility may be self-defeating for an investor looking for mispriced options, since by construction the investor will find that the implicit volatility assures that the option is correctly priced.

If the option formula is being used to compute the hedge ratios for strategies, however, it is a good method to use. And if several options are used, and their implicit volatilities used to set a weighted average of the implicit volatilities, the result will represent the best measure of the market consensus of the future stock volatility.

The estimate of volatility derived from the implicit volatility is illustrated in Figure 5–7. This figure uses the implicit volatility for all the options listed, all weighted by the elasticity of variance. (See Chiras and Manaster (1978) for an explanation of this.) The implicit volatility further improves the accuracy of the combined estimation technique illustrated in Figure 5–6. Since it requires no data collection, it may be more convenient to use.

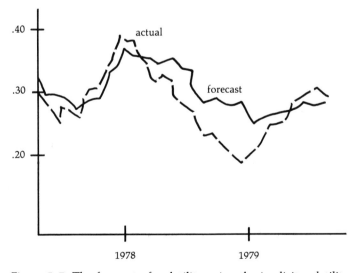

Figure 5–7 The forecast of volatility using the implicit volatility

EXTENSIONS OF THE FORMULA

The option pricing formula was originally derived under a set of restrictive assumptions. Further development of the formula has included research to relax many of these assumptions, thus making the formula comply more closely to actual market conditions. This section will consider some of the modifications that have been made.

Interest Rates

There are two restrictions for interest rates in the original derivation of the formula. First, the interest rate was assumed to be constant and known over time. Second, it was assumed that the same interest rate applied for both borrowing and lending. Of course, interest rates vary over time, and typically individuals face a premium over the riskless lending rate in borrowing funds.

If the interest rate varies from period to period, a separate interest rate will be used each period for the hedging strategy. As a result, the final interest rates in the formula will involve the product of various one-period rates rather than having the same interest rate used each period. This adjustment amounts to replacing the constant interest rate with the geometric average of the per-period interest rates.

If there is a difference between the borrowing and lending interest rate, the option price can only be established between the bounds dictated by the interest rates. If $C(r_l)$ represents the option formula value when the lending rate is used, and $C(r_b)$ represents the price when the borrowing rate is used, then the actual price C must be bounded by these two values:

$$C(r_l) \leq C \leq C(r_b).$$

If this condition does not hold, then there will be arbitrage opportunities. The option price may be between these two values without such opportunities existing, since then the option will be priced too high to use a strategy involving a long position in the riskless asset, but be priced too low for a short position in the riskless asset to be profitable. These bounds on the option price are far from clear-cut. Some investors will be able to borrow at very favorable rates, while others will have lending opportunities that are more favorable than those facing the typical investor. In an efficient market, one would expect the bounds to involve the lowest rate at which someone could borrow and the highest rate at which someone could lend.

Dividends

In the original formulation of the option pricing formula, it was assumed that there were no dividends or other payouts to the stockholders. If dividends are included in the analysis, the option formula must be adjusted, since the dividend payments will affect the price of the stock. Dividend payments may make it advantageous to exercise an American option early, and uncertain dividends may make the arbitrage argument of the pricing formula break down.

The stock price often drops due to dividend payments. If the option is not payout protected, the drop in the stock price will imply a decline in the option price as well. A holder of a call option may therefore find it advantageous to exercise the option just before the stock goes ex-dividend in order to capture the value of the stock before the decline. The problem of evaluation of the option must therefore take into account the possibility of early exercise. The problem is not intractable, however, since if the option is exercised early, it will be done immediately before the dividend payout is made. The option must thus be priced under two contingencies—that the option is exercised early, and that it is not. If the value of the option is greater in a particular situation when it is exercised early, then that value is used for the option in determining the option's formula. The problem is simplified further since only those options that are in-the-money will face the risk of early exercise. Out-of-the-money options will continue to be held unexercised, since they will be worthless if exercised early.

If the dividend payout is known, the discrete-case binomial model discussed in the previous chapter can be adjusted by replacing the stock price by the stock price minus the dividend in the formula. If dividends are assumed to be paid at a continuous rate, rather than in periodic lump sums, then the option formula can be easily adjusted to include dividend payouts. Let the dividend payout rate be δ. This rate, like an interest rate, represents the per-period earnings from dividends. For example, if the annual dividend on a $100 stock is $5, the δ will equal .05. To modify the Black-Scholes formula to include this rate, we replace the S in the first term of the formula with $e^{-\delta T} S$, and we replace the interest rate r in the d_1 and the d_2 terms with $r - \delta$.

Essentially these modifications reduce the stock price S by the amount of the dividend payout, and adjust the return from the riskless hedging strategy accordingly. Since dividends are paid quarterly in lump sums, this formula will be an approximation to the actual option price. It will overprice the option right before the stock goes ex-dividend, and underprice it just after the exdividend date. But when there are significant dividends, it will present a better approximation to the option price than the formula in Chapter 4.

If the dividend payment is not known, however, and may take on a number of values, the pricing technique can no longer be used. If the number of possible stock prices in the next period is greater than two, the investor cannot form a riskless hedge, so the arbitrage strategy will no longer be possible.

Taxes

Several models have adjusted the original option pricing formula to include taxes. If taxes must be paid on income, capital gains, or interest payments, the arbitrage argument proceeds as it has been outlined before, but now the return to the positions in the three assets must be adjusted for the tax payment. The option price, the stock price, and interest rate are corrected in the formula by their respective marginal tax rates. While the adjustment of the formula is straightforward, the existence of differential tax rates across investors causes difficulties for the arbitrage argument. If the option is priced according to one marginal tax rate, there will be another investor with a lower or higher tax rate for which the option will be mispriced. The three security values for the hedging strategy will be replaced by a number of prices, a different set for each tax bracket. In general, we cannot expect the option price to be correct for all tax brackets, and must resort to considering the correct option price for an investor in the "average" or "representative" marginal tax bracket.

Just as the formula can be modified for dividends, it can also be modified for taxes. Let us extend the option formula as modified for dividend payouts to include income tax as well. Taking the simple case of no tax on capital gains, and denoting the marginal tax rate on dividends and interest income by δ respectively and τ, the option formula will replace S by $e^{-\delta(1-\tau)T} S$, and will replace r in the d_1 and d_2 terms by $(r - \delta)(1 - \tau)$.

Stock Price Movement

The derivation of the continuous time formula assumed that the variance of the stock price was both constant and known. Our attempts at measuring the volatility of the stock price indicate that both of these assumptions are unrealistic. In theory, a changing variance poses no serious problem for the formula. In practice, however, the option formula becomes very complex when a nonstationary variance is introduced, and in general the formula cannot be solved in closed form. This means that numerical solution techniques, which require a computer to solve, must be used.

If the variance of the stock is unknown, the hedging argument breaks down because the hedge ratio cannot be determined exactly. The error in the measurement of the variance means that the hedge may not be riskless—the range of the stock movement may be more than what was expected. Since in practice the variance is measured with error, this means that the investor cannot in fact establish an arbitrage profit position. There will always be some risk that the hedge has been miscalculated, and thus there is always some risk to the investor's position. This problem hits at the heart of the theoretical argument of the option pricing technique. Rather than being founded on the opportunity for a riskless arbitrage profit, the formula becomes founded on the opportunity for an uncertain profit opportunity. While the profit potential is still there, the shift from an arbitrage profit to an uncertain profit substantially weakens the case for the option pricing.

There is a counterargument that may redeem the formula to its former strength. It is argued by some proponents of the formula that the risk the investor faces from the uncertain variance is diversifiable. That is, the changes in the variance of the stock are not correlated with stock market prices, and if the investor holds a large portfolio, the risk faced from the changing variance can be eliminated. This argument has not been empirically verified yet, and the behavior of the variances calls it into question. As has been seen in discussing the volatility of the stocks, there is a "market" term in the volatility: the variance of one stock is correlated with the variance of other stocks. This correlation makes sense since the uncertainty with respect to inflation, interest rates, and other macroeconomic variables will tend to affect many stocks in the same way. Furthermore, there is a relationship between stock prices and volatility. The stock price is inversely related to the volatility. This may imply a link between systematic price movements and stock volatility.

In deriving the original option pricing formula, the stock price was assumed to follow a binomial random walk, which in the limit was described by a diffusion process. The diffusion process assumes that the stock price moves smoothly or continuously from one value to another. There are no restrictions placed on the range of the stock price in any time period, but if the stock moves from one value to another, it must do so by taking on every value between the two prices, rather than jumping from the one price to the other. The alternative stochastic process is the jump process. With a jump process, the stock follows its mean path with occasional jumps in price. The two processes are compared in Figure 5–8.

If stock prices are described by a jump process, an alternative option pricing formula developed by Cox and Ross can be used. Their formula assumes the return to the stock is constant most of the time, and occasionally the

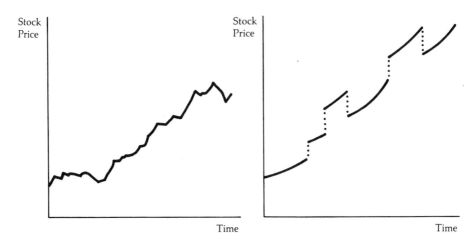

Figure 5–8 The continuous-time diffusion process (left) compared with the jump process (right)

stock price jumps up or down by a specified amount. It would be valuable to incorporate such a formula with the continuous-time formula that is based on a diffusion process, since stock prices are obviously described by both smooth price movements and occasional jumps in price.

One practical problem with doing this is large jumps in stock price are not frequent enough to obtain a good estimate of the expected size or frequency of the jumps. Another practical problem is that the Cox-Ross formula is very complex and difficult to evaluate when the jumps are allowed to vary in size, or when the jump size is treated as a random variable. But as we will discuss in the next section, the greatest problem posed is theoretical: if stock prices are described by a combination of a jump and a diffusion process, no general option formula based on the arbitrage argument is possible.

A CRITIQUE OF THE BLACK-SCHOLES OPTION PRICING FORMULA

The Black-Scholes option pricing formula has a number of attractive features that have made it popular within both the academic and the investment community. It is based on an elegant and persuasive arbitrage argument. It uses variables that are generally easily observable. And it does not depend on some important unobservable variables, such as the public's expectation of future stock changes.

The attractiveness of the formula has been widely discussed. Unfortunately, the problems with its applicability have not received such wide coverage. In this section we will present some of the drawbacks of the formula. The criticism can be drawn along three lines:

1. Is the formula correct?

2. If the formula is correct, can it be estimated accurately?

3. If the formula is correct and can be accurately estimated, does it imply the existence of profit opportunities for the investor?

The second question has been discussed in the previous section. In this section we will consider the other two questions.

Is the Formula Correct?

The formula depends on the assumptions underlying its derivation. If the assumptions are not reasonable, and yet are critical to the formula's derivation, then the formula is open to question. There are many simplifying assumptions involved in the derivation of the original Black-Scholes formula. Some of these have been relaxed in later derivations. We have already shown the modifications that are necessary when dividends, variable interest rates, and tax effects are included in the derivation. Relaxing these assumptions weakens the formula to some extent. Dividends present the possibility of early exercise, and if the dividends are uncertain, the arbitrage strategy upon which the formula is based can no longer be applied. Tax rates that differ from investor to investor mean that the degree of mispricing will also vary among investors, so there may not be one option price that will eliminate the profit opportunities for all investors. Uncertain interest rates and uncertain variance will cause uncertainty in the correct price of the option, and in the correct hedge ratio to use. Thus, the profit opportunities will no longer be riskless and the arbitrage argument will be violated. Two other assumptions that seem critical to the formula and at the same time are of questionable validity are the assumptions regarding no transaction costs and the underlying distribution of the stock price.

Is the Arbitrage Strategy Profitable When There Are Transaction Costs?

The use of the arbitrage strategy involves maintaining a dynamic hedge. To assure the hedge remains riskless, the position of the stock relative to the option must be constantly adjusted as the time-to-maturity decreases, and as the stock price changes. Each adjustment will involve transaction costs.

Empirical evidence by Galai (1975) suggests that even a 1-percent transaction cost will eliminate the profit potential from following the strategy. For the typical investor, this clearly makes the hedging strategy impractical. Even for the floor trader, whose transaction costs are very low (on the order of one dollar per contract), the implicit costs of the exchange seat, the computing and personal cost in following the hedge, and the cost of transacting in the stock may make the hedging strategy impractical.

If transactions costs prevent investors from profitably following the arbitrage strategy, then it is not clear how the investor can profit from the mispricing of the option. An investor can always simply buy or sell the option if it is mispriced, with the expectation that it will later move toward the correct price. But if the dynamic hedging strategy is not practical, it is not clear what mechanism will force the option toward the theoretically correct price. The formula's option price becomes a theoretical artifact, which may or may not obtain in actuality.

Is the Formula Valid When Stock Prices Do Not Follow a Diffusion Process?

A second serious problem with the formula is the assumption concerning the stochastic process driving the stock price. In the original Black-Scholes formulation, the stock is assumed to follow a stationary diffusion process. As we have already discussed, such a process restricts the stock to have smooth, continuous price changes. Also, the process is constant over time. It is clear that both of these assumptions are violated by actual stock movements. Stocks often exhibit jumps in price, sometimes by half a point, sometimes by several points.

If stock prices follow a smooth diffusion process, then the Black-Scholes formula can be used to price options. If the stock follows a jump process, then an alternative formula, the Cox-Ross formula, can be used to price options. Intuition would suggest that if options can be priced with either a diffusion or a jump process, then they should be able to be priced when both processes exist. However, Merton (1976a) has shown that when the stock price is characterized by a combination of the smooth time process and the jump process, it is impossible to derive a general pricing formula based on arbitrage profits. Rubinstein and Cox (1981) have also shown that the arbitrage argument for option pricing breaks down when the stock price is allowed to follow such a combination process. The pricing formulas thus lose strength when the actual behavior of stock prices is considered, since the arbitrage strategy on which the formulas are based is no longer possible.

Besides causing problems for the application of the option formula, the nonstationarity of the stochastic process driving the stock price opens up theoretical questions concerning the validity of the formula. Since the formula is derived for a stationary process, it will not be valid when the process is nonstationary. An option formula has yet to be operationalized that allows the volatility of the option to vary. The problem becomes increasingly complicated when the jump process is considered, since the use of a jump process which permits the volatility to vary is fraught with technical problems.

It may be that the option pricing formula would not differ significantly from the Black-Scholes formula if the assumptions of the stochastic process were relaxed. The Black-Scholes formula may be a good approximation in spite of the limitations on the type of stock price movement. However, it is impossible to evaluate the accuracy of such an approximation yet, since more general formulas have not been developed which allow us to measure the formula's error.

Is the Formula Valid When the Stock Volatility or the Interest Rate Is Uncertain?

We have already addressed the problem of changes in the interest rate and the stock volatility. But what if the interest rate or volatility not only changes over the period of the option, but that change is also uncertain? If there is either a stochastic interest rate or a stochastic volatility, then the arbitrage strategy is no longer valid, and the option pricing formula must be reconsidered. As with the question of the stock price following a nondiffusion process, the effect of stochastic interest rates and volatility on the accuracy of the formula are difficult to assess because of the great mathematical complexity involved. Analytical closed-form solutions for the option pricing formula are not available for processes with stochastic variations in volatility or interest rates. The best hope for considering these questions is the use of numerical analysis to solve the equations for the option formula once the assumption of known interest rates and volatility is relaxed, but this is an area of research that is still incomplete.

If the Formula Is Correct and Can Be Estimated, Does It Imply There Are Profit Opportunities for the Investor?

In an efficient market, all available information is used in obtaining the market price of a security. If the security is not priced fairly (i.e., so that it gives an expected return that is commensurate to its risk), there are profit opportunities, and those who detect the mispricing will move the price toward the correct price as they take advantage of the profit opportunities.

If new information becomes available that affects the price of the security, and if the information is widely known, then the security will adjust to the fair price given the new information without anyone profiting from the information. For example, if a firm makes an announcement before a group of investors that increases the investors' estimate of the fair price of the firm, all the investors will bid for the stock simultaneously. However, no one will sell the stock until the new fair price is reached. The stock price will rise to the new price without any trades being completed, and once at the new price, no profit opportunities will be possible. If only a few investors receive the information, they can bid on the stock and buy it from other investors who are still unaware. But if too many investors enter into the bidding, the price will move before any of them profit from the information.

The same principle applies to the profit available from the use of the option pricing formula. The formula is widely known and used. Most market-makers on the option exchanges subscribe to option services using the option pricing model, and major investment firms use an option pricing service in evaluating their option trades. Hence, the correct option price according to the option pricing formula is well-known information. And since it is widely known, any mispricing of an option will be immediately acted on by a large group of investors. With a large group bidding on the option simultaneously, it will adjust to the correct price before anyone can make a profit from the information.

Thus, the final barrier to the profitable use of the option pricing formula is its popularity. The formula can allow profit opportunities only when a small group of investors has that information. When a large group has access to it, the profit opportunities will be gone. And by any measure, the option formula is so well known and widely used that it has essentially become part of the market's information set.

Why, then, are there options that are not correctly priced according to the formula? The reason may be that although the formula represents part of the market's available information, it does not represent the entire information set. Investors, floor traders, and market-makers will combine the information from the option formula with other information in determining the market price of the option.

Given that the formula is well known, a divergence between the market price of the option and the formula's price implies one of two things. Either the market thinks the formula's price is correct, but has not yet adjusted, or the market does not think the formula's value is correct. The first possibility seems unlikely, since investors rarely stand by and let profit opportunities go unexploited. And given the previous discussion regarding the problems with the option formula, it seems reasonable that investors will not fully depend on the unmodified Black-Scholes option formula in making their option trading decision.

SUMMARY

The criticisms presented are meant to be constructive, providing the investor with a guide to the major problems that must be answered for the effective use of an option pricing technique. These criticisms can help to determine some of the important characteristics an option formula must have to be profitable. First, it must effectively meet the realities of the market which the original Black-Scholes option formula assumes away. In particular, it must include modifications to meet the effect of taxes, dividends, and variable interest rates and stock price volatility on option prices. It must also allow for a more general type of stock price behavior than the diffusion process model upon which the Black-Scholes formula is based. Second, the use of the formula must be based on an accurate estimate of the formula parameters, most notably the volatility of the stock. Third, the strategy for taking advantage of options that are found to be mispriced must be effective in substantially reducing the risk of the option position when transactions costs make continuous hedging impractical. Finally, the notion of efficient markets suggests that for any formula to allow profit opportunities it must not be widely known and used within the investment community.

REFERENCES

The modification of the option formula for taxes is presented by Scholes. Dividends are considered by Merton (1973b), Roll (1977), Geske (1979b), and Rubinstein and Cox (1981). Merton (1973b) also considers the effects of variable interest rates. The effect of different stochastic processes on the stock prices is discussed by Cox and Ross (1976a), and Merton (1976a, 1976b). These papers concentrate on deriving pricing formulas for alternative stochastic processes, especially for jump processes.

There is an increasing number of empirical papers that test the accuracy of the option formula or the existence of profit opportunities through the hedging strategy. Galai (1975, 1978) and Chiras and Manaster (1978) present studies of the profit potential from the use of the option formula. Galai finds such opportunities do exist if transaction costs are not considered, but in the face of even small transaction costs, the profit opportunities are lost. Trippi (1977), and Chiras and Manaster indicate that opportunities exist even when transaction costs are considered. One problem with these studies that may invalidate their result is their use of the closing price quotes to determine the market price of the options. But if the trading is thin in an option, the quoted price may not be the price at which the option would currently be purchasable. Since in practice the option may not be purchasable at the price of the last quote, it is difficult to evaluate whether their strategy would yield a profit under actual trading conditions.

The use of implicit volatility to estimate the stock volatility is considered by Latane and Rendleman (1976), and Chiras and Manaster. The sensitivity of option pricing to errors in volatility estimation is discussed by Boyle and Ananthanarayanan (1977). An empirical discussion of market volatility is presented by MacBeth and Merville (1979). Parkinson (1980) and Garman and Klass (1980) show how to improve the accuracy of historical estimates of volatility by using the opening, high, and low quotes of the day in addition to the closing stock quotes.

QUESTIONS

1. a. What will happen to the relative sensitivity of the option pricing formula to errors in the specification of the interest rate and volatility if the volatility is small relative to the interest rate?

   b. There has been some discussion of introducing options on short-term money instruments. These instruments have very low volatility. What does that imply about the difficulties in applying an option pricing formula in pricing these options?

2. The anticipation of announcements can have a significant effect on the volatility of a stock, even before the stock price itself changes in reaction to the announcement. How will the following affect the stock volatility:

   a. The outcome of a major lawsuit against the company is about to be announced.

   b. An oil company is about to announce the results of drilling operations in the area of a major oil lease.

   What other situations will affect the volatility of the stock before affecting the stock price? What does this imply about the accuracy of techniques which measure volatility through strictly quantitative techniques?

3. Suppose that rather than knowing the volatility of the stock price for certain, you have an estimate of the volatility that is expressed by a probability distribution. In particular, you think there is a .5 probability that
   the volatility is .2, and a .5 probability that the volatility is .3, for an expected value of .25. Compute the value of the option pricing formula
   when the expected value of the volatility, .25, is used. Compare that with
   the option value that results when the formula value is computed using
   the volatility of .2 and using the volatility of .3, and then these two values
   are averaged together. That is, compare $C(S, T, E, r, .25)$ with $.5C(S, T,
   E, r, .2) + .5C(S, T, E, r, .3)$. (Use any value for S, T, E, and r.) Why do
   the results differ? Which one is a more accurate indication of the fair
   price? What does this imply about the technique that should be used in
   pricing options when the estimate of the volatility is expressed by a probability distribution (such as a mean value and standard deviation)?

Chapter 6 THE APPLICATION OF OPTION PRICING TO OTHER FINANCIAL SECURITIES

Up to this point in the book, we have considered options on the stock of a firm. However, an option can be formed on any underlying security. For example, it is common for investors to write options to purchase land. An option on land would give the buyer the right to purchase the land at a specified price on or before the option's expiration date. Options have also become common on commodities and metals. There is a commodity option exchange in London that functions much like the stock option exchanges in the United States, but with a commodity contract (promising the delivery of a specified number of units of a commodity) as the underlying security. No matter what the underlying security, the theory in the previous chapters is still applicable.

Many financial instruments can also be considered as options. Thus, option theory has become of great interest in the academic financial community because the rich results of option theory can be applied to a wide range of financial instruments. Also, there is a practical payoff once these techniques become available for pricing the claims of the firm. In this chapter we will apply option theory to equity, debt, and convertible securities, and also consider other, more wide-ranging applications.

EQUITY

Consider a firm with a very simplified investment stream. The firm is financed through an equity issue and a debt issue. The debt issue is composed of a discount bond promising the payment of B dollars at maturity. When the debt issue matures, the firm is sold out at its market value V, and its value is distributed to the equity and the bondholders. The bondholders receive their promised payment B, and the stockholders receive the residual value of the firm, $V - B$. (If there are 1,000 shares outstanding, each share will be worth $\$(V - B)/1,000$.) If the value of the firm is less than the payment due to the bondholders, the firm goes bankrupt—the bondholders get the full value of the firm, V, and the stockholders receive nothing. The feature of limited liability protects the stockholders from any further claim by the bondholders beyond the value of the firm.

While in this example the debt corresponds to a one-period bond, in practice the debtholders receive coupon payments and a balloon payment consisting of interest and principal at maturity. In practice the equityholders also receive their payments in a stream, and not in one lump sum at the end. However, the present value of that income stream will equal the current market value of the firm since the equity is nothing more than ownership of the firm (less any senior claims such as debt).

At the time of maturity of the debt, the total value of the equity will be either $V - B$ or zero, whichever is greater. That is, at the end of the period, the value of the equity, E, will be Max $(0, V - B)$. This expression should look familiar. It is of the same form as the expression for the end-of-period value of a call option. In this expression, the value of the stock, S, is replaced by the value of the firm. The exercise price E is replaced by the bond payment B. The time-to-expiration is the time of maturity of the debt.

The similarity of these expressions illustrates the relationship between the equity of the levered firm and a call option. The holder of a call option has the right to the value of the underlying stock in excess of the exercise price. The holder of the equity of the firm has the right to the value of the underlying firm in excess of the claim of the bondholders. The equity of a firm is a call option on the value of the firm. When B is greater than zero, the value of the equity, like the value of an option with a nonzero exercise price, may be less than the value of the firm. The reasoning is the same as that for a call option on stock—there is a chance that the firm will be priced below the exercise price of B, in which case the equity will have no value at the time of the maturity of the debt. The possibility of having the equity be worthless when the value of the underlying firm is still greater than zero implies that the equity will not be worth as much as the firm.

Usually the value of the firm is much higher than the claim of the bondholders, so the equity of the firm will behave like an in-the-money option and follow the value of the firm very closely. But in the case of a firm near bankruptcy, the analysis of the equity as an option leads to some interesting results.

Option theory suggests that an option will be more valuable as the underlying security becomes more risky. Consider a firm with a current value of 50 million dollars and a debt obligation of 100 million dollars. If the firm has 1 million shares of equity outstanding, then each share can be represented as an option on one-millionth of the end-of-period value of the firm, with a striking price of $100, and with the underlying security's current value being $50.

What will each share of the firm sell for if there is a year before the debt becomes due? If the firm is in a very stable business where the probability of the value of the firm doubling in one year is small, the equity will be almost worthless now, since there is a high probability that in a year the firm will still be worth under the $100 million due the bondholders. The bondholders will then get claim to the firm and the present equityholders will get nothing. On the other hand, if the firm is in a volatile business, where there is a good chance that the firm will double or quadruple in value, then the equity may still have substantial value. Thus, we see in the valuation of the equity the same property that holds for stock options—the more volatile the underlying security, in this case the firm, the more valuable the option will be.

As the manager of the firm, hired by the equityholders, and with an interest in maximizing the value of the equity of the firm, what would be the best course of action to take?

If the firm is in a stable industry, the equity value will be increased by shifting the business of the firm into more risky, volatile areas. Of course, increased risk implies a higher possibility of the value of the firm declining even more. But, as with any other option that is out-of-the-money, there is no loss from further price decline. The more stable the firm is, the more certain the equity will be worthless once the debt becomes due. The value of the equity might even be increased if the manager liquidated the firm's current facilities, took the money to Las Vegas, and bet it all on a game of roulette. There would then be one chance in thirty-three of the firm being worth $1.6 billion at year's end. This prospect would give one chance in thirty-three of each share of stock being worth $1,500. It may be more attractive to the shareholder than the current prospects of the equity being almost certainly worthless, since then there will be a chance of it being worth $10 or $20 a share, after the debt claims are paid. Of course, the debtholders would be adverse to the firm shifting into a riskier business because it is essentially their money with which the manager is playing. Most bond indenture agreements have provisions to protect the bondholders against this possibility.

The prospect that equity may actually increase in value with an increase in the firm's risk, even if the expected return of the firm declines, seems counter to the risk-return tradeoffs we are familiar with in capital market theory. But as the value of the firm declines relative to the debt outstanding, the equity takes on the characteristics of an out-of-the-money option and an increase in risk will increase its value.

Pricing the Equity of the Firm

Just as one can replicate the stock of the firm by properly mixing the riskless asset with the option of the firm's stock, so also one can replicate the return structure of the levered firm by mixing the equity of the unlevered firm with the riskless asset. Essentially, an investor can produce "home-made" leverage by borrowing money through a no-recourse loan to purchase the stock. The investment will then have the same characteristics as a firm that levers its equity through a debt issue. Since the levered firm can be replicated in this fashion, the value of the levered firm must be the same as the value of the unlevered firm combined with the home-made levered position. One can create a hedging strategy between these assets in the same manner as the hedge is created between the option and the riskless asset to replicate the stock. The possibility of such a strategy suggests that the Black-Scholes approach might yield a pricing formula for the equity of a levered firm. The formula for the value of the equity is

$$F(V, T, B, r, \sigma^2) = VN(X_1) - Be^{-rT}N(X_2) \tag{6.1}$$

where

$$X_1 \equiv \left[\ln\left(\frac{V}{B}\right) + (r + \tfrac{1}{2}\sigma^2)\, T \right] / \sigma\sqrt{T}$$

and

$$X_2 \equiv X_1 - \sigma\sqrt{T}.$$

As would be expected from the previous discussion, this formula is the same as the call option formula derived in Chapter 4, but with the value of the firm, V, replacing the price of the stock, and with the debt payment B being used as the exercise price. Note that as B goes to zero, so that the firm approaches an unlevered firm, the value of the equity equals the total value of the firm.

The problem in applying this formula is that the value of the firm will generally be difficult to observe. If the firm has a number of claims outstanding (such as both equity and debt), then the value of the firm can be calculated as the sum of the value of all of the claims on the firm.

DEBT

A similar analysis can be done for the debt of the firm since the debt is complementary to the stock—what is gained by one is lost to the other. The terminal condition for the debt of the firm is $B = \text{Min}(V,B)$. That is, the debtholder gets either the amount due on the bond, B, or the value of the firm, V, which ever is less. The condition is illustrated in Figure 6-1. Because this condition differs from the terminal condition of the call option, the pricing of the bond will differ from that of the equity. However, since the debt is a contingent claim, its final value being contingent on the end-of-period value of the firm, the Black-Scholes methodology can be employed to price it.

Just as the unlevered firm can be replicated by the equityholder by forming a riskless hedge with the levered equity of the firm and the riskless asset, so also the debtholder can combine the debt of the firm with the riskless asset to replicate the value of the unlevered firm. Since the firm's value is given, it must be that the debt of the firm is priced so that such a replication will yield the value of the firm.

Merton (1974) has derived the formula for the value of the debt of a firm, which is written as

$$D(V, T, B, r, \sigma^2) = \qquad (6.2)$$

$$Be^{-rT}[N(h_1) + \frac{1}{d}N(h_2)]$$

where

$d \equiv Be^{-rT}/V$, the current debt-firm ratio,

$h_1 \equiv -[\frac{1}{2}\sigma^2 T - \ln d]/\sigma\sqrt{T}$

$h_2 \equiv -[\frac{1}{2}\sigma^2 T + \ln d]/\sigma\sqrt{T}.$

Equation (6.2) can be derived directly from Equation (6.1) since it is equal to $V - F(V, T, B, r, \sigma^2)$. Since the equity and debt divide the value of the firm according to a specified agreement, the value of one is directly computable from the value of the other. The claim that one gets is lost to the other. It should be stressed that this formula applies to debt in the context of this chapter, i.e., where the debt is paid off as one lump sum on a specified future date. However, the analysis can be extended to debt that has coupon payments and a balloon payment at the end.

To replicate the payoff of the equity of the levered firm, an investor would hold the equity of the unlevered firm on margin. That is, the investor would borrow some of the riskless asset to purchase the stock of the firm. To replicate the payoff of the debt of the levered firm, an investor would hold the

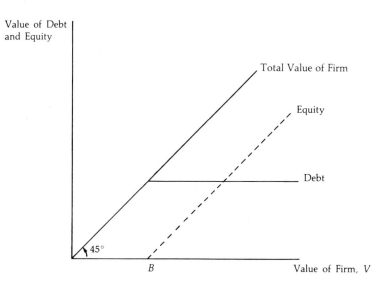

Figure 6-1 The value of the debt (solid line) and equity (broken line) of the firm as a function of the value of the firm

equity of the unlevered firm and take a long position in the riskless asset. Rather than borrow to purchase equity, and thus increase the risk of position, the investor only places a fraction of the investment in the equity, and places the rest in the riskless asset. The investor's position is then less risky than a position in the equity of the unlevered firm, which would be expected from the fact that debt is less risky than the firm on which it is written.

The weights of the unlevered firm and the riskless asset necessary to replicate the return structure of debt depend on the ratio of the end-of-period payment and the value of the firm. As the ratio of the value of the firm to the present discounted value of the payment B gets larger, the amount of the riskless asset held relative to the equity of the firm increases.

In the limit, the portfolio consists almost entirely of the riskless asset. In other words, the debt of a firm with V much larger than the present value of B is almost like the riskless asset. This result is hardly surprising, since in such a case the probability of default, and hence the probability of getting less than B back, is small. On the other extreme, if B is much larger than V, the debt is replicated by holding a majority of the portfolio in the equity of the firm. Thus, the debt of a firm in bankruptcy behaves much like the equity of the unlevered firm. This is reasonable because once the bond becomes due, there is a high probability that the bondholders will become the equityholders. In practice, as a firm gets closer to bankruptcy, the bonds of the firm take on the characteristics of the equity in the sense that they become as volatile as equity. And the equity of the firm starts to behave like an option, becoming increasingly sensitive to variations in the prospects of the firm.

The debt will always be less volatile than the firm itself. This is a logical result of the formation of debt as a combination of the unlevered equity and the riskless asset. The variance of the debt is a function of the ratio of the value of the firm to the present value of the debt. As was discussed previously, the smaller this ratio, the larger the proportion of equity in the replicating portfolio, and therefore the greater the variance of the debt will be. The variance of the debt relative to the variance of the firm is high when the value of the firm relative to the present discounted value of the bond payment, $V/e^{-rT}B$, is small. When the ratio is equal to one, so that the replicating portfolio is half equity and half the riskless asset, the debt will have a variance equal to one-half that of the firm. As $V/e^{-rT}B$ becomes small, the variance of the debt will approach that of the firm, since the debt will be very likely to have claim to the firm.

Option Theory and the Modiglianni-Miller Proposition

The Modiglianni-Miller proposition on the irrelevance of the financing decision of the firm is a central result of corporate finance. This proposition states that in the absence of taxes and bankruptcy costs the value of the firm will be independent of the debt-equity ratio. The former analysis can be used to illustrate this proposition even in the presence of bankruptcy.

Imagine that there are two firms that are identical, except that one firm issues debt and the other firm does not. The investor can create a security with the payoff structure of the levered firm by mixing the equity of the unlevered firm with the riskless asset. By borrowing the riskless asset to buy the equity of the unlevered firm, the investor can create the equity of the levered firm. And by mixing the equity of the unlevered firm with a long position in the riskless asset, the investor can create a position with the same return structure as the debt of the levered firm. Hence, the investor can create the same payoff as the payoff of the levered firm by mixing the riskless asset with the equity of the unlevered firm. The value of the debt of the levered firm must sell for the same value as that of the home-made debt, or else an arbitrage opportunity will exist.

Similarly, the levered equity must sell for the same price as it costs to create the equity position from the unlevered equity and the riskless asset. The net value of the home-made risky debt and home-made levered equity is equal to the value of the unlevered firm which was used to create it. Since the levered equity and debt must sell for the same price as their home-made counterparts, the value of the sum of the two, which is equal to the value of the levered firm, must also equal the value of the unlevered firm. Hence, the value of the levered firm is equal to the value of the firm without leverage, and the Modiglianni-Miller proposition holds.

CONVERTIBLE BONDS

A convertible bond, like an ordinary bond, promises the holder a specified payment, but a convertible bond also may be exchanged for a specified number of the shares of the firm's equity at the owner's option.

The value of a convertible bond at maturity is illustrated in Figure 6–2. If the value of the firm is less than the payment B due the convertible bondholders, then the value of the bond issue is the value of the firm V, since, like ordinary bondholders, they have the right to the assets of the firm if they do not receive the debt payment due. If the value of the firm is such that the value of

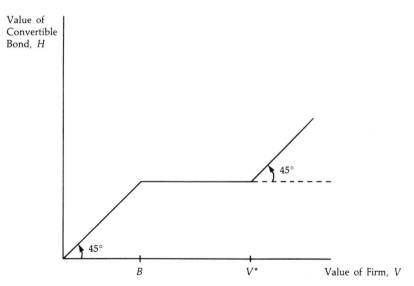

Figure 6–2 The value of a convertible bond at maturity as a function of the value of the firm

shares to which they have a right is greater than the value of the bond payment, then they will exercise. In particular, say the firm has N shares outstanding, and the bondholders have the option to acquire n shares of stock. If they
exercise their option, the firm will issue n more shares and distribute them to
the bondholders. The total number of shares outstanding in the firm will then
be $n + N$ shares. If the value of the firm at the time of exercise is V, the total
value of the convertible bonds will be $(n/(n + N))V$ (the total proportion of
the equity owned by the bondholders times the total value of the firm, if exercised). The quantity $(n/(n + N))V$ is called the *dilution factor*, and will be denoted by g. With this notation, the conversion value of the bond is then gV. If
they do not exercise their option at the end of the period, the convertible bondholders receive either the bond payment B or the value of the firm V, whichever is less. The convertible bonds will only be exercised if they are worth
more exercised than not. That is, a condition for exercise is that $gV \geq B$. This
implies that the convertibles will be exercised if the value of the firm is greater
than or equal to the critical value $V^* = B/g$. The value of the convertible on
the maturity date will then be

$$H(V, 0) = V \text{ if } 0 \leq V \leq B$$
$$= B \text{ if } B \leq V \leq V^*$$
$$= gV \text{ if } V^* \leq V.$$

The convertible bond is clearly a combination of a bond on the firm and
an option on the equity of the firm. The price of the convertible will thus reflect both of these features. If the value of the firm is very low, i.e., if V is
much lower than the value V^* which the firm must attain to make conversion
attractive, then the option portion of the convertible will be priced as a far out-
of-the-money option, and will have little value. The bulk of the convertible's
value will be represented by the bond feature. If the value of the firm is near
V^*, then the convertible is a combination of a near-the-money option and a
bond, and both will play an important part in determining the price of the
bond. The convertible will be priced more highly than a bond without the conversion feature, since the option in the convertible will hold a significant premium. And, if the value of the firm is much higher than V^*, so that the value of
the convertible will be worth much more as an option than as a bond, and will
almost certainly be exercised, then the convertible will be priced as an in-the-
money option, and may acquire some of the price features of the equity even
before it is exercised.

Since both the bond and the option features of the convertible can be priced using the Black-Scholes approach, one would expect that the convertible bond, as a combination of the two, can also be priced. Indeed it can, and its formula is given as

$$H(V, T, B) = D(V, T, B) + C(gV, T, B) \qquad (6.3)$$

where $D(V, T, B)$ is the value of the debt of the firm as stated in Equation (6.2), and $C(gV, T, B)$ is the value of an option with exercise price B, and with the underlying security having a value gV. Thus, the convertible bond is equal in value to a portfolio containing a discount bond as described earlier in this chapter and an option entitling the owner to purchase a fraction of the equity of the firm upon payment of the exercise price equal to the principal B of the bond. A convertible bond will thus be priced at a premium above a simple discount bond, with the premium being worth the value of the convertible's feature.

Convertible Bonds with Call Provisions

In practice, most convertible bonds are callable by the firm prior to maturity. That is, the bond contract specifies that the firm may re-purchase the convertibles for a specified payment to the bondholders of $K(T)$ at any given time before expiration. This feature of convertibles clouds the analysis somewhat, since now we are faced with a situation where the bondholders must take into account in their conversion decisions whether the firm will call the bonds if they do not exercise them. In Chapter 3 it was shown that a call option should not be exercised prior to maturity. The same proposition carries through here. The convertible bond will be worth more alive than dead, and optimally will not be exercised before maturity. But will it be in the best interest of the firm not to call the bond early? Intuitively, we would think they would have an interest in calling the bond if the value of the firm is sufficiently high, since if they call the bond they need pay only K, while if the bond is exercised, they may have to pay a larger amount if V is large. Such is the case. It is shown by Ingersoll (1977a) that if the value of the firm reaches $V^{**} = K(T)/g$, it will be in the firm's interest to call the bond. Thus, in practice, the maximum value of the convertible bond will be bounded and the bondholders will not enjoy the full benefits of the option feature.

Equation 6.3 can be modified to include a call provision. To do so, however, we must specify the functional relationship between the call price K and time. One natural specification to use, and the one that is used by Ingersoll in deriving the pricing formula for a callable convertible, is $K(T) = Be^{-\rho T}$, i.e., that the current call price is equal to the promised payment discounted at an interest rate ρ.

The larger ρ is, the larger the discount of the call provision will be. As a limiting case, when $\rho = r$, the price of a convertible bond with a call provision is

$$H(V, T) = D(V, T, B) + C(gV, T, B/g). \tag{6.5}$$

In this case, the value of the convertible bond is again simply equal to a portfolio containing an ordinary bond and a call option. This is similar to the valuation equation for the noncallable bond, except that the option in this case has an exercise price B/g. Since this exercise price is larger than that of the option for the noncallable convertible, the value of this option will be lower, illustrating again that the call provision reduces the value of the convertible.

FURTHER APPLICATIONS

The application of option theory is widespread, both in evaluating the financial assets of the firm and in understanding other financial practices. A few of these applications are outlined here. Others are mentioned in the references at the end of each chapter.

Pricing Financial Claims on the Firm

An option is a contingent claim—the claim of the optionholder is contingent on the price of the underlying security. Other financial instruments, including debt and equity, are contingent claims because their value is contingent on the value of the underlying firm. Thus the broader nomenclature of option theory is contingent claims theory.

We have shown how three of the contingent claims of the firm can be priced along the lines of the option theory we have developed. But the analysis can be extended past equity, debt, and convertible bonds, to any contingent claim on the firm—be it an income bond, mortgage bond, preferred stock, or whatever.

In many cases these securities cannot be analyzed as simply as the debt or convertible bonds can be, because the contract for their claim on the value of the firm is more complex. However, in principle, the price of any claim on the firm can be determined through the arbitrage argument that we have applied to the other securities in this chapter. Any asset on the firm can be replicated by a dynamic hedging strategy involving the equity of the firm and the riskless asset. The trick is to determine just what the proper hedging strategy is. Once that is known, then the price of the security can be determined on the basis of the arbitrage argument—the price must be set to equal the cost of replicating the security through the hedging strategy.

The solution technique for determining the value of contingent claims is outlined by Merton (1974). He derives a partial differential equation which, when solved according to the boundary conditions that are implicit in the contract for the contingent claim, will yield the correct price for that claim. There are several problems in extending the pricing techniques, however.

One problem with the use of this technique is that the differential equation cannot always be solved in closed form. In that case, numerical techniques must be used to solve the equation, and these techniques require considerable expertise and large computer capabilities to apply.

A second problem is that the arbitrage strategy is often not a real possibility. While with an option we have seen that an arbitrage hedge can be created, such a hedge may not be possible for other assets of the firm.

And finally, the only way to determine the value of the firm, which is a necessary input into pricing any contingent claim of the firm, is to compute the market value of the firm by adding up the sum of all assets that give a claim to the firm. This involves some circular reasoning since among the assets that must be included in this computation is the one that is being valued through the pricing technique. If the asset is mispriced, then the value of the firm that is obtained will be incorrect. And by using an incorrect input in the pricing formula, an incorrect price will come out. On the other hand, if the asset is correctly priced, then the input for the value of the firm will also be correct, but then the whole calculation is unnecessary, since the asset has been correctly priced by the market in the first place.

The pricing techniques will still be useful if it is assumed that the sum total of the assets of the firm leads to a correct valuation of the firm, but the division of the value of the firm across the assets of the firm is incorrect. The technique will also be useful if the objective is not to price the current assets of the firm, but rather to determine the correct price for a new offering. For underwriting purposes, then, this technique can be valuable in assessing the correct price for complex financial issues.

Loan Commitments

The recent volatility of interest rates has spurned the development of loan commitments, which guarantee the purchaser the right to obtain a loan at a specified interest rate on a given date in the future. These commitments are options on loans. If the going market rate for the loan is greater than the rate specified in the commitment, then the option will be exercised. On the other hand, if the rate drops by the maturity date of the commitment, then the commitment will be left to expire unused. Since these commitments are so similar to options, the same techniques that are used for evaluating the price of options can also be applied to them. Indeed, option theory provides one of the most accurate ways for determining the fair price of loan commitments.

Executive Incentives: The Case of Real Estate Investment Trusts (REITs)

The compensation package used widely by REITs lead to perverse results, which can be explained through option analysis. The analysts of REITs have often been given a compensation program that included a share in any net income of the firm above a preset amount. Their income stream is equal to a base salary plus a given percent of any net profit above some minimum level. If the salary is $15,000, and the package includes a 10-percent share of net income above $10 million, then the terminal value is similar to an option, $15,000 + \text{Max}\ (0,\ .1(N - \$10,000,000))$, where N is net income.

Unfortunately, in the case of REIT it turns out that the option portion of the contract is potentially far more valuable than the fixed salary portion, and the managers behave in a way that increases the value of the option with little concern for the fixed salary of $15,000. As was mentioned with the case of equity, the way to do this is to enter into highly volatile, but potentially highly profitable, enterprises. If they pay off, the return is high; if they do not, the downside risk is comparatively low—or at least it is low for the manager. With the incentive system designed in this way, it is not surprising that the REITs enter into highly speculative areas, and characteristically overextend themselves. The manager may act to maximize the value of an option, but to the detriment of the owners of the trust.

Exploratory Investment

Research and development, test marketing, mine surveying, and many other investments which are undertaken prior to the full scale implementation of a project may be analyzed as an option on that project. Categorized under the heading of exploratory investment, they help give the firm "strategic positioning" and further information on the profitability of the project. If the project is judged to have positive net present value (NPV) the option will be exercised and the project undertaken. It should be noted that the decision to take on the project should be based on the value of the project itself and not on the cost of the option since the option is a sunk cost. If the project has positive NPV it should be undertaken to help offset the option cost even if the NPV of the project plus the cost of the exploratory investment option is negative. Thus, the striking price of these options can be taken to be zero.

The use of a formal option pricing formula to evaluate exploratory investment is difficult. In principle, one can get estimates of the variance and value of the project (as viewed from the present), and the time period of the option is usually determined by the firm, but these estimates will usually be very rough. The greatest problem is that exploratory investment has value in addition to its strict financial value as an option since it provides information and expertise for the project. Although exact valuation is difficult, viewing exploratory investment as an option leads to two interesting observations.

First, since an option is more valuable the more volatile the underlying security (or in this case the underlying project), a given dollar expenditure on exploratory investment will be more valuable when it is spent on riskier projects, for a given present value. In practice this seems to be what happens—the more volatile industries spend the greatest amount on exploratory investment.

Second, treating exploratory investment as an option suggests a sensible way to evaluate these projects. One cannot correctly estimate the NPV of a project using traditional discounted cashflow methods if the costs of the exploratory investment are directly computed into the cashflow stream. This is because use of discounted cashflow assumes risk is resolved at a constant rate, and this assumption is violated when the risk of the exploratory investment is resolved at the expiration date, before the project itself even begins.

To illustrate this point, assume a firm is considering undertaking a project which requires $1,000 investment the first year and then will yield a return in perpetuity of either $250 or $0 per year, each with a probability of one-half. The firm decides to invest $125 in a year of test marketing after which it will be able to ascertain which outcome will result from further investment. Using traditional discounted cashflow calculations, one would compute NPV by taking the expected value of the project flows, in this case $125 the first year, $500 the second year, and +$125 each year thereafter. At a discounted rate of 15 percent, the NPV is approximately $70. Compare this result to the correct formulation of the problem, treating the first $125 as an option on the project. The project, if undertaken, has NPV of $666 (the present value of the perpetual $250 income stream is $1,666 from which we subtract the $1,000 initial outlay). Thus, at the expiration of the year of test marketing, the $125 option will have a 50-percent chance of being worth $666 and a 50-percent chance of being worth $0—for an expected value of $333—a far more attractive proposition than it would appear to be if analyzed with traditional methods.

REFERENCES

The original Black and Scholes (1973) option pricing paper contains some discussion of the application of their pricing techniques to other financial instruments. Merton (1974) presents a rigorous derivation of the pricing formula for various securities, including the equity and debt of a levered firm. He prices debt when it is in the form of a discount bond, and also when it is in the more usual form of a coupon bond with a terminal balloon payment. His derivation of these instruments is generally applicable to any contingent-claim security. He discusses the effect of the determinants of the variance and rate of return of these securities on their price and their relationship to the value of the unlevered firm. He also includes a discussion of the implications of the analysis to the Modiglianni-Miller proposition. The relevance of options to the Modiglianni-Miller proposition is also in Merton (1977b).

The application of option pricing techniques to convertible bonds is presented by Ingersoll (1977a, 1977b) and by Brennan and Schwartz (1977c). Merton (1977a) applies option theory to deposit insurance and Brennan and Schwartz (1976, 1979) apply it to equity-linked life insurance. Ingersoll (1976) uses option pricing techniques to analyze dual funds. Bartter and Rendleman (1979) discuss the application of option theory to bank loan commitments. Feiger and Jacquillant (1979) analyze multiple-currency bonds, a type of Eurobond that gives payment in any of a number of currencies at the bondholder's option, as an option that uses foreign currencies as the underlying security.

QUESTIONS

1. Suppose a silver mining company issues bonds that promise the holder a payment that has the following relationship to the price of silver: (1) If silver is below $20 an ounce, the mining company pays the bondholder $1,000 at the time of maturity. (2) If the price of silver at the time of maturity is between $20 and $50 an ounce, the company pays the bondholder

the current value of 50 ounces of silver. (3) If the price of silver is above $50 an ounce at the time of maturity, the company pays the bondholder $2,500.

a. Why might the company prefer to make such a contingent contract over the more conventional bond contract?

b. In what way is such a bond analogous to holding silver coins?

c. Use the binomial option pricing formula to derive a formula for this bond. (Assume the price of silver follows a binomial process.)

2. There has been some discussion of the government guaranteeing a price floor for oil produced from oil shale. Such a floor would give the producers of oil shale oil a price that is the maximum of the floor price or the market price. What would happen to the value of such an incentive to the oil shale producers if oil prices became more volatile?

3. In real estate limited partnerships, there is a general partner who selects a property to purchase (and who receives a front-end commission fee for finding and marketing the property), and limited partners who receive income and tax liabilities from the property. The property may be sold at any time at the option of the general partner. Once sold, any increase in the value of the property is divided between the general and limited partners. Any loss in the value of the property is completely absorbed by the limited partners. Describe this partnership arrangement as a set of option contracts. What incentives might the general partner have in the type of property he or she selects that will be against the interests of the limited partners?

4. U.S. Steel has recently issued a thirty-year bond which has interest rates that are set weekly to equal the higher of a) a fixed percentage of the thirteen-week Treasury Bill Discount Rate, or b) a fixed percentage of the thirty-year U.S. Treasury Bond Rate. The interest rate on the bond is allowed to fluctuate according to these rates within the bounds of 6 percent and 14 percent. Analyze this bond as a contingent claim on the underlying Treasury Bill Rate and Treasury Bond Rate. Show how option theory could be used to price the bond issue.

Chapter 7 TRADITIONAL OPTION TRADING STRATEGIES: SPREADS AND STRADDLES

Flying first class may be hard to justify in terms of the extra leg room and service, but in terms of the opportunities to meet people it can be quite worthwhile, even profitable. Besides meeting interesting people, one may become the beneficiary of valuable information. Once an investor recounted to me the events of a cross-country trip he had just taken. He could overhear the conversation of two gentlemen seated behind him. It was of little interest for most of the flight, dealing with technical matters of the computer industry. Then, toward the end of the flight, it started to get a bit livelier.

"The hardware is fully developed, but then our competitors have the hardware problems pretty much figured out, too."

The other man, seated directly behind him, said, "Well, then I wish you'd get the prototype developed and out. You know there's over half a billion dollars worth of defense contracts waiting out there if we can get the ECM system working."

Whenever the discussion mentions amounts in excess of a quarter of a billion dollars, I start to pay special attention. My friend does, too. He reclined his seat slightly, and while appearing to prepare for a nap, kept his ear tuned in through the crack between his seat and the adjoining cushion.

"I don't know why you guys don't move quicker," he continued. "If this thing comes out, Honeywell will take off. My options may even end up worth exercising," he added with a sarcastic mumble.

The other replied, "You must realize the problems we've been having with the software though. It hasn't even been clear whether our algorithm system is feasible for what we're doing. And we've had half our staff working on it for I don't know how long."

"I'm not the only one who knows that. If it doesn't come through, there will be a lot of disappointed investors. I know that Lockman Brothers is ready to unload all their stock if it doesn't work out."

"Well, you can stop living in suspense now. The feasibility studies for our software system have been completed. Six months ahead of schedule, I might add. And the results are conclusive that the system we've been working on is totally . . . " Just then the intercom drowned them out. "Ladies and gentlemen, we have just been cleared for landing. Please be seated, extinguish all smoking material, and return your seats to their original upright position."

Back to their conversation, it was apparent that my friend had missed a key remark. The man directly behind him said in an excited tone, "You're kidding! Has this been released yet?"

"No, as a matter of fact, I'm on my way to report it now. It will be public knowledge in three or four days. First we have to get our bases covered, if you know what I mean."

"Brother. When this hits the street, Honeywell is going to . . . " Once again the stewardess came on, and although he strained to do so, he could not hear the next critical word. "Ladies and gentlemen, we are ready for deplaning. Please check under your seats and into overhead compartments to make sure you do not leave any of your belongings. I hope you have enjoyed your flight, and thank you for flying with us."

They started to get up, and the one man wishfully commented, "Well, all I can say is I wish I weren't an insider. I could take care of my retirement on this one."

"You could always tell your mother-in-law, you know. Or should I say . . . "

"Yeah. Maybe my wife will take the tip in lieu of alimony."

The lady sitting next to him was too slow getting out, and they had exited before he could get off the plane. In reconstructing the conversation, there was no way he could discover whether the news was good or bad. While he knew that Honeywell was shortly going to either make a substantial increase or decline, he could not figure out which direction the move would be.

As he began to berate the bad timing of the flight attendant's announcements, I gave him some consolation. While some essential parts of the conversation were lost, I knew how he could use some option strategies to make a profit from the information no matter in which direction Honeywell turned. To find out how, read on.

STRADDLES

A *straddle* is a simultaneous transaction in both the call and put of a stock. When buying a straddle, the investor buys both a put and a call. When writing a straddle, the investor sells both a put and a call.

The straddle is an effective strategy if the investor has expectations concerning the future movement of the stock, but does not know the direction of the movement. The straddle is thus the perfect investment instrument for the eavesdropper in the start of the chapter. He has good information that Honeywell is going to have a large price change, but he does not know if the change will be up or down. If he buys a straddle on Honeywell, he will make money no matter which direction it moves, so long as it moves substantially.

Buying a Straddle

Consider the following quotes for the current Honeywell 70 calls and puts:

Honeywell

	Aug.	Nov.	Feb.	Stock price
Honeywell 70 call	2½	4½	6	70
Honeywell 70 put	2	4	4¾	70

With Honeywell trading at 70, he could buy an August 70 put for 2 and an August 70 call for 2½. His total initial dollar investment will be $450. If the company's announcement is favorable, and the stock in goes up to 80 by the August expiration date, the put will expire worthless, but the call will go up to 10. Since the initial cost of the position was 4½, his net gain will be the 5½ rise in his position, for a net profit of $550.

If the announcement is unfavorable, and causes the stock to drop to 60 by the expiration date of the option, the call will be worthless, but the put will now increase to 10, and again his net gain given the initial cost will be $550.

His maximum loss will occur if the stock stays unchanged at 70. Then both of the options will expire worthless, and he will lose the initial investment of $450.

These and other possibilities are laid out in Table 7–1. The profit profile for the straddle is shown in Figure 7–1 by plotting the value of the position (in hundred-dollar terms) as a function of the price of the stock at the time of the August expiration.

Table 7-1
Profit from Buying Honeywell August 70 Straddle

Stock price at August expiration	Initial value of position	Value at expiration		Net value of position (initial value − value at expiration)
		Value of Aug. 70 call	Value of Aug. 70 put	
60	− 4½	0	10	5½
65½	− 4½	0	4½	0 .
70	− 4½	0	0	− 4½
74½	− 4½	4½	0	0
80	− 4½	10	0	5½

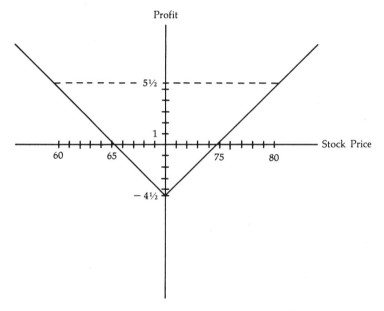

Figure 7-1 Profit profile at expiration from buying a Honeywell 70 straddle

The straddle allows investors to take a position based on their expectations of the volatility of the stock, as opposed to their expectations of the future price. If their estimate of the volatility is more accurate than the estimate currently imputed in the options' prices, the investors will be able to profit from their superior estimate by taking a position in a straddle.

Writing a Straddle

The example of the eavesdropper illustrates the benefits of buying a straddle when the investor expects the volatility of the stock to be greater than the expectations held by the market. Selling a straddle will be the correct strategy if the volatility of the stock is being overestimated.

For example, say a tender offer is announced on Avon at an offer price of 50 per share. The stock, which had been selling at 42, moves up to 50 immediately after the offer is made, so that the investor cannot take advantage of any price differential to make a profit. But, depending on the perceptibility of the market, profits may still be possible through the use of a straddle.

During the period of the tender offer, the stock will be far less volatile than it has been historically. It will not be likely to move far from the offer price. By writing a straddle on the stock, the investor can take advantage of this reduction in volatility. Once the stock rises to 50, say the Avon 50 call and put options are priced as follows:

Avon
Sept. 10

	Oct.	*Jan.*	*Apr.*	*Stock close*
Avon 50 call	2½	4⅝	5½	50
Avon 50 put	2	3⅞	4½	50

The investor writes a straddle by selling both an October 50 put and call. The net position initially is then the combined premium value of 4½. If the stock remains at 50 through the expiration date (which is likely to be the case if the tender offer continues for the duration), then both options will expire worthless, and the investor will make a $450 profit.

Of course, the investor need not hold the options to expiration. Over time both options will diminish in value, so if there is no price change, the investor could close out the position after a few weeks with a profit. Or, the market may come to realize, later than the investor, that the volatility of the stock has diminished. The option prices will drop as the market reprices them, based on this new estimate of the variance.

If the effect of the tender offer on the volatility of the stock is misjudged, and it moves out of the $50 range in either direction, the straddle writer stands to lose. If the Avon stock rises to $60, the put will be worthless, but the call will increase to 10. In order to cover the position, the investor will need to pay $1,000 for the call, and will face a net loss of $550.

The effect of various stock prices at the time of expiration are shown in Table 7-2, and the resulting profit profile is shown by the solid line in Figure 7-2.

As the profit profile suggests, writing a straddle is quite risky because the investor is writing both a naked call and a naked put. There is no protection against a large move in the stock price in either direction, so there is a potential for an unlimited loss. For example, if Avon rose to $150 a share, it would take

Table 7-2
Profit from Selling Avon October 50 Straddle

Stock price at October expiration	Initial value of position	Value at expiration		Net value of position (initial value − value at expiration)
		Oct. 50 call	Oct. 50 put	
40	4½	0	− 10	− 5½
45½	4½	0	− 4½	0
50	4½	0	0	4½
54½	4½	− 4½	0	0
60	4½	− 10	0	− 5½

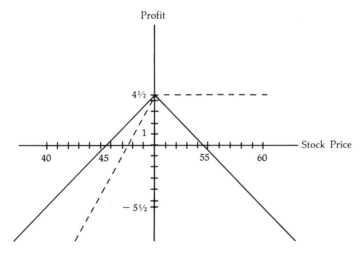

Figure 7-2 Profit profile at expiration from writing an Avon October 50 straddle naked (solid line) and covered (broken line)

$10,000 to cover the call option. A less risky method of employing this strategy is to write covered straddles. This is nothing more than writing both a covered call and a covered put on the stock. When writing a covered straddle, the investor is faced with one of three possibilities. First, the stock may not move from the exercise price, and the writer will keep both premiums and the stock. Second, the stock will increase in price, and the writer will keep both premiums but lose the stock and the value of the appreciation in the stock price. Third, the stock decreases in price, and the writer must buy 100 shares of the stock at the exercise price, thus ending up with the two premiums and 200 shares of the stock. The profit profile for the covered straddle is also shown in Figure 7-2 by the dotted line.

When to Use the Straddle

The overheard conversation and the tender offer are just two examples of when a straddle strategy will be useful. Any uncertainty in the firm that will have a significant effect on the stock price, and that will be shortly resolved, represents a potential profit opportunity. For example, during a merger or takeover attempt, the stock will usually be positioned between two price extremes and will move to one of the two extremes after the uncertainty regarding the success of the attempt is resolved. Or, if a firm is scheduled to make an important announcement, such as the success of a recent research project or the oil yield of a recently explored field, an increase in the future volatility of the stock may be expected—the stock going up if it is good news and down if it is bad. While immediately after the announcement the price will adjust without any unusual profit opportunities, a straddle position may allow the investor to profit no matter which direction the stock turns.

The following two examples illustrate the profit potential of these strategies.

Selling a Straddle When the Volatility Is Expected to Drop: Carrier Corporation

Carrier Corporation was subject to a takeover bid by United Technology Corporation. This announced takeover was made on September 19, 1978. United Technology offered $28 a share for all outstanding stock. The offer was to expire December 3, 1978. Stock and option trading was suspended on the U.S. Exchange on September 19, and trading was resumed on September 26. If a straddle was written on September 26, it would have been purchased for $550 on a December 25 option. The December 25 straddle was chosen because the insurance premium is the greatest on an option that is close to the money and has sufficient time to move. The option price varied slightly and always hovered close to the exercise price. In closing the position the day before expiration, the investor would have netted $362.50 (transaction cost ignored) on one contract of options. The merger had still not been resolved and so given the assumptions that another three months period of time would elapse before the completion of the takeover, and that the insurance price for the option was still overpriced, the investor could have written another straddle.

Carrier Corporation
December 25 Options

Date	Call	Put	Stock price
September 26	$4\frac{1}{4}$	$1\frac{1}{4}$	$27\frac{3}{4}$
December 14	$\frac{1}{16}$	$1\frac{13}{16}$	$23\frac{3}{8}$

Buying a Straddle When the Volatility Is Expected to Rise: IBM

In 1969 the United States Justice Department filed an anti-trust lawsuit against IBM. During the four years after 1969, nineteen companies also filed suits against IBM claiming damages caused by its monopoly powers.

The largest of the nineteen company suits against IBM was filed by Memorex. They claimed that IBM had violated the Sherman Act and the Clayton Act. Specifically, they claimed that IBM had made unnecessary product changes, manipulated prices, and altered tie-in arrangements for peripheral products after an extensive study of Memorex. This suit was for $306 million in damages, on which the judge could award triple damages, making it nearly a billion dollars. This was a pivotal trial—if Memorex were to lose this case the chances were high that all the other suits would also fail.

On July 6 the jury was deadlocked, 9 to 2 in favor of Memorex. The judge declared a mistrial because of a hung jury. Memorex asked for a new jury trial. IBM asked for a directed verdict from the judge in their favor. The judge had to rule on their requests by the next month.

The extreme importance of this case to IBM, and the fact that in about one month's time it could be concluded in their favor or against them, made this a volatile situation—and an excellent opportunity to buy a straddle. At the time the mistrial was declared and the two companies made their requests to the judge, the options were priced with only a small premium for volatility. Once the final decision on the case was made, the stock would be expected to make a drastic move.

The July options were not useful for this straddle as they would expire prior to the judge's decision. Therefore, an October 240 straddle would be advisable. The initial straddle position, taken on July 6, cost $2,662.50.

IBM
October 240 Options

Date	Call	Put	Stock price
July 6	22⅝	4	257½
August 14	53¼	⅜	289

Prior to the mistrial verdict on July 6, 1978, the market seemed to have been discounting IBM's stock in anticipation of a verdict against them by a jury that was favoring Memorex. When the mistrial was declared, the stock recovered the nearly three points it had lost. By mid-July the press was saying that IBM would probably win the directed verdict it had requested. The stock rose another ten points.

The press had indicated that the judge's verdict had to be given shortly after August 4, 1978. Apparently in anticipation of that, the stock jumped up twelve points on August 3. It fell a little on August 4, but remained high until August 14, when IBM won the directed verdict. Selling on that day gave a net return of $2,700.00.

The stock continued to go up to 297. Thus the more patient investor could have realized an even greater return from this strategy.

Of course, the profitability of these strategies depends on the investor having a better perception of the future variance than the market has already imputed into the option price. If the option price is efficient in correctly estimating and incorporating the future volatility of the stock, then profits cannot be made through the use of straddle strategies any easier than they can through estimation of the future course of the stock price. The efficiency of the market, as far as the stock price and expected stock price changes are concerned, has been extensively tested with mostly positive results.

No statements are yet possible with regard to the efficiency of option prices with respect to correctly estimating the expected stock volatility. Indeed, as was mentioned earlier, it is the estimation of the instantaneous variance of the stock price and the difficulties, both practical and theoretical, in allowing for changes in the variance over time, that are the weak point in the option pricing formula. And if a large enough portion of the market uses techniques based on the historical data to estimate the variance of the stock price or use pricing models which are based on the assumption that the stock variance is constant over time, then price discrepancies may well appear which the more astute investor can profit from.

To gain some insight into the straddle, recall that both the put and call give insurance against stock movements. The call protects the investor against a rise in the stock price, and the put protects the investor against a fall in the price. To insure against any movement in the stock, it follows that an investor should buy both a call and a put. In buying a straddle, the investor is buying this "full-insurance package." Profit comes from being able to buy the insurance for less than its true value. If the market is underestimating the risk of the stock, it will issue the insurance against that risk, the put and call options, at below the fair price. When the true risk of the stock is later realized, the price of the insurance in the market will increase. In other words, the value of both the put and call will increase, and the investor's straddle is worth more.

When writing a straddle, the investor is in effect issuing insurance against both upside and downside risk. That is, the investor is insuring the buyer of the straddle against any large movement in the stock. If investors in the market are overestimating the risk of a price movement in the stock, they will be willing to pay more for the insurance than it is worth, and the straddle writer, by issuing the insurance when it is overpriced, will make more than the fair return for issuing it.

SPREADS

A *spread* is the simultaneous purchase of one option and sale of another option on the same stock, with the two options differing in time to expiration or in exercise price.

A spread formed by buying one call option while selling another option on the same stock at a different exercise price is called a *vertical spread*. A spread formed by buying one option while selling another option on the stock with a different expiration date is called a *time spread*, *calendar spread*, or *horizontal spread*. The terms *vertical* and *horizontal* come about because options differing according to exercise price are listed vertically in the published option quotations, while the price quotes on options differing in terms of time to expiration are listed horizontally.

Horizontal Spreads

A horizontal spread involves buying one option while selling another option on the same stock with a different expiration date but with the same exercise price. For example, the investor can establish an Avon January–October 45 spread by buying a January 45 call for $4\frac{1}{2}$ while simultaneously writing an October 45 call for 3.

Avon

September 20

	Oct.	Jan.	Apr.	Stock close
Avon 45	3	$4\frac{1}{2}$	6	46

The initial cost of the position is $150, the difference between the $450 call that is bought and the $300 call that is written. If the stock price remains at 45 at the October expiration date, then the October option will expire worthless. The investor will retain the $300 premium on that stock free and clear. The January option will have reduced in price as well, since it now has less time-to-expiration. The time deterioration on an option is less severe the longer its time-to-expiration. Although the October option declined three points over the time period, the January option, with three more months left to expiration, will still have a premium remaining. Say the January 45 drops to 3 by the time of the October expiration if the stock price remains at $45. This represents a $1\frac{1}{2}$ point decline in its time premium. A profit of $150 will be netted if the investor's spread is liquidated: the $300 value of the January 45 option minus the $150 initial cost of the position.

If the stock moves away from the 45 exercise price, the profit will be reduced. For example, if the stock drops in value to $30, the October option will again expire worthless, but the January option will be priced far below the 3 it would have been worth if the stock had remained at 45. If the January option drops to $\frac{1}{4}$ with the sharp decline in the stock, the investor will realize a $125 loss: the $150 initial cost less the $25 value of the January 45 option that is held. This is shown in Table 7–3.

Similarly, if the stock increases in value, the spread will be less profitable. If the stock goes up to $60 a share, the October 45 will be worth $15 at the time of expiration, and the January 45 will have only a small premium because it is so far into the money. If the January 45 is at $15\frac{1}{2}$, the investor will lose $100 in the transaction.

The profit profile for this spread is shown in Figure 7–3. The maximum loss is the difference between the value of the long and short position, which is called the *basis* of the spread. This maximum loss will occur if the option stock

Table 7-3
Profit from Avon January–October 45 Spread

Stock price at October expiration	Initial value of position	Value at expiration		Net value of position (initial value − value at expiration)
		Value of Oct. 45	Value of Jan. 45	
30	− 1½	0	¼	− 1¼
40	− 1½	0	1	− ½
45	− 1½	0	3	1½
50	− 1½	5	6	− ½
60	− 1½	15	15½	− 1

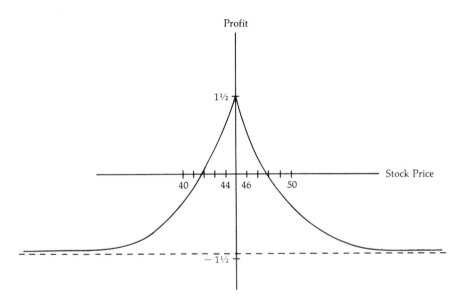

Figure 7-3 Profit profile at October expiration from an Avon January–October 45 spread

price drops substantially, so both positions become nearly worthless, or if the stock rises substantially, so both options have nearly the same value.

The central tradeoff in this strategy is between the change in the basis with the change in the time-to-expiration and the change in the basis with a change in stock price.

The time premium deteriorates at an increasing rate as the time-to-expiration is approached. Thus, there is a negligible change in the price of an option over a one-week period when there are months left to expiration, but a significant change in the price if there are just a few weeks left to expiration. The time spread takes advantage of this since the value of the shorter maturity option will decrease rapidly and the premium gained from writing it will accrue to the investor through a short position, while the value of the longer maturity option will stay virtually the same. Buying a horizontal spread will be more attractive the closer the shorter-term option is to expiration and the closer the price of the two options or the narrower the basis of the spread. If the two options are selling at the same price, a profit is assured, since when the shorter-term option expires, the longer-term option will still have a premium.

While the passage of time will increase the spread between the premiums of the two options, a movement in the stock price away from the exercise price will tend to decrease the spread. The premium on the option decreases as the option goes further into the money, and an increase in the stock price will thus diminish the premium gained on the longer option. Similarly, if both options go far out-of-the-money, the premium on the longer option will diminish relative to the premium on the shorter option. However, since the premium on the shorter-term option cannot exceed that of the longer-term option, the total loss is limited to the cost of the investor's long position minus the premium gained from the short position or the basis of the spread.

The maximum loss on a spread may be contrasted with the unlimited loss possible on a short position when a position on the longer maturity option is not also taken. The investor will then have simply written a naked option. He or she will still gain from the decrease in the time premium, but is highly exposed to an increase in the stock price. By adding the long position on the longer maturity option and creating a spread, the investor has reduced this risk. The long position in the spread essentially acts as a hedge to limit the maximum possible loss.

The alternative horizontal spread is to buy the shorter-term option and sell the longer-term option. In this case, the investor will benefit from a rise or decline in the stock price, and will lose money if the stock remains near the exercise price. Using the Avon example, the investor buys the October 45 call and sells the January 45 call. The investor collects the basis of 1½ if the two options become equal in value, which will occur either through both going far into the money, or through dropping far out of the money. The profit profile for this spread is the reverse of that for buying longer term and selling the shorter term.

This spread is not as common as the other horizontal spread. There is a margin requirement because the long position does not cover a short position on an option with a longer time to maturity, and there is a greater risk of exposure on the short side.

Other Spreads

The number and variety of spreads are almost limitless, since a spread of some sort can be formed by shorting and longing any two options on the same stock. They all have two things in common: by limiting the risk from the short side, they concentrate on the range of the future stock price rather than its direction, and by generating large commissions, they assure ready advocates for just about any strategy the investor can create. We will mention several of the more common spreads which seem to present a useful return structure for some strategies.

Vertical spread. A vertical spread involves buying an option at one exercise price while selling another option on the same stock at a different exercise price but with the same maturity date. For example, as is illustrated in Figure 7–4, an investor could form a vertical 50–60 spread on Polaroid by buying the January

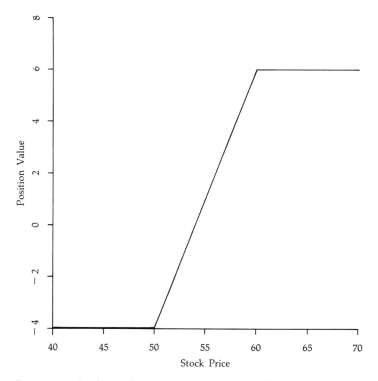

Figure 7-4 Profit profile at expiration for a Polaroid January 50–60 spread

50 for 8 while selling the January 60 for 4. If Polaroid goes above 60, both options are into the money, and the investor will gain the 10-point differential in the exercise prices, for a net profit of 6. If both options drop out-of-the-money, the investor will lose the net investment of 4 points that was invested to create the spread. If the stock price falls between 50 and 60, net profit will simply be the difference between the stock price and the exercise price of 50 minus the investor's basis of 4.

As the profit profile for this spread suggests, the vertical spread is like writing a covered option, except that the maximum loss from the spread is limited. Rather than covering the option with a position in the stock, the investor covers the stock position with a long position on another option. So, if the stock has a large decline, only the premium of the long option is lost. This strategy thus has the same application as writing covered options. The investor will be better off employing this strategy than simply holding a long position in the stock if the stock price is expected to make only small price movements during the holding period of the option. But forming a vertical spread will be preferable to writing an option with the stock as a cover if the investor wants to be protected against the possibility of a large decline in the stock price.

The alternative vertical spread is to sell the option with the lower exercise price and buy the option with the higher exercise price. For example, a vertical 60–50 spread with Polaroid involves buying the 60 for 4 while selling the 50 for 8. If the stock drops below the 50, the investor will keep the basis of $4. The maximum loss occurs if both options of the stock is above the 60 exercise price, since then the shorted option will be worth ten points more than the long option, and the investor will have a net loss of the ten-point difference in the exercise price less the four-point basis, for a net loss of six. The profit profile for this spread is the reverse of that for the other vertical spread. Because the potential loss is greater than the intrinsic value of the position, this spread requires that the investor put up margin. There is a margin requirement for this spread.

This spread will be profitable if the stock declines in value. It represents a short position on the stock, but with an option taken out to partially cover that position, and thereby puts a floor on the maximum possible loss that can be incurred.

Butterfly spread. This spread involves selling two options, one with a high exercise price and one with a low exercise price, and buying two options at the exercise price in between the two. For example, a butterfly spread on Polaroid could be formed by selling the Polaroid 40 and 60 for 14 and 4 respectively, while buying two Polaroid 50's for 8. The investor receives a net inflow of 2 from the premiums.

The option price is a convex function of the exercise price. That is, the sum of the prices of an option with a high exercise price and a low exercise price will exceed the price of two options with an exercise price halfway in between. In this example, this means the combined value of the Polaroid 40 and 60 will be greater than the value of the two Polaroid 50 options.

This property of option pricing assures that the two short positions in the butterfly option will be worth more than the long position in the intermediate options, so that initially the butterfly spread will yield a net inflow. The hope of the investor is to establish the spread when the basis is large and then have the basis diminish. This will occur if the stock moves substantially away from the intermediate exercise price.

If the stock drops below the lowest exercise price of 40, all the options will become worthless, and the investor will gain the difference of 2. If the stock rises and all the options go into the money, the premiums will diminish, in the limit going to zero, so that again the investor will gain the whole difference of 2. The maximum loss occurs if the stock is at 50 on the expiration date, since the investor must then cover the short position on the 40 call, with a net loss of 8. The profit profile of Figure 7–5 shows the value of the spread on expiration date. Large movements in the stock price will increase the value of

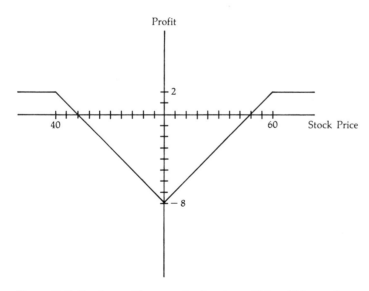

Figure 7–5 Profit profile at expiration for a Polaroid butterfly spread

the spread before this date, since even before the expiration date the premia on the options will diminish as all the options either go far into the money or far out of the money.

Sandwich spread. The sandwich spread is the opposite of the butterfly spread. While with the butterfly spread the investor hopes to catch the stock price in the wings of the butterfly formed by the spread, with the sandwich spread the investor hopes to sandwich the stock between two prices. To put a sandwich spread on Polaroid, the investor would buy the 40 and 60 options and sell two 50 options. This spread will cost money to form and will be profitable if the stock stays near the price of the intermediate exercise price. Profit will be maximized if the stock trades at 50, since then the investor will have the value of the 40 option while the two 50 options will be worthless. The maximum loss is limited to the initial net investment, the basis of the spread, since the value of the two short positions cannot exceed the value of the two long positions. The profit profile for this spread is shown in Figure 7–6. Note that its return structure is the negative of the butterfly spread.

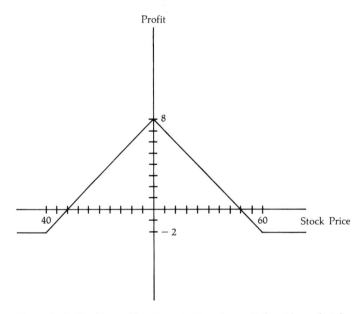

Figure 7–6 Profit profile at expiration for a Polaroid sandwich spread

The sandwich and butterfly spreads will yield an investor profits under the same conditions that buying or writing a straddle will. The butterfly spread will earn a profit if the volatility of the stock increases, while the sandwich spread will be profitable if the stock becomes less volatile. They present the investor a good strategy when there is no put traded on the stock.

The sandwich spread also has the advantage of limiting the possible loss if the stock makes a large move. It is thus a more prudent strategy than writing a naked straddle. However, as with the other spreads, the commissions can be significant and wipe out an apparent profit.

Diagonal spread. This is a combination of a vertical and a horizontal spread. The option written differs in both maturity and exercise price from the option that is bought. Such a spread seems to add more complication than anything else to the choice of option strategies, because it is difficult to compute the return structure and the value of the hedge.

One possible diagonal spread is to buy the longer-term low exercise price option and sell the shorter-term high exercise price option. For example, with Polaroid selling at 55, one would buy the January 50 for 8 and sell the October 60 for $1\frac{1}{2}$. The net position is, naturally, a cross between a horizontal and a vertical spread. As October approaches, the premium on the October option diminishes, and the investor gains the premium.

The investor's net exposure is greater than with simply a vertical or a horizontal spread since the investor's basis is larger. And if the stock rises in price, the difference between the price of the two options will narrow, with the minimum difference being the ten points that separate the exercise prices. If the stock drops, the difference in the price of the two options will also narrow, with the prices both going to zero. Thus, the investor faces a maximum gain from the change in the time premium of $1\frac{1}{2}$, a maximum gain of 2 from the exercise price differential of 10, and a maximum loss of $6\frac{1}{2}$ if both options drop out of the money. As can be seen from the profit profile (Figure 7–7), the maximum gain possible exceeds the ten-point differential in the exercise price because the investor is also earning the premium of the shorted option if it expires worthless.

With both the exercise price and the time to maturity as variables, there are many other possibilities for diagonal spreads. One could sell the longer-term high exercise price option and buy the shorter-term low exercise price option, sell the longer-term low exercise price option and buy the shorter-term high exercise price option, and so on.

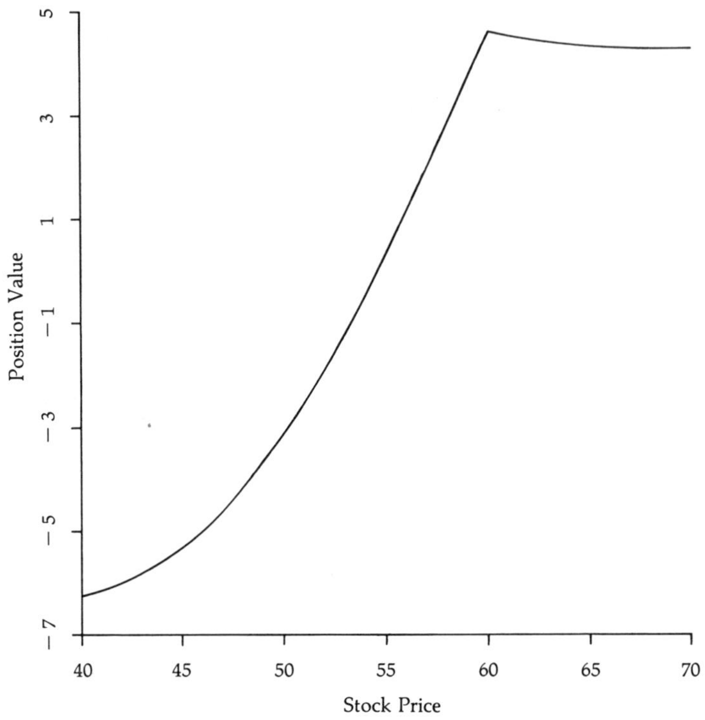

Figure 7–7 Profit profile at October expiration for a Polaroid 50–60 diagonal spread

Box Spread. To illustrate the great variety of option strategies, consider the following box spread that one broker has used profitably on several occasions. In a box spread, the investor holds the stock, buys a put with a low exercise price, buys a call with a high exercise price, and writes two calls with an exercise price in between the other two. To illustrate this, consider the following prices for Aetna:

Aetna

	January	*April*	*July*	*Stock close*
Aetna 25 call	6¼	6½	6¾	31
25 put	½	1	1¾	31
30 call	2½	2¾	3½	31
30 put	1½	2	2⅝	31
35 call	1	1½	2	31
35 put	5	5¼	5¾	31

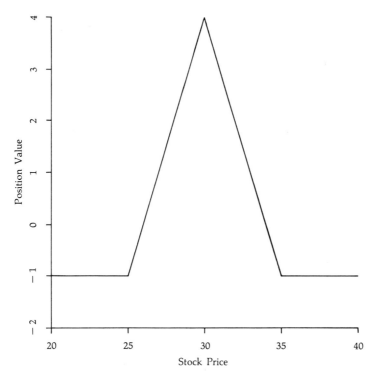

Figure 7-8 Profit profile for the Aetna January box spread

To create a January box spread on Aetna, buy a January 25 put for ½, a 35 call for 1, hold 100 shares of stock, and write two January 30 calls for 2½ each. The put protects the downside of the position, while the two written calls will counteract any profits on the stock and the 35 call from a substantial price rise. As Figure 7-8 shows, the box spread boxes the investor in—this strategy turns a profit as long as the stock stays within the prescribed range. The box spread has a profit profile like the sandwich spread, but may have tax benefits that the sandwich spread does not, and will also be preferred to the sandwich spread when the investor holds the underlying stock.

A Few Other Considerations in Trading Spreads

The profit margin for each spread is small, so spreads are usually transacted in large blocks with ten or twenty options in each position. This brings practical problems to option spreading.

First, there is difficulty in executing large blocks simultaneously, so the investor may be partially exposed, with short positions not fully covered. Or, he may not have all contracts transacted at the quoted price.

Second, spreads involve large transactions costs. A short and a long position taken on a large block of options, and later closed, make the commissions a very important consideration in determining the profitability of a spread. The spread is undoubtedly the stockbroker's favorite strategy, but careful analysis must be used by the investor in determining its potential.

WHAT THESE STRATEGIES TELL US ABOUT OPTION TRADING

The traditional option strategies discussed in this chapter contain the essential points of the more sophisticated option strategies which will be discussed later. First, the initiation of the strategy is usually based on the mispricing of options, not on anticipations about the future direction of the stock price. Second, the position provides some protection against stock movements. While the hedge is imperfect, it gives some protection against the direction of the stock change, although not against the magnitude of that change. With the exception of the vertical spread and the diagonal spread (which in part is a vertical spread), the investor's loss depends on the size of the stock price movement and not on the direction of that movement. Thus, while betting on the volatility of the stock, the investor is not betting on which way the stock will go. When buying a straddle, the investor is betting the options are underpriced. If the market underestimated the future volatility, both the call and the put will be selling at too low a price. In writing a straddle, the options are thought to be overpriced, with the market overestimating the volatility of the stock. The investor profits from this mispricing by writing both the put and the call. Of course, the investor can take advantage of the mispricing by taking a position in just the call or just the put, but profit may be jeopardized by an unfavorable turn in the direction of the stock. The investor has a sort of hedge by transacting in both of the options. Profit will be independent of the direction (though not the magnitude) of any stock price change.

The popular horizontal spread is another example of this, and it provides the best model for the option strategies which will be discussed later. The motivation for initiating a horizontal spread is usually an excessive time premium for an option that is close to expiration. The investor writes that option to get the premium. Rather than be in the position of writing a naked option, the investor covers the position by buying another option. This second option is a hedge to eliminate some of the risk from an unfavorable shift in the stock price. If the stock rises in value, the investor will lose on the option he or she wrote, but make up for it on the option that was bought. The options may not be held in the ideal hedge ratio, so that protection from shifts in the stock price may not be complete. And if the hedge position is not adjusted over time or as the stock price changes, then the protection will be further eroded. But the objective of the strategy—writing an overpriced option and buying another option to hedge the position—is correct.

REFERENCES

The Chicago Board Option Exchange and the American Stock Exchange have a number of booklets that present a practical guide for option spreads and straddles. These guides are available through most brokerage houses that trade on the option exchanges. Books by Bookbinder (1976), Clasing (1978), Gastineau (1979), and Henin and Ryan (1977), all contain several chapters on the use of the traditional strategies. These books do not make full use of the recent findings on option pricing in forming or in explaining the strategies, however.

Chapter 8 OPTION TRADING STRATEGIES: PROFIT POTENTIAL AND RISK

The option strategies discussed in the previous chapter dealt with the traditional tools of option trading. The recent developments of option analysis permit us to extend these strategies to a more general framework. We can consider the profitability of option positions that are closed before the expiration date and that use a variable option hedge. We can also determine the risk of an option position and the sensitivity of an option hedge to changes in the stock price.

These techniques, which help us assess the risk and the profitability of option positions as the time-to-expiration and the stock price change, provide the tools for successfully evaluating alternative option strategies.

This chapter relies on the option analysis covered in the first part of the book. We use the results of the option pricing formula to introduce a method for evaluating option positions that in practice is more effective than the methods commonly used. In the next section, we will show how to evaluate option positions, and how the value of the positions will change with changes in the stock price or the time-to-expiration. We will then show how to determine the correct hedge position for an option strategy. In the final section, we will show how the risk and the exposure of the strategy is affected by changes in the stock price.

EVALUATING THE PROFIT POTENTIAL

Consider two options with prices C_1 and C_2. The number of the first option held is n_1, and the number of the second option held is n_2. If the option is held long, n is positive; while if the option is written, n is negative.

The value of the option position V will equal the value of each of the options multiplied by the size of the position in each of the options:

$$V = n_1C_1 + n_2C_2. \tag{8.1}$$

We can compute the value of C_1 and C_2 from the option formula, and since the size of the position in each option is known, the value of the position can be determined for any time-to-maturity and for any stock price. This will be useful for the investor who is considering liquidating position at some time before the option's expiration date. To illustrate this method of evaluating the option position, consider some of the strategies covered in the last chapter.

Time Spread

Suppose we hold a time spread on Polaroid. We write the April 50 and cover the short position by buying a July 50. The hope is that Polaroid will stay near the exercise price of the option, and as the time to the April expiration approaches we will gain the premium on the April 50 option. If we hold 10 options in each position, the value of the position will be

$$V = -10C_1 + 10C_2$$

where the subscript 1 denotes the April 50 option and the subscript 2 denotes the July 50 option.

If we are interested in what the value of the position will be with one month to expiration and if the stock price at that time is 45, we use these values in the option pricing formula for the two options to compute the value of C_1 and C_2. Let the interest rate, r, equal 6 percent, and the volatility of the stock, σ, be .3. Then the value of the options, written explicitly as a function of the stock price, time-to-expiration, exercise price, interest rate, and volatility will be:

$$C_1 = C(45, .0833, 50, .06, .3) = .25$$
$$C_2 = C(45, .3333, 50, .06, .3) = 1.63.$$

The time to expiration is expressed in annual terms, so the April option, with one month to expiration, has .0833 years to expiration, and the July option has one-third of a year to expiration.

Using these values in Equation (8.1), we find the value of the position when there is one month to the April expiration and the stock price is 45 to be

$$V = (-10 \times .25) + (10 \times 1.63) = 13.80.$$

Measuring Profit Potential with the Profit Profile

The same exercises can be done for other values of the stock price and for other times-to-expiration. If there is one month to expiration and the stock price is at $50, the value of the position will be

$$V = -10C(50, .0833, 50, .06, .3) + 10C(50, .3333, 50, .06, .3).$$

Computing the value of the options with the Black-Scholes pricing formula, we have

$$V = (-10 \times 1.85) + (10 \times 3.93) = -18.50 + 39.30 = 20.80.$$

By going through the same procedure for other values of the stock, we can tabulate the value of the option position as shown in column 4 of Table 8–1. This column shows the value of the position as a function of the stock price when there is one month to the April expiration. By subtracting the initial cost of the option position, we can tabulate the profit from the position if the option position is liquidated with one month to April expiration. This can then be used to plot the profit profile.

If the April 50 options were 1 when written, and the July 50's were 1½ when bought, then the cost of the investor's position would be

$$(-10 \times 1) + (10 \times 1\frac{1}{2}) = 5.$$

Table 8–1
Value of Position with One Month to April Expiration

(1) Stock price	(2) C(S,.0833, 50,.06,.3)	(3) C(S,.333, 50,.06,.3)	(4) Position value (column (3 − 2) × 10)	(5) Profit from position (column 4 − $5 initial position cost)
45	.25	1.63	13.80	8.80
46	.41	1.99	15.80	10.80
47	.64	2.40	17.60	12.60
48	.95	2.87	19.20	14.20
49	1.36	3.38	20.20	15.20
50	1.85	3.93	20.80	15.80
51	2.44	4.54	21.00	16.00
52	3.11	5.18	20.70	15.70
53	3.85	5.87	20.20	15.20
54	4.66	6.59	19.30	14.30

Subtracting this cost from the value of the position, we obtain the values in column 5, the net profit from the position with one month to April expiration. This profit is plotted against the stock price in Figure 8-1 to give the profit profile.

Figure 8-1 has the same interpretation as the profit profiles used in the previous chapter. However, here the value of the position is given for a time before the expiration date.

If we go through the same process for a different time to the April expiration, we can get a second graph. In Figure 8-2, the profit profile of the time spread is drawn for several times to expiration. Besides the one month to expiration we have already derived, Figure 8-2 also graphs the value of the position as a function of the stock price for three months and for the date of expiration.

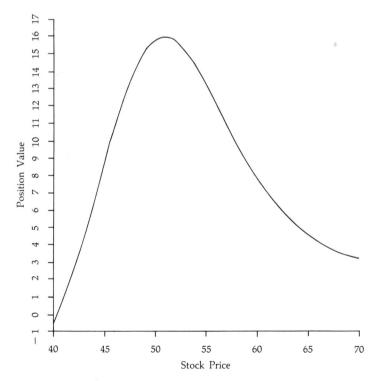

Figure 8-1 Profit profile for a Polaroid April–July 50 spread with one month to April expiration

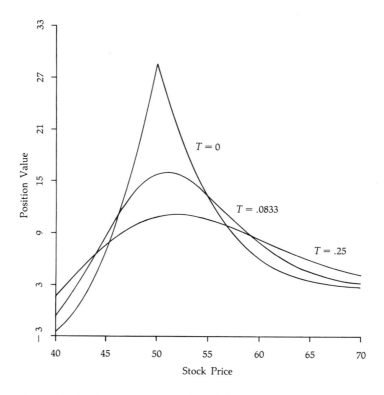

Figure 8-2 Profit profile for a Polaroid April–July 50 spread (*T* denotes the time to April expiration)

Vertical Spread

For the vertical spread, the time-to-maturity for the two options is the same, but the exercise prices of the two differ. Let us compute the value of a vertical spread on Polaroid. Suppose the investor buys an April 50 and sells an April 60, at a net cost of $4. The value of the investor's position with one month left to expiration will be

$$V = C(S, .0833, 50, .06, .3) - C(S, .0833, 60, .06, .3).$$

By using various values for the stock price in the formula, the investor can plot out the profit profile of the position. The position is assumed to cost 4 to put on. The profit profile for six months, three months, and one month to maturity, as well as the value of the position at maturity is presented in Figure 8-3.

Table 8–2
Value of Vertical Spread, Three Months to Expiration

(1) Stock price	(2) C(S,.25, 50,.06,.3)	(3) C(S,.25, 60,.06,.3)	(4) Position value (column 3 − 2)	(5) Profit from position (column 4 − $4 initial position cost)
46	1.51	.15	1.36	− 2.64
47	1.89	.22	1.67	− 2.33
48	2.32	.22	2.10	− 1.90
49	2.81	.41	2.40	− 1.60
50	3.35	.54	2.81	− 1.19
51	3.95	.71	3.24	− .76
52	4.59	.91	3.68	− .32
53	5.29	1.14	4.15	− .15
54	6.02	1.42	4.60	.60
55	6.79	1.74	5.05	1.05
56	7.60	2.11	5.49	1.49
57	8.44	2.52	5.92	1.92
58	9.31	2.97	6.34	2.34
59	10.19	3.48	6.71	2.71
60	11.10	4.02	7.08	3.08
61	12.03	4.62	7.41	3.41
62	12.97	5.25	7.72	3.72
63	13.92	5.92	8.00	4.00
64	14.88	6.63	8.25	4.25

Sandwich Spread

The sandwich spread involves a position in options with three different exercise prices. The investor buys two options, one with a high exercise price and one with a low exercise price, and sells two options with an exercise price between the other two. Using the Polaroid example again, the investor could form a sandwich spread by selling the April 40 and April 60 option and buying two April 50 options. The value of the position will then be

$$V = C(S,.0833,40,.06,.3) - 2C(S,.0833,50,.06,.3)$$
$$+ C(S,.0833,60,.06,.3).$$

The 40 and 60 options enter with a positive sign since they are being bought, while the two 50 options enter with a negative two, since they are being written.

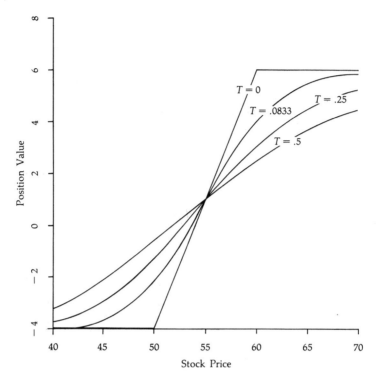

Figure 8–3 Profit profile for a Polaroid April 50–60 vertical spread (*T* denotes the time to April expiration)

As before, we can draw the profit profile by computing the value of the spread for various stock prices. These are listed in Table 8–3. The resulting profit profile is presented in Figure 8–4. We have also drawn the profit profile for six months and three months to expiration, and also the value of the position at the time of expiration.

As the sandwich spread example illustrates, the evaluation of option positions can be done when more than two types of options are being used.

Straddle

The option position can be evaluated when put options are combined with call options. In a straddle, the investor buys a call and a put. Using a *P* to represent the put option, the value of the position will be

$$V = C + P.$$

Table 8–3
Value of Sandwich Spread, One Month to Expiration

(1) Stock price	(2) C(S,.0833, 40,.06,.3)	(3) C(S,.0833, 50,.06,.3)	(4) C(S,.0833, 60,.06,.3)	(5) Position value (column 2 − 2 (column 3) + column 4)	(6) Profit from position (column 5 − $2 initial position cost)
30	.00*	.00	.00	.00	− 2.00
35	.10	.00	.00	.10	− 1.90
40	1.48	.01	.00	1.46	− .54
45	5.33	.25	.00	4.83	2.83
50	10.20	1.85	.04	6.54	4.54
55	15.20	5.53	.46	4.60	2.60
60	20.20	10.28	2.22	1.86	− .14
65	25.20	15.25	5.76	.46	− 1.54
70	30.20	20.25	10.37	.07	− 1.93

*Values less than ½ cent shown as zero.

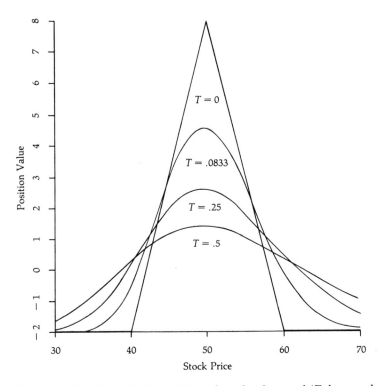

Figure 8–4 Profit profile for a Polaroid sandwich spread (T denotes the time to April expiration)

While the value of the call option can be computed using the option pricing formula, an exact closed-form solution to the price of a put option has not yet been developed. But the price of the American put can be approximated by using the call option formula to obtain the value of a European put. As was shown in Chapter 3, the value of a European put, p, is

$$p = C - S + Ee^{-rT}.$$

Since the value of C can be obtained through the Black-Scholes formula, we can substitute that value into this equation to get an expression for the put option as well.

If the investor buys both a Honeywell August 70 put and call with one month to expiration, then the position is

$$V = C(S, .0833, 70, .06, .3) + C - S + Ee^{-rT} = 2C - S + Ee^{-rT}.$$

Using the option formula to compute the value of C for various values of S, we obtain the profit profile in Figure 8–5. Again, the value of the position at other times to expiration are also drawn.

Variable Strategies

In most of the more common option strategies, the number of options held short equals the number of options held long. That is, $n_1 = -n_2$. But as we will see in the next section, it may be advantageous for the investor to enter into a strategy where the size of the position in the two options differs. The option position at any point in time may involve a different number of options held short than are being held long. Since the number of the options held is flexible in the valuation formula, such a strategy can also be evaluated using the methods described previously.

If an investor forms a time spread in Polaroid by writing four April 50 calls and buying only one July 50, the value of the position with one month to the April expiration date will be

$$V = -4\ C(S, .0833, 50, .06, .3) + C(S, .3333, 50, .06, .3).$$

If the stock price is $45 with one month to expiration, the value of this position will be

$$V = (-4 \times .25) + 1.62 = .62.$$

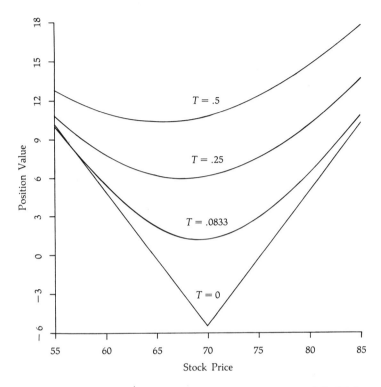

Figure 8-5 Profit profile for a Honeywell August 70 straddle (*T* denotes the time to August expiration)

By computing the value of the position for various *S*, a profit profile for this variable strategy can be obtained, as is shown in Figure 8-6.

As a second example of the generality of this approach to evaluating option strategies, take another look at the box spread described in Chapter 7. To put this spread on Aetna, buy a January 25 put, a 35 call, hold 100 shares of stock, and write two January 30 calls. The value of this spread for one month to expiration can be calculated as

$$V = P(S, .0833, 25, .06, .3) + C(S, .0833, 35, .06, .3)$$
$$+ S - 2C(S, .0833, 30, .06, .3).$$

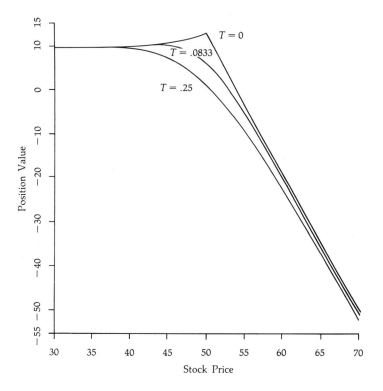

Figure 8-6 Profit profile for a Polaroid variable spread (*T* denotes the time to April expiration)

Subtracting the cost of putting on the position, $26, we trace out the profit profile in Figure 8-7 for four months, three months, and one month to expiration, and for the time of January expiration.

EVALUATING THE HEDGE POSITION

The straddles and spreads discussed in Chapter 7 use an equal number of options in both the long and the short positions. However, the best strategy may involve a variable hedge, where the number of options in one position differs from the number in the other.

The objective of the long position in the spread is to protect the investor against a large loss if the stock price rises unexpectedly. Ideally, the long posi-

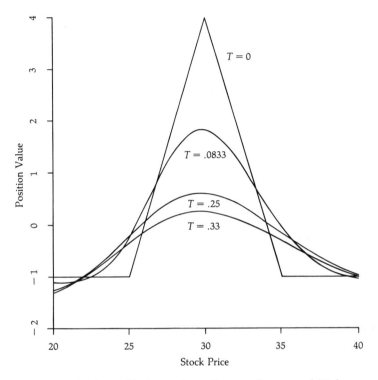

Figure 8-7 Profit profile for an Aetna January box spread (*T* denotes the time to January expiration)

tion should gain in value just enough to offset the loss incurred in the short position. If the long position gains more than the short loses when the stock rises, then it will also lose more than the short position gains if the stock drops in price, resulting in a net exposure to the investor from a stock decline. Similarly, if the long position does not gain as much as the short position loses when the stock rises in price, the investor is faced with a net exposure from a stock rise, and the spread is not fully meeting its objective.

Spreads with a one-to-one ratio of long to short positions will represent the best spread only if the options that are held long move just as much with a change in the stock price as the options that are held short. However, such a relationship cannot be expected to hold in general.

An option will react more to a stock price change in dollar terms the longer it has to expiration. For example, if the stock price increases, a July 50 will increase more in dollar terms than an April 50 will. If the long position in the time spread is held on an option with more time-to-expiration, it will increase more than the short position will. This means that if the investor holds as many options long as are held short, the value of the position will increase if the stock price increases, and decrease if the stock price decreases. The investor's position thus has net exposure to changes in the stock price.

The same holds true with other strategies. An option will move more with a change in the price of the stock the more in-the-money the option is. As the option gets far enough into the money, a one-point change in the stock price will bring almost a one-point change in the option price as well. If an option is far out-of-the-money, it will hardly move at all with a change in the stock price. This implies that in a vertical spread the option with the lower exercise price will change by more than the option with the higher exercise price as the stock price changes. Thus, a straight one-to-one spread with the long position on the option with the lower exercise price leaves the investor exposed to a loss if the stock drops in price. A better spread may be to hold less than one option long for each option held short.

The Hedge Ratio Revisited

The purpose of the hedge is to protect the investor from stock price movements. We need to know what hedge ratio will eliminate any exposure to stock price movements. For the case where the stock is used as a hedge, we saw that the hedge ratio that gives the investor a riskless position is $h = -N(d_1)$, where $N(d_1)$ is from the first term in the Black-Scholes option pricing formula of Chapter 4. If the investor holds h shares of stock for every option written, then a change in the stock price will exactly offset any change in the option price. The investor will thus be fully hedged against stock price changes.

A similar hedge ratio can also be established for two options when one option is used to hedge another option. This hedge ratio, called the *position hedge ratio*, determines the proportion of one option that must be held against another in order to eliminate the risk from stock price changes.

To see how we can determine the hedge ratio for a position in two options, let us return to the expression for the value of the option position:

$$V = n_1 C_1 + n_2 C_2.$$

The objective of the hedge ratio is to choose n_1 and n_2, the number of the options held, in the proportions that will keep the value of the position unchanged should the stock price change. The position hedge ratio means that the change in V caused by a change in S is zero. Using Δ to denote the change in the variable, this can be written as

$$\Delta V/\Delta S = 0.$$

Carrying this through to the other side of the equation, we have

$$\Delta V/\Delta S = n_1\Delta C_1/\Delta S + n_2\Delta C_2/\Delta S = 0.$$

From Chapter 4, we know that $\Delta C/\Delta S$, the change in the option price caused by a change in the stock price, is simply $N(d_1)$, or $-h$. The change in the value of the first option with a change in the stock price is simply equal to the negative of the hedge ratio of the first option:

$$\Delta C_1/\Delta S = -h_1.$$

Similarly, the change in the second option's price with a change in the stock price is

$$\Delta C_2/\Delta S = -h_2.$$

So denoting options 1 and 2's hedge ratios by h_1 and h_2, we can write

$$- (n_1 h_1 + n_2 h_2) = 0,$$

as the equation that must be fulfilled to have the position value be unchanged by shifts in the stock price. Using a little algebra, this can be reexpressed as

$$n_1/n_2 = -h_2/h_1.$$

If n_1 and n_2 are chosen to equal the inverse of the ratio of the options' hedge ratios, then we will have a hedged position. Denoting the position hedge ratio as h_p, i.e., defining h_p as

$$h_p = n_1/n_2$$

(so that h_p equals the number of the one option held relative to the other option in order to obtain a riskless hedge), the position hedge ratio will be

$$h_p = -h_2/h_1. \tag{8.2}$$

If h_p is -3 and the investor holds nine of the first option long, then three of the second option must be held short. Since the hedge ratio of the two options is easily computed, the hedge ratio for the position, h_p, can be established.

To illustrate the use of the hedge, let us take the example of the Polaroid time spread we worked with in the last section. Let us compute the hedge ratio for an April 50 written against a July 50, when there is one month to April expiration, and when the stock price is at $45. Denoting the two options by a subscript 1 and 2 respectively, the hedge ratios for the two options are

$$h_1 = -N_1(d_1) = -N((\ln 45/50)$$
$$+ (.06 + \frac{1}{2} \times .3^2 \times .0833))/.3\sqrt{.0833} = -.132$$

$$h_2 = -N_2(d_1) = -N((\ln 45/50)$$
$$+ (.06 + \frac{1}{2} \times .3^2 \times .333))/.3\sqrt{.333} = -.342$$

Using Equation (8.2), the position hedge ratio will then be

$$h_p = -2.59.$$

If a change in the stock price causes the April 50 option to move one point, then the July 50 option will move 2.59 points. Therefore, if 2.59 April options are written for each July option held long, then the spread will be unaffected by small stock price changes. If the ratio used is 1, so that each April option is covered by one July option, then the investor is exposed to stock movements. A one-point drop in the stock price will cause a loss in the position, since the long position will lose .342 points while the short position will gain only .132. If the hedge ratio used is greater than 2.59, the investor is again exposed; a rise in the stock price will cause a loss.

This hedge ratio, like the hedge ratio used when the option is covered by the stock, will protect the investor from changes in the stock price. Indeed, the stock hedge fits right into this framework. If the investor holds the stock to hedge the position in an option, the position hedge ratio is equal to the ratio of the hedge ratio for the option divided by the hedge ratio for the stock. Since the stock moves one-to-one with itself, the hedge ratio for the stock is always one. The hedge ratio, h_p, is then equal to the option hedge ratio divided by one, which is simply the hedge ratio for the option. Thus, if one option is held long, then h shares of stock must be held short.

The same caution applies here that applies for the use of the stock as a hedge; the hedge position must be reevaluated often, since changes in it will change with time and will also change with changes in the stock price. Also, it is only a local protection from small changes in the stock price. If the stock price suddenly jumps five or ten points, the investor will not be fully protected.

Limits to Hedge Protection: Changes in Time and in Stock Price

The effect of a change in the stock price on the protection of the hedge is illustrated in Figure 8-8. When the hedge is initiated with one month to the April expiration, a small movement in the stock price leaves the value of the position virtually unchanged. However, a large stock price move will still expose the investor to the stock price, since the hedge ratio only gives protection against small price changes. If the stock were to move significantly, the investor would need to reevaluate the hedge position.

Even if the stock price remains unchanged, the hedge ratio needs to be reevaluated as the time-to-expiration decreases. While the hedge ratio gives pro-

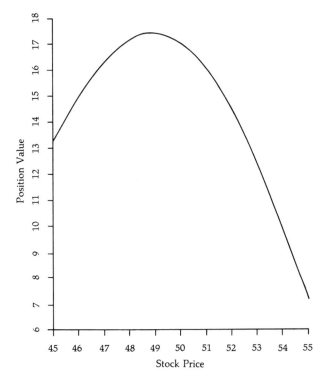

Figure 8-8 Profit profile for a Polaroid April–July 50 spread (hedge ratio is set for $S = 49$)

tection when there is one month to expiration, it no longer gives protection when there are just two weeks to expiration. And the exposure of the investor increases as the time to expiration comes closer. The hedge ratio that applies when there is one month to expiration will not be the correct ratio when there are two weeks left to expiration. The ratio must be reevaluated, and the option hedge updated, as the stock price changes and as the time-to-maturity expiration decreases.

This is illustrated in Figure 8–9, which gives the profit profile not only for one month to April expiration, but for two weeks and for one week to April expiration as well. The slope of the profit profile for $S = 49$ is no longer zero, indicating that the hedge is losing its effectiveness as the time to expiration changes.

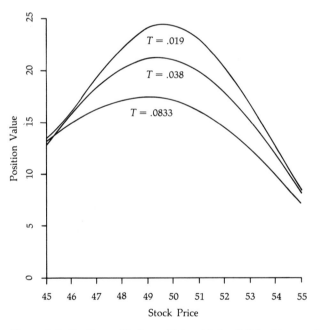

Figure 8–9 Profit profile for a Polaroid April–July 50 spread (the hedge ratio which eliminated the exposure for $S = 49$ with one month to April expiration no longer eliminates the exposure with just two weeks or one week to expiration)

EVALUATING THE POSITION RISK

The investor who forms the riskless hedge still faces risk if the stock suddenly jumps in price, or if he or she is away in Bermuda for a few days and cannot adjust the position while the stock price changes. If the options are not held in the correct hedge ratio, then the investor faces risk from the stock price for any size of movement. In this section we present methods that permit the investor to measure this risk.

The first measure is the exposure ratio. The *exposure ratio* tells the investor how the value of the position will be affected by a change in the stock price. For investors who do not hold the options in the prescribed hedge ratio, the exposure ratio is a valuable tool to help them evaluate the risk they face from the stock.

The second measure is the sensitivity ratio. The *sensitivity ratio* measures the effect of a stock price change on the hedge. Depending on the option used in forming the hedge, changes in the stock price will have varying effects on the risk of the hedge. The sensitivity ratio shows how sensitive the riskless hedge is to shifts in the stock price; that is, it shows how the risk of the hedge is affected by stock price changes.

The Exposure Ratio

If options are not held in the correct hedge ratio, then the investor will be exposed to risk from the stock price. This risk can be measured by using the exposure ratio. The position exposure ratio, x_p, measures the change in the value of the position with a change in the stock price:

$$x_p = \Delta V / \Delta S = n_1 \frac{\Delta C_1}{\Delta S} + n_2 \frac{\Delta C_2}{\Delta S}.$$

The change in the position is simply equal to the change in the price of the position in the first option caused by a change in the stock price, plus the change in the value of the position in the second option caused by a change in the stock price. The change in the value of the total position is then

$$x_p = -(n_1 h_1 + n_2 h_2).$$

Of course, if the investor holds the two options in the proportions dictated by the hedge ratio, exposure will be zero. By choosing n_1 and n_2 in the ratio dictated by the position hedge, we will have x_p equal to zero. But if that ratio is not maintained, either because of the cost of shifting the option position, or because of expectations of the future course of the stock price, then the investor will have exposure to the stock price. By using the exposure ratio, both the direction and the size of that exposure may be determined.

To illustrate the use of the exposure ratio, consider an investor who holds a Polaroid time spread, with an April 50 option written and a July 50 option held long. If the stock price is at 49 and there is one month to April expiration, then the hedge ratios for the two options will be

$$h_1 = -.447$$

and

$$h_2 = -.533$$

The exposure ratio will be

$$x_p = -(.447 - .533) = .086.$$

This ratio is positive, which means that if the stock price increases, then the value of the position will increase. If the stock increases by one point, the value of the position will increase slightly less than one-tenth of a point. This hedge position will therefore be preferred if the investor is bullish on the stock.

Measuring Exposure with the Profit Profile

To illustrate the exposure ratio further, consider the profit profile for the Polaroid time spread discussed previously with one month to April expiration. This profile is shown in Figure 8–10. It is the same as that of Figure 8–1. At a stock price of 49, the profile is upward sloping—an increase in the stock price brings about an increase in the value of the position. Indeed, the slope of the profile at this point is .086—*the slope of the profit profile is identical to the exposure ratio for the investor's position.* This makes sense, since the slope of the profile is the change in the position value resulting from a change in the stock price, which is exactly what the exposure ratio measures.

The slope of the profile is increasing until the stock price reaches 51. At that point the slope is zero—the change in the position resulting from a change in the stock price is zero. This amounts to a zero hedge; if the stock price is 51, then $\Delta V/\Delta S = 0$, and the investor will be fully hedged. From the profile, it is apparent that if the stock price changes slightly, from 51 to 50.5, the value of the position will be virtually unchanged. But, as we have warned before, this hedge is a local measure, and if the stock price changes significantly, dropping to 50 or 49, then the hedge will not give complete isolation from the stock move.

Once the stock price passes 50, the slope is negative. If the stock price is above 50, then the hedge will result in negative exposure. The investor will

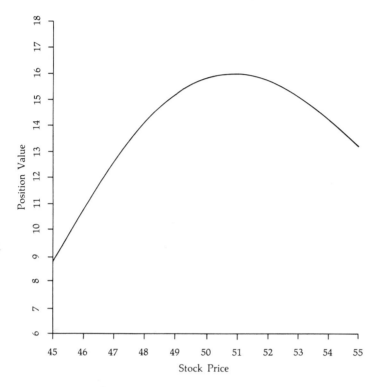

Figure 8-10 Profit profile for a Polaroid April–July 50 spread with one month ($T = .0833$) to April expiration (this profile is identical to that of Figure 8-1)

gain if the stock price drops, and will lose if the stock price rises. The determination of a bullish or a bearish hedge, whether the exposure ratio is positive or negative, corresponds to finding out if the slope of the profit profile is upward or downward sloping at the stock price in question.

Thus the profit profile provides a useful method for determining the exposure to the stock price.

Sensitivity Ratio

If options are held in the proportions dictated by the hedge ratio h_p, then the value of the investor's position will be unaffected by small changes in the stock price. But if the stock price moves sufficiently, the position will no longer be riskless, and the investor may be subject to a loss.

To illustrate the effect of large stock price changes on the hedge ratio, consider two hedge positions. Let the April 50 option be covered by a July 50 option in the one case, and by an October 50 option in the second case. If one April 50 is written, and if the stock price is 49, then the proper hedge ratio when the July 50 is used is $h_p = -1.19$ (for each April option written, .84 July options must be bought). For the October 50, the hedge ratio is $h_p = -1.28$ (for every April option written, .78 October options must be bought).

The profit profile for these two option positions is presented in Figure 8–11. Both options have a zero slope at the stock price of 49. This is the characteristic of the riskless hedge: for an option position to be riskless at a given stock price, the profit profile must have a zero slope at that stock price. In this case, both options have a zero slope at the stock price of $49, so that the value of the position will be unchanged for a small change in the stock price.

It is evident from the profit profile that the position using the October option is more sensitive to changes in the stock price than a position with the July option. If the stock price changes by one point, from $49 to $50, then the option position created with the July hedge changes in value by less than the position created with the October option. The investor's hedge will be less sensitive if the July option is used to hedge the position.

The sensitivity ratio shows how quickly the slope of the position changes from the zero slope as the stock price changes. The sensitivity ratio will thus be equal to the change in the exposure ratio with a change in the stock price $(s_p = \Delta x_p / \Delta S)$ and is the second partial derivative of C with respect to S. The sensitivity ratio can be estimated by measuring the change in the exposure of the option position with a one point change in the stock price:

$$s_p = |x_p(49) - x_p(50)|$$

where $x_p(49)$ is the exposure ratio of the position when the stock price is at $49, and $x_p(50)$ is the exposure ratio of the position when the stock price is at $50. (Recall that $x_p(49)$ is zero for both positions since the positions were determined by the position hedge ratio.)

In the above example, the sensitivity ratio for the July–April position is:

$$s_p = |(1 \times .540 - .84 \times .580)| = .053$$

while for the October-April position the sensitivity ratio is:

$$s_p = |(1 \times .540 - .78 \times .893)| = .085.$$

The lower the sensitivity ratio, the wider will be the effective range of the hedge.

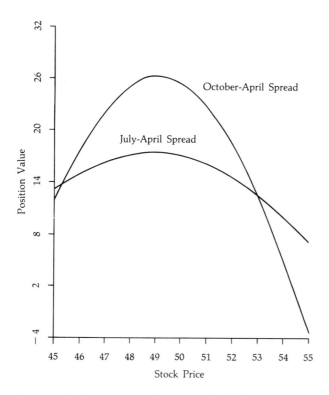

Figure 8-11 Comparison of a Polaroid April–July 50 spread with an October–April spread (the October–April spread has a steeper slope, and is thus more sensitive to changes in the stock price)

As with the exposure ratio, the sensitivity of the position can be determined from the profit profile. The greater the change in the slope of the profile, the greater the sensitivity of the position changes in the stock price.

Thus, while both the April 50–July 50 spread and the April 50–October 50 have zero exposure at a stock price of 49, the October 50 will be a more sensitive hedge—the hedge will entail more risk if the stock price changes.

COMPARING THE PROFITABILITY OF OPTION STRATEGIES

The previous sections of this chapter have described how to measure the risk and reward of option positions. The next question we address is how to choose between two option strategies when both of them have attractive profit potential.

In most investment decisions, the choice between investment alternatives is determined by the relative risk-reward tradeoffs of the two opportunities. In choosing between two option strategies, the tradeoffs are more subtle because if properly taken, an option position can be formulated to provide zero exposure—the risk to the profitability of the position from small changes in the stock price can be eliminated. If both positions have zero exposure, then the measure of risk must be determined by the relative sensitivity of the two positions.

To compare two option positions, we adjust the size of each position to yield the same maximum profit, and then compare the sensitivity of the two positions.

Consider the two option strategies discussed in the previous section, the April–July 50 spread and the April–October 50 spread. As is apparent from Figure 8–11, the April–October spread is far more sensitive to changes in the stock price. It has a much steeper slope, so that if the stock price moves from the zero-exposure value of 49, the profit of the April–October spread will deteriorate more quickly than will the profit of the April–July spread. But, the maximum profit from the April–October spread is greater than that of the April–July spread, so while it has greater risk, the April–October spread provides greater profit potential. It is therefore difficult to compare the two and say which is superior on a risk-reward basis.

In order to better compare the two strategies, we need either to set the sensitivity of the two positions equal and then compare the relative profit potential, or set the profit potential of the positions equal and then see which of the two has the greater sensitivity. By properly choosing the amount of the two options that are held, this can be accomplished.

As long as the options in the respective positions are held in the proportions prescribed by the hedge ratios (−1.19 for the April–July spread, and −1.28 for the April–October spread), the strategy will have zero exposure at the current stock price of $49. The absolute amount of each option that is held is still open. For example, the correct hedge ratio can be maintained for the April–July spread with 50 April options written and 42 July options bought, or with 100 April options written and 84 July options bought.

In order to compare the two strategies, we choose the absolute amount of options in each of the positions so as to equilibrate the profit of the positions at the current stock price. Suppose we write 100 April options and buy 84 July options to hedge the position. The maximum profit potential will be

$$V = -100 \ C(49, .0833, 50, .06, .3) + 84 \ C(49, .333, 50, .06, .3) - 26$$
$$= \$121.9.$$

We must choose the proper amounts of the April and the October option to give the same profit potential. That is, we must choose the n_1 and n_2 of the April–October spread to give $V = 121.9$ when the stock price is 49, and also have the amount of the options held fulfill the hedge ratio

$$h_p = n_1/n_2 = -1.28.$$

Substituting the second equation into the first, we have:

$$121.9 = -1.28\, n_2 C(49,.0833,50,.06,.3)$$
$$+ n_2 C(49,.5833,50,.06,.3) - c.$$

Noting the values for C_1 and C_2,

$$C(49, .0833, 50, .06, .3) = 1.36$$
$$C(49, .5833, 50, .06, .3) = 4.81$$

we can solve first for n_2, and then from the hedge solve for n_1. The amount of the two options to hold is:

$$n_1 = 62.7$$
$$n_2 = 49.$$

The profit profile for these values of the options is presented in Figure 8–12. By the proper choice of the number of options, the two strategies both have zero exposure at $S = \$49$, and further, both have the same maximum profit potential of $121.9.

Since the return of the two strategies is now set to be equal, and with both strategies giving zero exposure at the current stock price, it is obvious that the strategy will be preferred which has the lowest sensitivity to the changes in the stock price. It is apparent from the profit profile that the April–October spread is preferred to the April–July spread. When both the spreads are adjusted to give the same maximum return, the April–October spread has less sensitivity to the stock price since it has less slope. This may be because the October option, trading at 2½, is more underpriced than the July option, and therefore in combining it with the overpriced April option a more attractive spread results. The important point is that until the two spreads were adjusted, it was not apparent which of the two was the best.

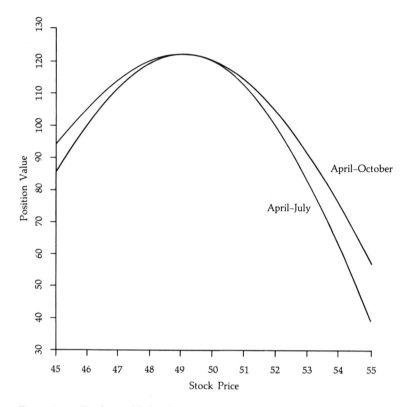

Figure 8–12 Profit profile for the April–July and the April–October spreads adjusted to yield the same maximum profit

The April–July and the April–October spread actually shifted in relative sensitivity when the level of the position was changed. To see the transformation that occurred, the April–July spread is shown in Figure 8–13 for various levels of n_1 and n_2 which give the required hedge ratio of -1.19. Note that as the value level of the hedge increases from $n_1 = -25$ and $n_2 = 21$ to $n_1 = -100$ and $n_2 = 84$, the sensitivity of the spread increases. Thus while the April–July spread appeared less sensitive in Figure 8–11, once the level of the spread is increased to give a profit potential equal to that of the April–October spread, its sensitivity exceeds that of the April–October spread.

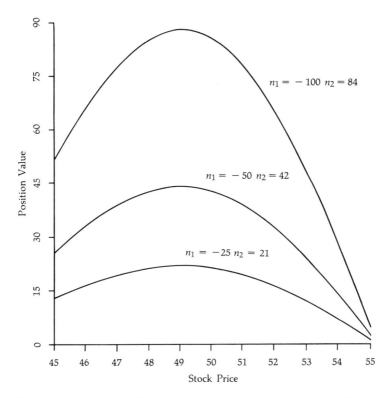

Figure 8-13 Profit profile for the April–July spread for various levels of n_1 and n_2 (note that the sensitivity increases as the level of the hedge increases)

The Profit Profile: A Simple Method for Evaluating Option Strategies

The investor must know the profit potential and risk of the option position to critically evaluate any investment strategy. Besides looking at the profit potential, we have shown how to evaluate the riskiness of the option position to changes in the stock price through the exposure ratio, and how to evaluate changes in exposure with changes in the stock price through the sensitivity ratio.

The added dimension of the effect of time on the profit potential and risk can also be determined by looking at the profit potential and the exposure and sensitivity ratios at specific times to expiration. There is great flexibility in these measurement techniques, and they can be adjusted to evaluate the option position for any time up to expiration.

A shortcut to the application of these techniques is provided by the profit profile. The profit profile contains all of the information necessary to evaluate the profit potential, as well as the exposure and sensitivity of the position, at a glance. This has already been demonstrated, and it deserves repeating here:

---

1. The *height* of the profit profile shows the profit potential of the position.

2. The *slope* of the profit profile shows the exposure of the position to changes in the stock price.

3. The *rate of change in the slope* of the profit profile (the curvature of the profile) shows the sensitivity of the position hedge to changes in the stock price.

4. A comparison of the profit profile over two times to expiration shows the effect of changes in the time to expiration on the option position.

QUESTIONS

1. Show that the position hedge ratio, h_p, reduces to the option hedge ratio, h, when the stock is used as the hedging security.

2. One method of determining the attractiveness of a mispriced option is to take the difference between the market value and the formula value of the options. The greater this difference is in absolute terms, the more mispriced the option is, and the more attractive a profit opportunity it presents. Another alternative is to divide the difference between the market price and the formula price by the option's hedge ratio. This alternative is called the *profit measure.* Why would the profit measure be a better indicator of the profit potential of an option than simply looking at the absolute difference between the market and formula price?

3. In profiting from a mispriced option, will a hedge with nonzero exposure ever afford greater profit opportunities than are possible by pursuing the zero exposure hedge? Will an investor ever prefer to maintain nonzero exposure in an option strategy?

Chapter 9 STRATEGIES FOR OPTION TRADING

In Chapter 7 we discussed some of the common option strategies, and found that many of them had a common objective—to exploit options that were not correctly priced relative to the stock, and then to hedge the position in that option by taking a position in a second option.

In Chapter 8 we showed how to evaluate option positions that were more complex than those presented in Chapter 7, and how to evaluate the position at times before expiration. We also gave the hedge ratio for option positions that will eliminate the risk from uncertain stock price changes.

The next item is to decide what option position to take. In this chapter we cover the trading rules that the investor should follow in making trading decisions and in constructing option positions. The four trading rules for option trading are:

1. Take a position in a mispriced option. If an option is overpriced, sell it. If an option is underpriced, buy it.

2. Hedge the position in the mispriced option to reduce or eliminate the risk from stock price movements.

3. Adjust the hedge over time and as the stock price changes to maintain the proper hedge ratio.

4. If the option returns to the correct price, liquidate the position.

These simple rules represent the basis of a sound option trading strategy. All the strategies covered in the previous chapters are special cases of these rules. We will discuss these rules one by one.

TAKE A POSITION IN A MISPRICED OPTION

The objective of option trading strategies is to take advantage of mispriced options. In any option strategy, an option position is taken because the investor feels the option is not priced correctly. Naturally, if it is felt the market is overpricing the option, the investor will sell the overpriced options to the market. If it is thought the market is selling the option for less than the correct price, the investor will buy the underpriced option.

For example, consider an investor who is taking on a time spread by writing an option close to expiration and covering the position with an option with a longer time to expiration. There will usually be one of two reasons for taking such a position. The time premium for the option being written is too high given the time-to-expiration, and the investor is writing the option to take advantage of the excessive time premium. Or the investor may feel the stock is very stable for the short term, and there is a good chance that the option will expire worthless, since the stock will probably not rise above the exercise price for the option in the short time to maturity.

Both reasons amount to the investor feeling that the option is mispriced. In the first case the market is misestimating the premium associated with the time-to-maturity. In the second case the market is overestimating the volatility of the stock. The investor takes advantage of the mispricing by writing the overpriced option and hedging the position with another option which is assumed to be not overpriced.

Of course, a key factor is knowing when an option is mispriced. The option pricing formula presents one way to do so, but it is just one method available. There are modifications of the formula, and various methods for measuring the inputs of the formula. And there are more subjective methods for evaluating the option prices—following the market to get a "feel" for the correct value of options. We have leaned heavily on the use of the option formula to price options because it is a method that has generated interest in the investment community. However, it is not the only way to determine if options are mispriced.

As an example of the use of the option trading strategy, consider the following option prices for Avon, taken three weeks before April expiration:

Avon
Three Weeks to April Expiration
Stock Price = 50

		April	July	October
45	Market price	5½	6½	7⅝
	Formula price	5.19	6.48	7.63
	Hedge ratio	−.98	−.83	−.80
50	Market price	3	3¼	4½
	Formula price	1.28	3.22	4.54
	Hedge ratio	−.53	−.58	−.61

Just looking at the quotes, it appears that the Avon April 50 is over-priced. The stock is at $50 per share, and there are only three weeks to the April expiration. Yet that option has a premium of 3. Further, the July option, with three more months to expiration, is only at 3¼. The spread between them is unusually low.

Taking the Black-Scholes value of the option prices confirms this suspicion. Using a volatility of .25 and an interest rate of 6 percent, we have calculated the formula price for the options listed on Avon. The April 50 option is overpriced; its correct price is 1.28. The first step to exploiting this is to write the overpriced option:

Step 1: Write 10 Avon April 50 calls.

HEDGE THE POSITION

Option prices move with the stock price. Whenever the investor buys or sells an option, there is a possibility of a loss if the stock moves adversely. Even if the investor has found an option that is overpriced and has gained the premium from writing it, the profit will be wiped out if the stock rises enough.

The investor needs to be able to "purge" himself or herself from the risk of the stock price. Trading should be done on the basis of relative mispricing, not on the basis of the future stock price.

How Much the Investor Should Hedge

The hedge position allows the investor to reduce or eliminate the risk faced from the stock price movement. The selection of the proper hedge ratio has been discussed in the previous chapter. The investor can use the exposure ratio presented there to evaluate the net exposure of the position, and can adjust it accordingly.

The investor may not wish to totally eliminate exposure to stock price changes. If basically bullish on the stock, for example, the investor may wish to have a position that will increase in value with an increase in the stock price. A hedge will then be taken that will give a positive rather than zero exposure. That is, the position will have an exposure ratio that is greater than zero.

The investor who takes on an option position because of relative option mispricing and does not fully hedge that position is also taking on a position on the underlying stock whether it is desired or not. Such an investor is playing two investment games—playing on beliefs about the option and also playing on beliefs about the future direction of the stock itself. The zero hedge is designed for the "option purist" who only wants to play on the option mispricing. Because our interest in this book is options, we are concentrating on this zero hedge. But it is simple to adjust the hedge to simultaneously play the stock simply by holding a position that on net is long on the stock or option if bullish, or is short on the stock or option if bearish.

How the Hedge Should Be Established

A number of securities can be used to hedge the option position. The stock itself can be used, as was illustrated in Chapter 4. Or another option can be used to facilitate the hedge. If a call is believed to be overpriced, and the investor sells it, the position can be hedged by buying the stock, by buying another call option, or by selling a put. Not all hedges will be equally effective, however.

There are several criteria to consider in choosing the security to use to hedge the option position.

First, *select a security that will closely match the movement of the mispriced option*. If an April 50 is being written, then generally an April 45 will be preferred to an April 40 as a hedge, since the April 45 will move more closely with the April 50 as the stock price changes. Similarly, a July 50 will generally prove to be a better hedge than a July 60 or an October 50. The objective is to form a hedge with the least sensitivity to the stock price.

Second, *determine whether the option that is used as a hedge is also mispriced*. If two call options are mispriced in the same direction, that is, both are overpriced or both are underpriced, then the two calls should not be paired up in a hedge. If both the April 50 and April 45 options are overpriced, then the profit gained by writing the overpriced April 50 will be lost by buying the overpriced April 45. When an investor chooses to use a horizontal spread rather than a vertical spread, it may be justifiable on the grounds that all options on the stock that are close to maturity are overpriced, so that if the April 50 were covered by another option with an April expiration date, the profits would be eliminated.

On the other hand, if they are mispriced in opposite directions, so that one is overpriced and the other is underpriced, then pairing the two in the hedge will accentuate the investor's profit.

For example, if the April 50 is overpriced while the July 50 is underpriced, then in writing the April 50 the investor gains the excess premium, and in using the July 50 to hedge the position an option is bought at below its fair price. The investor thus gains on both sides of the transaction.

A last consideration is to *determine whether the stock or option is preferred in forming a hedge.* If all the options are mispriced in the same direction, then the stock may be the only security that can be used to create the hedge. (If a put is available, it can be used to hedge a call since the position will be in the same direction for both options.) But outside of this case, the stock will generally not be preferred to an option in creating a hedge. One reason for this is that usually the position hedge ratio is less sensitive to the stock price when a second option is used in the hedge.

A second reason is that the commission for hedging with options will usually be less than the commission for the stock. This is especially true when the investor is dealing in large lots of options.

And third, when two options are combined in forming the hedge, there is less error in the hedge ratio than when the option is combined with the stock. Since the hedge ratio of both options is obtained from the Black-Scholes formula, any miscalculation in the variables of the formula or in the specification of the formula will be partially cancelled out. For example, say the investor overestimates the volatility of the stock in deriving the hedge ratio of the two options, and the hedge ratio used for the two options is too large. When the two hedge ratios are combined to form the position hedge ratio, the net effect of the overestimation may be reduced. If the true hedge ratios are $-.8$ and $-.7$ respectively, but an overestimation of the volatility results in estimated hedge ratios of $-.85$ and $-.74$, then the computed position hedge ratio will be $-.85/.74 = -1.15$, compared to the actual ratio of $-.8/.7 = -1.14$. Although the error in both of the option ratios is significant, most of the error is eliminated when they are used to obtain the position hedge ratio.

Since most errors in computing the hedge ratio occur because of inaccurate estimation of the volatility of the stock or because the formula is not correctly specified, errors in the option hedge ratio will be in the same direction for all the options, and the error will be reduced when they are used to calculate the position hedge ratio.

In summary then, we can add several corollaries to the trading rules presented at the start of the chapter:

2a. If all other options are correctly priced, the hedge should be provided with the option that is most similar to the mispriced option in terms of the expiration date and the time to exercise price.

2b. If other options are also mispriced, hedge the option with an option that is mispriced in the opposite direction. Do not hedge with an option that is mispriced in the same direction.

2c. If all the options are mispriced in the same direction, hedge with the stock or use a put-call position.

Continuing with the Avon example, we now will consider how to hedge the position taken in the Avon April 50. Using the rule that the most similar option should be used to hedge the mispriced option, we can choose an option with the same expiration date but a different exercise price, the April 45, or with a different expiration date and the same exercise price, the July 50. Both are similar to the mispriced April 50, one differing slightly by exercise price, the other differing slightly by expiration date.

Notice that the April 45 is also overpriced slightly. Its correct price is 5.19 while its market price is 5.50. If we use that as a hedge, then we will be taking a long position in an overpriced option. This will partly negate the premium from the short position in the April 50, and reduce the profit. Instead, we choose the July 50 as a hedge. It is correctly priced, and since it is similar to the April 50, it will move closely with the April 50 as the stock price changes, thereby reducing the need to revise the hedge too frequently.

The hedge ratios for the options are listed under the formula price. The hedge ratio for the April 50 is $-.53$, and for the July 50 is $-.58$. The position hedge ratio is then

$$-0.58/.53 = -1.1: \frac{n_1}{n_2} = \frac{-h_2}{h_1} = -1.1.$$

This means that for the ten overpriced April 50 we write, we hedge by buying nine July 50 options.

Step 2: Hedge the 10 April 50 calls by buying 9 July 50 calls.

ADJUST THE HEDGE

Since the hedge ratio changes as the time to expiration decreases and as the stock price changes, the hedge ratio must be constantly revised. The question of determining when to adjust the hedge involves the tradeoff between the transactions cost of changing the hedge ratio and the risk of increased exposure if the hedge is not changed. In order to keep a riskless hedge, the ratio would have to be continually adjusted. But the existence of any transactions cost would make a continuous adjustment strategy unprofitable.

The optimal frequency of readjustment is a function of the investor's desires to eliminate risk, and the size of the transactions cost the investor faces. The risk from the stock price may not be of concern if the investor is bullish or bearish on the stock, and wants to maintain a position that permits profit if the stock price moves in the anticipated direction. Or, if the investor has a well-diversified portfolio, the risk from the stock price may be diversified away. If the investor maintains a hedge that is close to the riskless hedge, then the loss from the position will be the same whether the stock goes up or down in price. Since only the size of the stock move, and not the direction of the move, matters, this risk may not be correlated with the systematic risk of the investor's other investments which depends on the direction of the stock move.

The investor's exposure to stock price movements can be determined by the exposure ratio discussed in Chapter 8, which compares the ratio of position with the riskless hedge ratio. If the riskless hedge ratio is $-.8$, then a one-point movement in the one option will be balanced out by a $-.8$-point movement in the other option. When the one option gains one dollar, the other will lose eighty cents. If a ratio of $-.7$ is used, so that the investor holds ten of the one long to seven of the other short, then the investor has positive net exposure to the stock. When the stock goes up and the long position gains one dollar, the other position loses less than a dollar. On net, the investor gains from a stock rise.

When deciding to readjust the hedge, the investor may do so by changing position in either of the securities. For example, if the stock is held long as a hedge against a short position in an option and the hedge ratio increases, the investor can either buy more stock or reduce the short position in the option.

If the option is overpriced, the best method for adjusting the hedge will be to buy more stock. If the investor adjusts by reducing the short position in the option, some overpriced options will need to be bought back. But the investor should *sell* overpriced options, not *buy* them. By adjusting the position through the options, the investor will reduce profit.

On the other hand, if the hedge ratio decreased, so that the investor must either write more options or else sell some of the stock, profit can be augmented by writing more options. Since the options are still overpriced, the investor will be selling more of the overpriced options.

The same reasoning holds for underpriced options. If the adjustment of the hedge involves buying more underpriced options, then the adjustment should be made through the option. If the adjustment would involve selling some of the underpriced options, then the adjustment should be made through the stock or other hedging security. Thus, the following is a corollary to the trading rules for adjusting the hedge:

3a. When possible, adjust the hedge by buying underpriced options or by selling overpriced options. Do not adjust the hedge by selling underpriced options or by buying overpriced options.

The value of the Avon option with two weeks to expiration is shown below:

Avon
Two Weeks to April Expiration
Stock Price = 50 ¾

		April	July	October
45	Market price	5¾	7	8
	Formula price	5.86	7.03	8.16
	Hedge ratio	−.99	−.86	−.82
50	Market price	2¼	3½	5
	Formula price	1.48	3.55	4.91
	Hedge ratio	−.65	−.62	−.64

The stock has risen three-quarters of a point over the week, and the stock change, combined with the decreased time-to-expiration, has resulted in a shift in the hedge ratio. The new position hedge ratio is now −.65/.62 = −1.05. The correct hedge now requires ten July 50's bought for the ten April 50's written. But the difference between the new and old hedge does not involve much risk for the investor. The new hedge ratio means that a one-point rise in the April 50 will be met by a one-point rise in the July 50. With the ratio currently held, the investor's July 50 position will rise only .9 if the April 50 drops by one point. The total net loss from a one-point change in the April 50 is only $1 per option, for $10 total. It would take nearly a two-point move in the stock to bring about a one-point move in the April 50 option.

Given the commission in adjusting the hedge, the investor would thus be well advised to continue to hold the original hedge position.

Step 3: Continue with the initial hedge.

CLOSE THE OPTION POSITION

Once the mispriced option returns to the correct price, the position should be closed out. If the option remains mispriced throughout the duration of the option contract, the investor may not be able to realize the full potential profit of the position until the expiration date. At expiration, the value of the option is set at its intrinsic value by contract, so that even if there is continued mispricing before then, the investor can always claim profit at the time of the expiration date.

However, generally an option will not remain mispriced for very long. The mispricing will almost always correct itself after two or three weeks, and often in just a few days. When the option has returned to the correct price, there is no reason to continue in the option strategy. The investor should take the profit and get out. From the time the option returns to its correct price, the investor is holding a position in a correctly priced option; a profit cannot be obtained from following the hedging strategy in that case. An investor who continues to hold the option position after the mispricing is eliminated is in the same situation as an investor who buys an underpriced stock at $40, and once it rises to its fair price at $50, continues to hold it. Once it reaches the fair price, any speculative profit has been fully realized. Return from that point on will just be the fair return given the risk the investor is bearing.

With one week left to April expiration, the stock is at 52, and the price of the options is:

Avon
One Week to April Expiration
Stock Price = 52

		April	July	October
45	Market price	7	8	9¼
	Formula price	7.05	8.04	9.13
50	Market price	2⅛	4¼	5½
	Formula price	2.16	4.25	5.64

The April 50 option is now correctly priced, and the investor should close out the position. The amount of $3,825 will be received for the long position in the July 50, and $2,125 will be paid to cover the April 50's that were written. The value of the position at closing is $1,700. Adding the value of the initial position, $75, net profit is $1,775.

If the April 50 had been written without the July 50 hedge, the investor would have had an initial position of $3,000 in writing the calls, and after closing out for $2,125, would have netted a $875 profit. This profit is less than with the hedge in the July 50, since profit from the April 50 is diminished by the two-point rise in the stock price. Thus the hedge, in reducing the risk from the stock price moving, also leads to a higher profit.

Three Weeks to April Expiration:

Write 10 April 50 calls	$ 3,000
Buy 9 July 50 calls	(2,925)
Net initial position	75

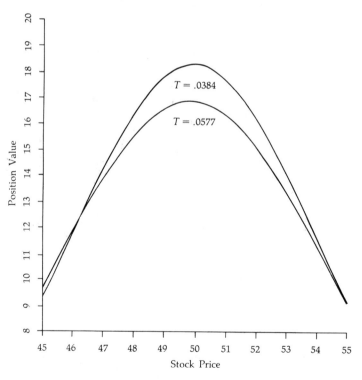

Figure 9-1 Profit profile for the Avon spread with three weeks and two weeks to expiration

One Week to April Expiration:

Buy 10 April 50 calls	2,125
Sell 9 July 50 calls	3,825
Net final position	1,700
Total profit	1,775

The profit profile for the Avon strategy is presented in Figures 9–1 and 9–2. In Figure 9–1, the profit profile for the initial hedge ratio is pictured for both three weeks and two weeks to expiration. With the stock at 50¾, the investor has a slight negative exposure to the stock price—if the stock price rises above 50¾, the value of the position will drop. However, as this profile indicates, the degree of risk is small. If the stock shifts slightly, the value of the position is still virtually unchanged.

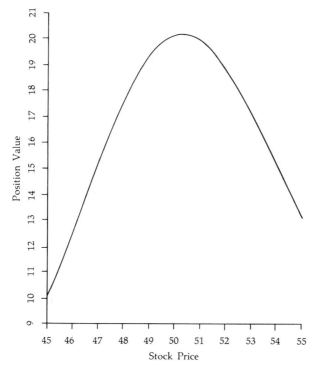

Figure 9–2 Profit profile for the Avon spread with two weeks to expiration using the optimal hedge ratio

In contrast, the optimal hedge ratio with two weeks to expiration is −1.05 (9.6 July options held long for the ten April options held short). The profit profile for this strategy is shown in Figure 9–2. The slope of the profit profile is zero at 50¾, but as is evident in comparing Figure 9–2 with Figure 9–1, there is little difference in the sensitivity of exposure of the two hedge positions.

By way of contrast, consider the profit profile if the investor had used the October 45 option to hedge the position in the April 50. Figure 9–3 shows the profit profile for this hedge compared to the profit profile for the July 50 hedge, with three weeks to the April expiration. Although both hedges give zero exposure at the then-current stock price of $50, the sensitivity is greater for the October 45 hedge. If the stock price takes an unexpected move, the investor will face more risk of a deterioration in the position with the October 45 option as a hedge.

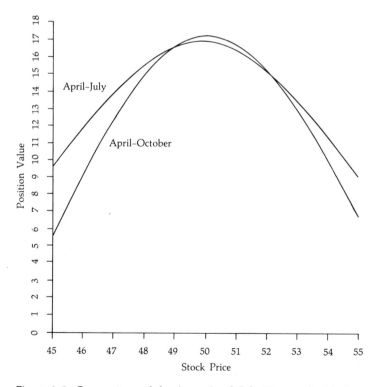

Figure 9–3 Comparison of the Avon April–July 50 spread with the April–October 50 spread (Note that the sensitivity of the position is greater for the April–October spread)

OPTION TRADING STRATEGIES: FURTHER EXAMPLES

Polaroid

Here is another example of the option strategy discussed previously. It involves a time spread to take advantage of the mispricing, but in this case the hedge is adjusted a few weeks after the position is initiated. The initial option prices and hedge ratios are presented in Table 9-1.

Table 9-1
Polaroid Option Prices with Two Months to April Expiration
(Listing the Formula Price, the $S = 45$ Market Price, and the Hedge Ratio)

E		April	July	October
40	Formula price	5.79	7.07	8.16
	Market price	5.75	7.00	8.25
	Hedge ratio	− .865	− .798	− .778
45	Formula price	2.42	4.01	5.24
	Market price	3.00	4.00	4.88
	Hedge ratio	− .557	− .589	− .614
50	Formula price	.73	2.04	3.16
	Market price	.68	2.13	3.25
	Hedge ratio	− .236	− .375	− .443

Taking a position in the mispriced options. While most of the options are close to the formula value, two of the options, the April 45 and the October 45, are substantially mispriced. The April 45 is overpriced by nearly sixty cents, while the October option is underpriced by nearly forty cents. Once the mispricing is recognized, the next step is to determine the best way to profit from the mispricing.

The first rule is to sell overpriced options and buy underpriced options. The investor will therefore sell the April 45 and buy the October 45.

The second rule is to hedge the position in the options. The best hedge will generally be formed by using the option that has a hedge ratio that is the closest to the hedge ratio for the mispriced option. In forming a hedge position with either of the options, the July 45 would seem to be the best candidate. However, since the April option is overpriced and the October option is underpriced, an even more profitable hedge position can be created by combining the two mispriced options. The best strategy is to have the overpriced April 45 written against the underpriced October 45. The investor will then profit from both sides of the position.

Determining the best hedge. The correct hedge ratio in holding the two options is determined from the position ratio:

$$\frac{n_1}{n_2} = h_p = \frac{-.614}{.557} = -1.1.$$

If eleven April options are written, then ten October options should be bought. The cost of the initial position will then be

$$V = -11 \times 300 + 10 \times 488 = 1,580.$$

The profit profile for this hedge is shown in Figure 9–4. The profile has zero slope at $S = \$45$. The value of the position will remain virtually unchanged even if the stock price moves up or down a point.

Over the next two-week period, the stock price increases to 48, and the investor's position increases in value. Using the market values for the options

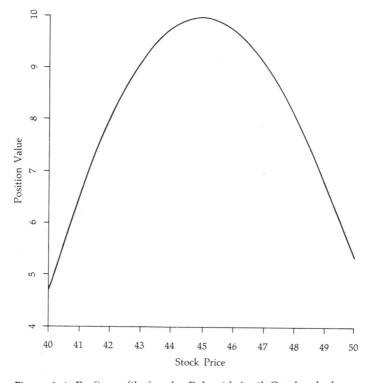

Figure 9-4 Profit profile for the Polaroid April–October hedge

Table 9-2
Polaroid Option Prices with Six Weeks to April Expiration
$(S = 48)$

E		April	July	October
40	Formula price	8.35	9.40	10.42
	Market price	8.25	9.50	10.50
	Hedge ratio	− .970	− .887	− .853
45	Formula price	4.02	5.71	7.00
	Market price	4.33	5.50	6.75
	Hedge ratio	− .771	− .714	− .708
50	Formula price	1.31	3.09	4.43
	Market price	1.50	3.25	4.25
	Hedge ratio	− .393	− .496	− .541

in Table 9-2, the value of the position with six weeks to April expiration can be computed:

$$V = -11 \times 433 + 10 \times 675 = 1,987.$$

The change in the stock price has affected the value of the position slightly, but the greater part of the increase in the value is due to the market price of the options moving closer to their correct values. As is shown in Table 9-2, the April option is now only overpriced by about thirty cents, and the October 45 option is only underpriced by twenty-five cents. This adjustment in the market price means a profit to the investor. And as other investors in the market realize that the options are mispriced, the option prices will adjust further to their correct values, and the investor's position will show an increased profit.

Adjusting the hedge. Over time, and as the stock price changes, the initial position will leave the investor exposed to stock price changes. The investor will need to revise the position to remain unaffected by the stock price. Two weeks after initiating the position, with six weeks left to April expiration, the investor reevaluates the position, and wishes to reduce exposure. (The position exposure is indicated in Figure 9-5.) The new position hedge ratio is $-.708/.771 = -.918$.

To adjust to the new position hedge ratio, the investor must either increase the long position in the October 45 or reduce the short position in the April 45—either October options or April options must be bought. If April options are bought, the investor will be buying overpriced options, while if the position is adjusted by buying more October options, the investor will be buying underpriced options. Profits will be increased by buying more of the underpriced October 45 options. If two more October 45 options are bought, then the ratio of the position is $-11/12 = .916$, which is the correct ratio.

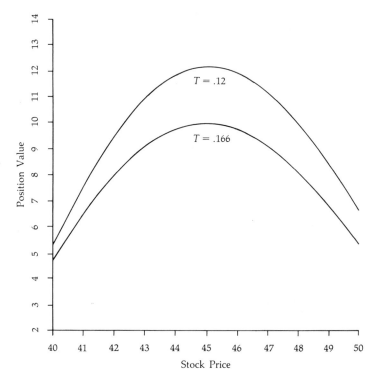

Figure 9–5 Comparison of the initial hedge position with two months ($T = .166$) and six weeks ($T = .12$) to April expiration

The value of this position becomes

$$V = -11 \times 433 + 12 \times 675 = 3{,}337.$$

The additional cost in adjusting the position, the cost of the two options, is $2 \times 675 = 1{,}350$.

The profit profile for this new hedge position is shown in Figure 9–6.

Closing out the position. With one month to the April expiration, the stock price has risen to $50. The associated option prices are shown in Table 9–3. The investor could hold on to the position until expiration, but since the April 45 and October 45 options have moved back to near their correct value, most of the profit can be realized by liquidating now. If the position is liquidated, the investor will realize the value of the position, which is

$$V = -11 \times 550 + 12 \times 825 = 3{,}850.$$

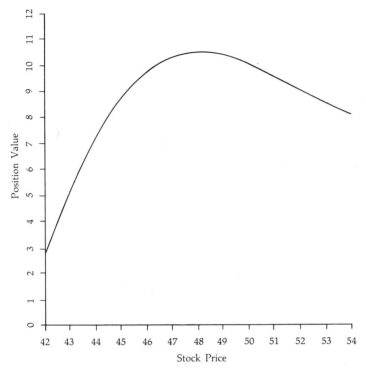

Figure 9-6 Profit profile of the adjusted Polaroid April–October hedge position (note that the position has zero exposure at $S = 48$)

Table 9-3
Polaroid Option Prices with One Month to April Expiration
($S = 50$)

E		April	July	October
40	Formula price	10.20	11.06	12.02
	Market price	10.25	11.00	12.00
	Hedge ratio	− .996	− .932	− .893
45	Formula price	5.42	7.00	8.31
	Market price	5.50	7.00	8.25
	Hedge ratio	− .906	− .791	− .766
50	Formula price	1.85	3.93	5.39
	Market price	1.75	3.75	5.50
	Hedge ratio	− .540	− .580	− .605

The cost of the position is the $1,580 from the first trade, plus the $1,350 from adjusting the hedge, for a total cost of $2,930. The investors' net profit is $3,850 − $2,930 = $920. This represents over a 30-percent profit during a one-month period. An outline of the steps of the strategy is presented in Table 9–4.

Table 9–4
Steps in the Polaroid Option Strategy

1. *Sell overpriced April 45*
   Buy underpriced October 45
   $(T = .166, S = 45)$
   hedge ratio:

   $$h_p = \frac{-.614}{.557} = -1.1$$

   position value:

   $$V = -11 \times 300 + 10 \times 488 = 1,580$$

   cost of position:

   $$C = 1,580$$

2. *Adjust position to maintain riskless hedge*
   $(T = .12, S = 48)$
   hedge ratio:

   $$h_p = \frac{-.708}{.771} = -.918$$

   position value:

   $$V = -11 \times 433 + 12 \times 675 = 3,337$$

   cost of adjustment:

   $$C = 2 \times 675 = 1,350$$

3. *Options are near their correct value; liquidate position*
   $(T = .083, S = 50)$
   position value:

   $$V = -11 \times 550 + 12 \times 825 = 3,850$$

   total cost:

   $$1,580 + 1,350 = 2,930$$

   profit after liquidation:

   $$3,850 - 2,930 = \underline{\underline{920}}$$

Honeywell

We now return to the Honeywell example of Chapter 7 to show how straddle positions can be established and adjusted when both the put and the call are underpriced. In taking on a position in Honeywell, the investor believes that the market has underestimated the future volatility of Honeywell stock. All of the options on Honeywell, both puts and calls, are accordingly underpriced. When all of the options are mispriced, the appropriate position is either to hedge with the stock, or if there is a put option listed, to initiate a straddle position.

Based on the overheard conversation that was presented at the start of Chapter 7, our friend is convinced that the Honeywell stock will be far more volatile in the next few days than is generally believed by the market. While he does not know the direction of the future stock move, he thinks it will move significantly one way or the other. He therefore thinks that all of the options are below the correct price. He can take advantage of the mispricing by buying the underpriced options.

The Honeywell option prices thirty days before the August expiration are listed in Table 9–5. The stock is at 70, and the formula price and related hedge ratios are computed based on an expected future volatility of .5.

The price for the put is computed from the call price using the formula $P = C - S + e^{-rT} E$, and the hedge ratio for the put is equal to the hedge ratio for the call plus one.

For example, if the August 70 call is 4.19, the formula price for the August 70 put is $4.19 - 70 + .9950(70) = 3.84$. The hedge ratio for the August 70 put is $-.54 + 1 = .46$. Recall that the hedge ratio for the put option is positive; a long position in a put is used as a hedge for a long position in the stock or in a call option, since the put changes in the opposite direction of the stock.

Table 9–5
Honeywell Option Prices with Thirty Days to August Expiration
$(S = 70)$

E		August	November	February
70	Market price	2½	4½	6
	Formula price	4.19	8.66	11.66
	Hedge ratio	− .54	− .58	− .61
70p	Market price	2	4	4¾
	Formula price	3.84	7.28	10.28
	Hedge ratio	.46	.42	.39

Taking a position in the mispriced option. Let us follow the strategy that was used in this example in Chapter 6. All of the options are underpriced. With the announcement expected within a few days, the August options would be the best to use since they will change the most in percentage terms with a change in the stock volatility. The investor buys the August 70 call, and hedges it with the 70 put.

Determining the best hedge. The correct hedge ratio in holding the two options will be:

$$\frac{n_1}{n_2} = h_p = \frac{.46}{.54} = .85.$$

This position hedge ratio can be fulfilled by buying 17 calls and 20 puts. Then the ratio h_p will be $17/20 = .85$. The cost of the initial position will be

$$V = 17 \times 250 + 20 \times 200 = 8,250.$$

After three days, with twenty-seven days to the August expiration, Honeywell makes an announcement that they are dropping out of the race for the development of the ECM system. (See Table 9–6.) The stock drops three points to 67. The option prices also drop, but not as much as might be expected. The August 70 call, for example, only drops half a point, and the February 70 call actually increases in value even with the three-point drop in the stock. This may be because the stock market is starting to adjust its estimate of the stock volatility upward.

The profit profile of the straddle is shown in Figure 9–7 for thirty and twenty-seven days to expiration.

Table 9–6
Honeywell Option Prices with Twenty-Seven Days to August Expiration
($S = 67$)

E	August	November	February
70	2	4	6½
	2.514	6.87	9.8
	− .41	− .52	− .57
70p	4¼	6⅞	8
	5.11	8.47	10.30
	.59	.48	.43

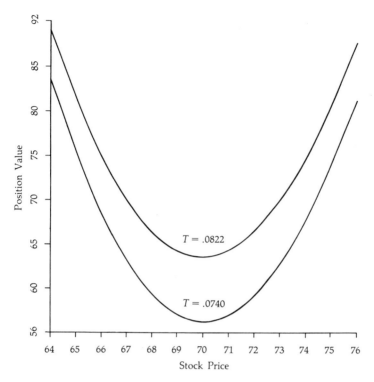

Figure 9-7 Profit profile of the Honeywell 70 straddle with thirty days ($T = .0822$) and with twenty-seven days ($T = .0740$) to August expiration with the initial hedge position

Adjusting the hedge. With the change in the stock price, the appropriate hedge also has changed. The exposure ratio for the hedge is

$$x_p = -(17 \times -(.41) + 20 \times .59) = -4.83.$$

If the stock drops another point to $66, the position will gain nearly $500. But if the stock rises, then the current value of the position will decrease.

The new position hedge ratio is

$$h_p = .59/.41 = 1.44.$$

To adjust the hedge, twelve more call options must be bought; then the ratio of calls to puts will be $29/20 = 1.45$, and the investor will have a nearly perfect hedge. (The alternative adjustment is to sell eight puts, to give a ratio of

$17/12 = 1.42$, but since this would involve selling underpriced options, the first alternative is preferred.)

Adjusting the position to reduce the exposure from any movement in the stock, the investor buys twelve more August 70 calls. (Note that the investor may want to maintain negative exposure. If it is thought that the stock will continue its decline, the investor may wish to maintain the current hedge, which is bearish on the stock. Then the investor will profit from the decline in the value of the stock even more than if a zero hedge is held.)

With the adjustment, the value of the position is now

$$V = 29 \times 200 + 20 \times 425 = 14,300,$$

and the cost of adjusting the hedge is $12 \times 200 = 2,400$.

The adjusted profit profile is shown in Figure 9–8. Note that the adjustment now gives zero exposure at $S = 67$.

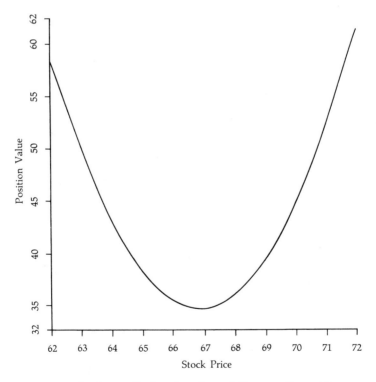

Figure 9–8 Profit profile for the adjusted Honeywell straddle

Honeywell continues to drop: readjust or close out. With 25 days to the August expiration, Honeywell has dropped another two points to $65 a share. (See Table 9–7.) It has now dropped five points since the position was initiated, and has had three trading days to adjust to the announcement. The current option prices reflect a higher market estimate of volatility on the market. Even though the stock has declined by two points, the November and February 70 calls are priced higher than they were two days earlier. Indeed, they are even higher than they were five days earlier when the stock stood at 70.

The investor must now reassess the estimate of the volatility and consider the likelihood that the market has discounted the announcement into the option volatility. The market price is still too low given the investor's estimates of the true market price. But those estimates are based on the belief that the volatility is .5. Was that too high, or is the market still not fully aware?

The investor can continue to hold the position, possibly readjusting again for the change in the position hedge ratio, or the investor can get out. If the investor does get out now, the value of the position will be

$$V = 29 \times 100 + 20 \times 550 = 13,900,$$

and the total cost of the position will be the initial cost of 8,250 and the cost of the adjustment in the hedge ratio of 2,400. The total cost will be $10,650, giving a profit from the transaction of $3,250—over a 30-percent return on investment over a five-day period. (See Table 9–8.)

One important point in this example is that the investor is trading on the option mispricing, and not on the stock price movement. While profit coincided with a sharp change in the stock price, it was not predicated on the stock price changing. Rather, it was based on the market assessment of the stock volatility being incorrect. To see that this is so, consider the following scenario.

Table 9–7
Honeywell Option Prices with Twenty-Five Days to August Expiration
$(S = 65)$

E	August	November	February
70	1	4⅜	6⅝
	2.35	6.80	9.73
	− .40	− .52	− .56
70p	5½	8	9¼
	6.95	10½	12.28
	.60	.48	.44

Assume Honeywell had reported publicly that it will have an important announcement to make on the success of its ECM system in the next few days. Many investors realize that this report drastically increases the volatility of Honeywell stock in the short term, and bid for the Honeywell options accord-

Table 9–8
Steps in the Honeywell Option Strategy

1. *Buy underpriced August 70 call*
   Buy underpriced August 70 put
   (30 days to August expiration, $S = 70$)
   Hedge ratio:

   $$h_p = \frac{.46}{.54} = .85$$

   Position value:

   $$V = 17 \times 250 + 20 \times 200 = 8,250$$

   Cost of position:

   $$c = 8,250$$

2. *Adjust the position to maintain riskless hedge*
   (27 days to August expiration, $S = 67$)
   Hedge ratio:

   $$h_p = \frac{.59}{.41} = 1.44$$

   Position value:

   $$V = 29 \times 200 + 20 \times 425 = 14,300$$

   Cost of adjustment:

   $$c = 12 \times 200 = 2,400$$

3. *Close out position*
   (25 days to August expiration, $S = 65$)
   Position value:

   $$V = 29 \times 100 + 20 \times 550 = 13,900$$

   Total cost:

   $$8,250 + 2,400 = 10,650$$

   Profit after liquidation:

   $$13,900 - 10,650 = 3,250$$

ingly. The options will adjust for the market's increased expectation of Honeywell stock volatility. The options will become correctly priced given the increased future range of Honeywell stock prices.

If the investor takes the position in the option before the report of the pending announcement, then profit from the position will be made even before the stock moves. The investor can close the position out once the options move upward in conformity with the higher future stock volatility. Once the options become correctly priced, the full potential profit will be realized. On the other hand, if the report is made public before the investor can initiate the position, then the profit opportunity will be gone. With the options correctly priced for the increased volatility in the Honeywell stock, the profit opportunity from the option strategy will be gone, even though the announcement has not yet been made, and the stock has not yet moved.

Chapter 10 THE USE OF OPTIONS IN PORTFOLIO MANAGEMENT

The use of option trading strategies can alter the return structure on a portfolio. An investor can use options to lock in the return gained on the stock, to minimize the possible loss on investment, or to accentuate the gains from an increase in the stock price. While these strategies have been discussed in reference to a single stock, they can also be applied to a portfolio of stocks.

The return structure of an investor's portfolio can be modified in the same way that the return structure of any one stock can be modified. The return distribution of the portfolio can be molded to minimize the risk of loss, or to maximize the probability of receiving a certain range of returns. As would be expected, evaluating the end result of combining an assortment of positions on a variety of stocks is more complex than dealing with just one stock. However, the general strategies involved are the same as those that have already been covered.

The ability to mold the return distribution will be appealing to many investors, particularly to portfolio managers who have specific investment objectives in mind. For example, a pension or trust fund manager may be expected to achieve a return of 8 to 10 percent on the portfolio. It is not expected to double the client's money, but if there is a significant loss, the manager may lose the client or his or her job. The typical method of diversification to reduce this risk will not completely serve the manager's purpose, since there is always a chance that the market will decline enough to present such a loss.

The manager would like to enter an insurance arrangement that would eliminate the left-hand tail of the return distribution. The manager would be willing to pay another investor an insurance premium if the investor would absorb the loss should the portfolio decline too far. Options provide a way for the investment manager to buy that protection.

THE ROLE OF OPTIONS IN EFFECTIVE PORTFOLIO STRATEGY

The investment strategy of modern portfolio theory is concerned with two variables: risk and return. The investor is faced with a tradeoff between the two and can gain a higher expected return only by accepting a greater risk of falling higher or lower than that return. Conversely, for each level of risk, there is a given expected return possible. The investor's choice is simply to select the desired level of risk and then receive the expected return associated with that level of risk. (Alternatively, the investor can choose the desired level of expected return, and the corresponding risk will be given.)

This approach locks the manager into a particular structure of returns. It is conventionally assumed that the rate of return to stocks is normally distributed. The investor is then forced into a return distribution such as that shown in Figure 10-1. The shape of this distribution is symmetric and is totally described by the mean and the variance of the portfolio's return. The mean specifies the center of the distribution, and the variance determines the spread around the mean. The tails of the distribution never hit the axis, so that there is some possibility of enormous returns. And, there is some possibility of losing everything.

If the investor is uncomfortable with the risk implied by this distribution, the variance of the portfolio can be reduced by levering it down. Less of the portfolio will be held in stocks and more of the portfolio in bonds, or a larger

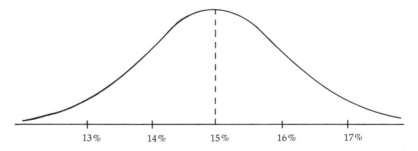

13%   14%   15%   16%   17%

Figure 10-1 The distribution of the return to a portfolio of stocks

*The return is normally distributed. The mean return is 15 percent. The probability of receiving a particular return is represented by the height of the figure at that return.

proportion of the portfolio will be held in the more stable stocks. In lowering the variance of the portfolio, the manager also lowers the mean or expected return, and ends up with a return distribution as shown in Figure 10–2. It is still a normal distribution, however, so there is still some chance of receiving a return that is far from the mean return. The chance of receiving a negative return, measured as the area under the curve to the left of $r = 0\%$, is lower than it is in the portfolio described by Figure 10–1, but there still is that chance.

Let us compare the return distribution depicted in Figures 10–1 and 10–2 with the sort of return distribution that the pension fund manager would most prefer. If willing to forgo some potential for a large return to eliminate the possibility of a negative return, the manager might have a distribution such as that in Figure 10–3. In this figure, the probability of having a negative return is zero. For the fund manager, this may translate into having a zero probability of being out of a job.

A striking feature of this distribution is that the expected return for the portfolio depicted by Figure 10–3 is the same as the expected return for the portfolio depicted by Figure 10–2. The risk of a negative loss has been eliminated with no loss in the level of expected returns. For those accustomed to the traditional risk-return tradeoff this may seem impossible, since the investor must have to give up something to get the benefit of having no chance of a negative return. But in this case the tradeoff is between the right-hand tail and the left-hand tail of the distribution rather than between the mean and the variance of the distribution. As Figure 10–3 shows, the investor has not only lost

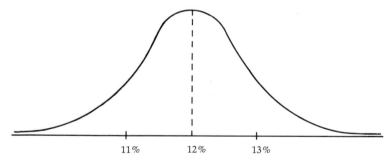

Figure 10–2 The distribution of the return to a portfolio of stocks

*The distribution of the stock return is again normally distributed, but the variance of the return is lower than the return represented by Figure 10–1. The price paid of a lower variance is a lower mean return. Note that there is still the possibility of receiving a return less than 0 percent.

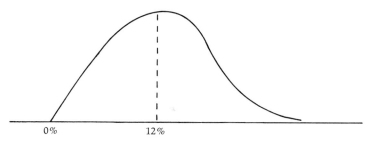

Figure 10-3 The distribution preferred by the portfolio manager

*There is no risk of receiving a negative return. The mean return is the same as in Figure 10-2. The price paid to eliminate the chance of a negative return is a lower chance for a large return.

all probability of having a return below a negative return, but has also substantially reduced the upward potential of the portfolio. Essentially, the option position the investor has taken involves selling another investor the upward potential of the portfolio on the terms that all risk of any negative return is also taken. If the portfolio does extremely well, the option position will transfer that gain to the other investor. The price the other investor pays for this chance at the high return is to take any loss that would result in a negative return. (In the particular example of the pension fund manager, the loss of the upward potential may not be altogether undesirable. Too high a rate of return may be counterproductive, since the actuarial rate may be increased and the manager judged against a higher standard.)

When dealing with stocks, the only tradeoff is between the mean and the variance. The investor can lever the portfolio up or down, and in doing so alters the shape of the distribution as depicted with Figures 10-1 and 10-2. When options positions are added to the investor's arsenal, other desirable features of the distribution besides the mean return can be traded away to get rid of undesirable features. To eliminate a portion of the undesirable left tail, the desirable right tail may be traded away. Essentially, the option position allows the investor to package up the two tails in a certain proportion and sell it for a certain price.

This is just one of many possible strategies that the manager could have taken to modify the return distribution. Rather than selling off the potential for large returns to eliminate the left tail, the left tail could have been sold off for a lump sum insurance option premium. The variety of positions and the possible variations in the return distribution are endless. In the next section, we will illustrate just a few of the most useful ones.

THE EFFECT OF OPTION POSITIONS
ON PORTFOLIO RETURNS

The return on an option position can be plotted as a function of the underlying stock price. These plots were used in the previous chapters to derive the profit profile for various option strategies as a function of the stock price. But such a relationship does not follow through when a portfolio of options is plotted against a portfolio of stocks. Given a particular value for the portfolio, there is no way to know exactly what the value of the option position on the portfolio will be.

One reason for this is that generally not all the stocks in the portfolio will have option positions. Some stocks may not even have options listed. There is then a chance that there will be a change in the value of the stocks that have no option positions without there being a similar change in the stocks that do have options. The portfolio as a whole will then change in value without a concomitant change in the value of the options.

For example, say an investor has a portfolio of fifty different stocks, and buys puts on ten of the fifty stocks. This position will give protection against a drop in the price of any of the ten stocks, but it will not give full protection against a decline in the overall portfolio. It is conceivable that the majority of the stocks in the portfolio will decline in price while the ten that have the puts remain unchanged or even increase in value. Only if the puts are placed on stocks that are perfectly correlated with the portfolio will a decline in the portfolio always be counteracted by an increase in the value of the puts.

The investor in this case is in the same position as a firm that only insures several of their stores. If the store that is insured burns down, the firm is covered for the loss. But, there is always the risk that the other stores will burn down. It would be less risky for the firm to insure all the stores for half their value than to insure half the stores for their full value. Options are like insurance. By using the options correctly, the investor can buy insurance that protects the firm from downside risk in the case of buying a call, or sell insurance to other investors and gain the value of the insurance premium.

As the number of different stocks that are involved in the put strategy increases, the probability that the option position will react to changes in the value of the portfolio will also increase. If the investor covers every stock in the portfolio, then protection from a decline in the portfolio is assured. No matter what combination of stocks leads the decline, they will be covered.

An important principle in using options, then, is to be highly diversified in the types of stocks that are covered by options. The objective is to get the option position as closely correlated with the stocks as possible, so that a change in the stock portfolio is met by the desired change in the options. If the portfolio is heavily weighted toward electronics stocks, then the options should also be in electronics stocks. If there are not many stocks which have options available, then options should be taken on stocks that are closely correlated with the stocks that are held.

Ideally, the option position should be taken on each stock in the portfolio, with the weight of the position on a given stock being proportional to the weight of the stock in the portfolio. But even then, the investor cannot be certain how the value of the options will react to changes in the portfolio's value.

This can be illustrated by the simple case of an investor who holds one hundred shares of two stocks, each with one option written on it. Say both stocks are initially at 45, and each has an option written at an exercise price of 50. Say the stock portfolio increases in value from $90 to $100 at the options' maturity date. If the increase in the value of the portfolio is due to one stock rising to 55 while the other stock remains at 45, then the investor receives only $5 of the $10 increase in the portfolio's value. On the other hand, if the increase in the portfolio is due to both stocks rising to 50, then the investor receives the full $10 increase in value. Without knowing the value of each individual stock at the end of the period, it is impossible to know which options have been exercised, and what the return to the investor is. See Table 10-1.

Alternatively, say the investor buys one put at 40 on each of the two stocks, and the value of the stock portfolio at the maturity date is 70. If the de-

Table 10-1
Own 100 Shares of Stock A and Stock B

When purchased:

Price of A = $45
Price of B = $45
Value of portfolio = $9,000
Write option on both stocks with $E = $50

At maturity:

Value of portfolio = $10,000

Price of A = 55 ⎱	Receive $500 from
Price of B = 45 ⎰	stock appreciation
Price of A = 50 ⎱	Receive $1,000 from
Price of B = 50 ⎰	stock appreciation

cline in value is due to both stocks dropping to 35, then the investor gains a return of $10 from the put position. But if the decline is due to one stock drop-
ping to 25 while the other remains at 45, then the return from the put position
is 15. See Table 10–2.

These problems make it more difficult to assess the effect of an option
position on the return distribution of the portfolio. Given a particular return
on the portfolio, there may be any number of different stocks that are above
the exercise price. But if we know the probability that the portfolio of stocks
will have any particular return, and we know the option position on the portfolio, there are mathematical methods available that describe the return distribution.

However, as the number of optioned stocks in the portfolio increases, the
complexity of determining the return distribution goes up dramatically. For
example, to determine the return distribution of a portfolio of stocks when
options are written on twenty stocks, over one million (2^{20}) probability statements must be evaluated, with each probability statement in turn being calculated by a twenty-one-fold iterated integral. Such a computation is cum-
bersome for even the latest generation computers. It is no wonder, then, that
portfolio managers interested in the use of options have had difficulty assessing the exact effect of the option positions on their portfolio returns!

Table 10–2
Buy put option on both stocks with $E = \$40$

At maturity:

Value of portfolio = $7,000

Price of A = 35 } Receive $1,000 from put
Price of B = 35 }

Price of A = 25 } Receive $1,500 from put
Price of B = 45 }

Expressing the Optioned Portfolio in Terms of Share-Equivalents

The return distribution of an optioned portfolio can be determined by translat-
ing the option position into share equivalents through the use of the option
hedge ratio. The hedge ratio for the option tells how the option will move with
a small change in the stock price, and therefore tells the investor how many
shares of stock will give the same amount of "play" as the option.

For example, if an option has a hedge ratio of .5, then it will move half a point when the stock moves by one point. Thus the option gives the same amount of play as holding fifty shares of stock. In terms of share-equivalents, the option has a fifty-share equivalent. By converting all of the options in the portfolio into their share-equivalents, the investor can translate the current option position into a portfolio of stocks which has a risk and reward potential that is equivalent.

This technique will be valuable for seeing what the risk of the position is over the very short term. However, it does not eliminate the difficulties of determining the return distribution of the portfolio over a reasonable time period. This is because the hedge ratio, and hence the share-equivalent, will vary as the time-to-expiration of the option approaches, and as the stock price changes. For example, in order to assess the return distribution of the portfolio over the next month, the share-equivalent for each option must be calculated for each possible stock price that might exist in one month. And that calculation must be made conditional on all the possible stock prices of all of the other stocks held in the portfolio. The same problem then exists that was previously outlined—an enormous number of possibilities must be covered.

To illustrate this, suppose an investor holds one hundred shares of Stock A and Stock B, which are currently trading at $45 a share. The investor writes options on both stocks with an exercise price of $50. Assuming the options have four months to expiration, the riskless interest rate is 10 percent, and the stocks both have a volatility of .3, the hedge ratio for both stocks will be .37. In terms of share-equivalents, each option position will be equivalent to a short position of thirty-seven shares in the underlying stock. In terms of *instantaneous* return, the optioned portfolio contains sixty-three shares of each stock.

Of course, investors are interested in returns over a finite time period, not instantaneous returns. And unfortunately, the share equivalent will change over any given time period as the time to expiration of the options and as the value of the underlying stocks change. Table 10–3 illustrates two of an infinite number of combinations of share equivalents that are possible for one particular value of the underlying stock portfolio after one month.

There is a way around this problem, however. Although the analytical solution to the return distribution is extremely complex, there are computationally efficient algorithms that give close approximations to the return distribution. These algorithms are beyond the scope of the book, but a description of them, and a computer program for applying them, is available from the author. The algorithms are based on the use of the expected value of the op-

Table 10–3
Own 100 shares of stock A and stock B

When purchased:

Price of A = $45
Price of B = $45

Value of portfolio = $9,000

Write option on stocks with $E = $50
Hedge ratio for both options = .37
Share equivalent for both option positions = − .37 share

In one month:

Value of portfolio = $10,000

| Price of A = $55 | Share equivalent of Option A | = 81 shares |
| Price of B = $45 | Share equivalent of Option B | = 32 shares |

The share equivalent portfolio is:
    19 shares of Stock A
    68 shares of Stock B

| Price of A = $50 | Share equivalent of Option A | = 60 shares |
| Price of B = $50 | Share equivalent of Option B | = 60 shares |

The share equivalent portfolio is:
    40 shares of Stock A
    40 shares of Stock B

tioned portfolio conditional on the return to the stock portfolio. Asymptotically (that is, as the number of optioned stocks becomes large), these algorithms will approach the same distribution as the analytical solution and will take a computer seconds, rather than the hours that would be required to compute the returns by the analytical method.

OPTION STRATEGIES IN PORTFOLIO MANAGEMENT

The emphasis of the strategies presented in this chapter is on the role of options for diversification or risk minimization. In previous chapters we have considered the use of options in active strategies where the investor takes advantage of a particular market situation. This chapter looks at the use of options to achieve a particular return distribution under the efficient market assumption that the investor has no advantage in predicting the future course of the market.

Buying Call Options

Call options are usually considered to be speculative instruments because they are volatile and because there is a reasonable chance that they will lose all their value in the few months to expiration. However, if used judiciously, trading in options is less risky than trading in the underlying stock. Indeed, buying call options is actually the most efficient way to reduce or eliminate the left tail of the return distribution. It is thus the most conservative investment strategy when used correctly.

To illustrate this point, consider an investor who has $4,800 to invest, and is contemplating buying one hundred shares of Upjohn at $48 per share. Compare this investment with buying a nine-month 50 option in Upjohn for $400 and putting the remainder of the money in treasury bills earning 6 percent. If the stock goes up ten points, the investor will earn $1,000 on the stock. On the option, the investor will gain just $400. Also nine months worth of interest on the $4,400 in the treasury bills will be gained, for a total return of $600.

What will be the return on the two portfolios if the stock drops ten points? If the stock is held, $1,000 will be lost. If the option portfolio is held, the initial cost of the option will be lost, but the interest on the remaining $4,400 will be gained, for a net loss of $200. The option portfolio is clearly less risky than holding the underlying stock. If the stock price increases, the return on the option portfolio is lower (although it will approach the return on the stock for large increases in the stock price). But if the stock price decreases, the loss on the option portfolio is also lower: no matter how low the stock drops, the option portfolio will never lose more than $200. The contrast in the return distribution for these two portfolios is illustrated in Table 10–4 and in Figure 10–4. The stock has a normal return distribution, while the option portfolio has a return distribution that eliminates the left tail.

Of course, if we compared the stock purchase with the option purchase, the return distribution for the option would look much less favorable than the return depicted here. But comparing the $400 option position with a $4,800 stock position gives a distorted picture of the alternatives facing the investor. If an investor has a given amount of money to invest, a complete comparison must ask how he or she invests the full amount. And given any initial amount of funds, those funds can be invested in an option position that will remove much of the risk of loss that would be entailed if the same funds were placed directly in the underlying stock. This should not be surprising when we recall that an option is in part an insurance contract.

Table 10-4

Comparison of Return from Buying the Stock and from Buying a Call on the Stock
(Initial Stock Price = 48; Cost of Option = 400)

(1) Stock price at expiration date	(2) Option value at expiration date (E = 50)	(3) Return to treasury bills (r = 6%)	(4) Return from stock position ((column 1 − 48) × 100)	(5) Return from option position ((columns 2 + 3) − 400)
35	0	200	− 1,300	− 200
40	0	200	− 800	− 200
45	0	200	− 300	− 200
50	0	200	200	− 200
55	500	200	700	300
60	1,000	200	1,200	800

More of the tail of the distribution is removed the higher the exercise
price of the options. If the investor in the preceding example had chosen an
exercise price of 45 rather than 50, the maximum possible loss from the option
position would have been $400. The option position may have cost $600 rather
than $400, and any decline in the stock price down to 45 would have to be
absorbed. But while a higher exercise price gives more protection, it also requires a higher risk or insurance premium. The insurance premium for the option with the 50 exercise price is the full $400, since the option is out-of-the-

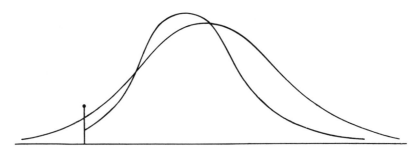

Figure 10-4 The return to the portfolio of stocks and the return to the portfolio composed of call options and treasury bills

*The return to the stock portfolio is represented by the normal distribution as used in
Figures 10-1 and 10-2. The return to the option portfolio has a minimum possible
return of −4 percent. The right tail of the option distribution is lower than the right tail
of the stock distribution, indicating that the option portfolio has a smaller probability of
a large return.

money and has no intrinsic value. The insurance premium for the 45 option is only $300, since the option is in-the-money by 3, and has an intrinsic value of $300. The insurance value increases with the exercise price because the probability that the stock will drop below the exercise price increases. As the option gets further into the money, the probability that the stock will drop below the exercise price becomes smaller, and the insurance premium drops to zero. The value of an option that is far into the money approaches the difference between the stock price and the exercise price of the option.

Since the cost of downside protection increases with an increase in the exercise price, the lowest exercise price for options should be chosen that will fulfill the investor's purpose. If the only concern is eliminating the probability of a loss of 10 percent, then the investor should buy options with an exercise price that is about 10 percent below the current stock price. If options with a higher exercise price are bought, the investor will be paying for more insurance than needed. The options with a lower exercise price will cost more, but a greater portion of that cost is the intrinsic value of the option. The investor will be paying less for the actual insurance package that is implicit in the option price.

A higher exercise price may look attractive since the cost of the option is lower, and thus more of the initial funds are available for other investment opportunities. But from a practical standpoint, an investment manager may be in a precarious position if too high an exercise price is chosen.

An exercise price that is higher than necessary reduces the prospects for a moderate positive return. Say the investor in Upjohn bought an option with an exercise price of 60. Then there is the chance that the stock would increase by over 20 percent, going from 48 to 60, while the investor would have a loss on the option position. For the portfolio manager, there may be some embarrassment when the option position is worthless while the underlying stock has increased substantially in value. A lower exercise price will still give protection from a decline in the stock while reducing the prospect of having a loss when the market is rising.

One may be hesitant to hold nothing but options, either because it would be difficult to persuade clients that it is not a highly speculative strategy, or because one wishes to invest in certain firms that do not have options listed. In that case, the minimum level of return cannot be derived as accurately. The portfolio may yield a return below the benchmark case of all options expiring worthless, since the other stocks may drop by any amount. The principle is still the same, however. The left tail can be reduced in proportion to the amount that the investor utilizes call options rather than buying the stock outright.

Writing Call Options

Buying call options allows the investor to sell off the left-hand tail of the return distribution at the cost of the option premium. Writing call options allows the investor to sell off the right-hand tail of the distribution and gain the value of the option premium. Since the right-hand tail of the distribution is desirable, other investors will be willing to pay a premium to the investor for the right to receive any returns in that tail. The premium is received when the option is written and added to the initial value of the portfolio. Since the initial value of the portfolio is increased, the return for the portfolio will be higher for any strategy as long as the stocks do not exceed the exercise price of the options.

The tradeoff in writing a call option is basically to increase the expected return of the portfolio in exchange for selling off the potential for large returns. The distribution of the portfolio for various levels of option writing is shown in Figure 10-5. These figures show the return distribution as the percent of stocks covered by the options goes from 0 percent to 75 percent. Figure a of 10-5 shows the return distribution when there are no options held. This distribution is similar to that presented in Figure 10-1. The following figures show the return when there are options held on 25 percent of the stock, on 50 percent of the stock, and on 75 percent of the stock.

The left tail of the distribution is unchanged in shape, but the distribution is shifted over to the right by the amount of the premium gained. The right-hand tail of the distribution shrinks as the size of the option position increases. The maximum return to the portfolio is limited by the event that all the options are exercised. When combined with a portfolio position, writing options is riskier than the option buying strategy previously described. The investor is still subject to the risk of very low returns, while the upward potential is reduced. However, the probability of receiving a moderate return is increased.

Two of the pitfalls of option writing bear mentioning here. First, investors tend to overestimate their expected return when writing options. They see the immediate gain from the option premium, but forget that they are still subject to declines in the stock for the duration of the option contract. Writing options properly can earn an initial premium equal to over 10 percent of the value of the underlying stock, but that return is by no means guaranteed.

Second, investors feel that any loss in the value of the stock over the duration of the option can be made up by repeated option writing. They feel that if they continue to write options as the stock declines, they will reclaim the loss on the stock through the option premia. A simple example will illustrate the fallacy of this approach. Say the investor writes a 45 Upjohn call and receives a premium of $6. By the maturity date, the stock has declined to 40,

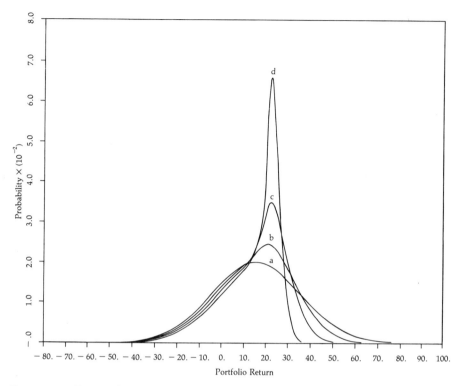

Figure 10-5 Return distribution on a stock portfolio when call options are written on 0 percent (figure a), 25 percent (figure b), 50 percent (figure c), and 75 percent (figure d) of the portfolio of stocks

and the investor again writes an option, this time at 40, and receives a $4 premium. The stock decline has been met with a net loss of zero. The stock declines again, this time to 32. The investor writes a 30 call for 4, and by the expiration date the stock has increased to 40. The option is exercised at 30, with a net loss of 6. By writing options with the decline in the stock, the investor is forced to sell at 30 rather than have ownership of the stock at 40. The loss is modest in this case, but it takes little imagination to find situations where this strategy will expose the investor to substantial losses.

Put Options

The put is an obvious tool to use to gain protection against decreases in the portfolio's value. As the stocks decline in value, the puts will increase in value. If every stock is covered by a put, the investor will be fully protected against a market decline. What the stock loses in value will be gained back in the value of the put. And the investor will realize any increase in the portfolio less the initial cost of the puts.

Figure 10-6 shows the return distribution of the portfolio for varying weights of puts being bought. The portfolio with no puts held, shown in Figure a of 10-6, has a normal return distribution like that shown in Figure 10-1. In the extreme case with one put held for each stock, the portfolio loses all probability of a decline, and the expected return of the portfolio is reduced by the cost of the puts. As the ratio of puts to stock increases beyond this point, the puts become counterproductive. Too many puts leaves the investor exposed to an increase in the value of the stocks. In the extreme case where the proportion of puts to the stocks becomes large, the investor may have enormous gains if

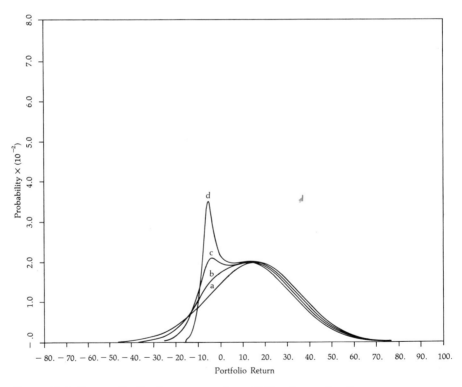

Figure 10-6 Return distribution on a stock portfolio when put options are purchased on 0 percent (figure a), 25 percent (figure b), 50 percent (figure c), and 75 percent (figure d) of the portfolio of stocks

the value of the stocks declines, while losing most of the investment if the portfolio increases in value and the puts become worthless.

The use of puts allows the investor the same sort of protection from low returns that the call option strategy does. Also it may be more attractive than the call strategy because it is a less drastic step from the usual portfolio. With the call strategy, the investor needs to sell all the stocks and start buying call options in their place. With puts, the investor can take the current portfolio of stocks and augment the holdings with put options.

Ideally, the investor should hold puts on all the stock in the portfolio with the weight of the put position in each stock being the same as the weight of the stock in the portfolio. If the investor holds four times as many shares of Polaroid as he or she does of IBM, then the investor should have four times as many put options on Polaroid as on IBM. The problem is that the put options are not available on many stocks, so it will be likely that many of the stocks that the investor holds will not be able to have this protection. The more stocks that are unprotected, the greater the chance that those stocks will decline in value without the protected stocks also declining, and the investor will have a loss in the portfolio without the put options compensating for it. The investor can minimize this problem by selecting put options in such a way that the option position is highly correlated with the stock position. The investor should maximize the probability that when the value of the portfolio of stocks declines, the value of the stocks that have put options also declines. In practice, it is possible to get an option position that is closely correlated even if none of the stocks in the portfolio have put options listed.

Combining Puts with Writing Covered Calls

If the investor shares the pension fund manager's preference for a high probability of a moderate return while eliminating the probability of receiving a very low return, the best strategy to follow is to use the proceeds of writing calls to buy puts. The investor then has the protection from a decline in the portfolio. By using the proceeds from writing call options the investor's initial capital is conserved. Since the investor's funds are augmented by the call option premium, the expected return to the fund will be higher. The price the investor pays to receive the premium on the calls is a reduction in the chance of receiving high returns. With this strategy the investor sells off the right tail of the distribution, and uses the proceeds to sell off the left tail of the distribution. The chances of a large loss or a large gain are both reduced, and the chance of a moderate return is increased.

Writing an option at the money leaves the investor with a high chance of losing the stock, which may be undesirable because of transaction costs. A better strategy is to write the option at an exercise price somewhat higher than the current stock price, and buy the put at an exercise price that is an equal distance below the stock price. Then some gain will be made on the stock to offset the commissions if it is called away. The premium from the call will still more than meet the cost of the puts.

This strategy will give the investor an initial profit on the option transaction as long as the exercise price for the call is as far above the current stock price as the exercise price of the put is below the stock price.

The effect of writing calls and buying puts is shown in Figure 10-7. As in previous figures, Figure a of 10-7 shows the return distribution of the portfolio

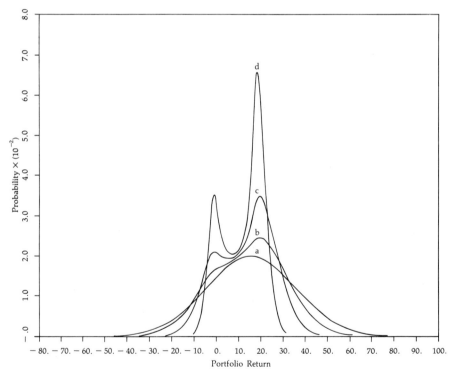

Figure 10-7 Return distribution of a stock portfolio when call options are written and put options are bought on 0 percent (figure a), 25 percent (figure b), 50 percent (figure c), and 75 percent (figure d) of the portfolio of stocks

when there is no option position taken. The following figures show the return distribution as the percent of the stock position that has a put and a call position taken increases, first with 25 percent of the stocks covered by the joint put-call position, then with 50 percent and 75 percent of the stock held having both a put bought and a call option written. In the extreme case of all stock being covered, the maximum downside risk is determined by the exercise price of the put, while the upside potential is completely cut off by the exercise price of the call (which is greater than the exercise price of the put).

CONCLUSION

The potential for molding the return structure of the portfolio by taking option positions is limitless. The difficulty is determining just what the effect of any given option position will be. While the examples presented give some insight into the direction and magnitude of these effects, the precise effect will differ from portfolio to portfolio, and according to the particular option used in the strategy.

As with the option strategies discussed earlier in the book, the four strategies we have discussed in this chapter are just the start of the option strategies that are available in altering the return distribution of a portfolio. For example, rather than holding a number of puts equal to the number of calls written, one may allow a bit more upside potential by writing puts on 50 percent of the portfolio while writing calls on only 25 percent. Or one may use a long call position to increase the leverage of the portfolio along with a put position to improve the downside protection.

The use of options in portfolio management is one of the most recent areas explored, and is clearly an area of option theory that has great practical application.

REFERENCES

The use of options to expand the types of return distributions available to the investor was first considered by Ross (1976). Papers by Breeden and Litzenberger (1978), Arditti and John (1980), Banz and Miller (1978), and Hakansson (1978) also consider the theoretical argument for using options to increase the number of contingencies that can be covered by investment strategies. These studies present theoretical arguments, but give no insight into just *how* options positions can be used to achieve a desired result.

An empirical study by Merton, Scholes, and Gladstein (1978) uses historical return data to show how the return distribution is affected by various option positions. However, as Gastineau and Madansky (1979) point out, these simulations that use historical data are of little value in determining the future effect of the same strategy should the investment climate change. Gastineau and Madansky present a discussion of the case of share equivalents in determining the risk of an optioned portfolio.

Appendix A COMPUTER PROGRAMS

The calculations for the option pricing formula, the hedge ratio, and the related measures of profit potential and volatility are tedious and time consuming to do by hand. To be of practical use in option trading, these must be calculated quickly and repeatedly. Accordingly it is essential that the option trader have computer facilities available.

A set of computer programs has been developed to prepare the tables and figures of the book. One program calculates the value of call and put options, the hedge ratios for options and for positions, and the exposure and sensitivity of option positions. When coupled with a graphic display, it also will plot the profit profile for option positions. The program was used in Chapters 8 and 9. A second program provides the graphics for determining the return distribution of a stock portfolio with option positions. This program was used in Chapter 10.

These two programs are available from the author in both Fortran and Basic languages.

For those who do not have access to a computer, this appendix provides a pocket calculator program that does many of the calculations necessary for using the option strategies. This program is written for the Texas Instruments T.I. 59 calculator. This program will compute:

1. The call option formula value, C
2. The call option hedge ratio, h
3. The put option formula, P

4. The put option hedge ratio, h
5. The position value, V
6. The position hedge at ratio, h_p
7. The position exposure ratio, x_p.

The procedure for using the program is presented, followed by the programming steps.

PROCEDURE

To calculate the Black-Scholes call option value:

Step	Procedure	Press	Display
1	Enter value for S	A	S
2	Enter value for T	B	T
3	Enter value for E	C	E
4	Enter value for R	D	R
5	Enter value for σ	E	σ
6	Compute value of $C(S,T,E,r,\sigma)$	1 2nd E	$C(S,T,E,r,\sigma)$

To calculate the call option hedge ratio, complete steps 1–5:

7	Compute call hedge ratio h	2 2nd E	h (call option)

To compute the put option value, complete steps 1–5:

8	Compute value of $P(S,T,E,r,\sigma)$	3 2nd E	$P(S,T,E,r,\sigma)$

To compute the put option hedge ratio, complete steps 1–5:

9	Compute put option hedge ratio	4 2nd E	h (put)

To calculate the value of a position with two options, complete steps 1–5:

10	Enter number of options in first position, n_1	$x \gtrless t$	
11	Enter number of options in second position, n_2	2nd A	n_1
12	Enter time to expiration for second option, T_2	2nd B	T_2
13	Enter exercise price of second option, E_2	2nd C	E_2
14	Enter cost of the position, c	2nd D	c
15a	If first option is a call, enter 1	$x \gtrless t$	

Step	Procedure	Press	Display
15b	If first option is a put, enter 3	$x \gtrless t$	
16a	If second option is a call, enter 1	SBR SBR*	
16b	If second option is a put, enter 3	SBR SBR	
17	Compute the value of $V = n_1 C_1 + n_2 C_2 - c$	5 2nd E	V

*SBR SBR means to press the SBR key twice

To calculate the position hedge ratio:

18a	If second option is a call, enter 2	$x \gtrless t$	
18b	If second option is a put, enter 4	$x \gtrless t$	
19a	If first option is a call, enter 2	SBR SBR	
19b	If first option is a put, enter 4	SBR SBR	
20	To compute the position hedge ratio h_p	6 2nd E	h_p

To calculate the exposure ratio complete steps 18 and 19:

21	Compute the exposure ratio x_p	7 2nd E	x_p

If the values of the inputs have already been entered (i.e., if the pre-requisite steps have already been completed), they do not need to be reentered before continuing. To recalculate any of the calculations with different inputs, only the necessary new input needs to be reentered. The other input will remain stored.

Programming Steps

Program step number	Key code	Key	Program step number	Key code	Key	Program step number	Key code	Key
000	91	R/S	010	00	00	020	71	SBR
001	53	(	011	18	18	021	01	01
002	71	SBR	012	65	X	022	11	11
003	00	00	013	71	SBR	023	94	+ / −
004	25	25	014	00	00	024	85	+
005	65	X	015	48	48	025	71	SBR
006	43	RCL	016	54	)	026	00	00
007	10	10	017	92	RTN	027	80	80
008	75	−	018	53	(	028	54	)
009	71	SBR	019	53	(	029	68	NOP

Program step number	Key code	Key	Program step number	Key code	Key	Program step number	Key code	Key
030	68	NOP	072	94	+ / −	114	65	X
031	68	NOP	073	85	+	115	43	RCL
032	68	NOP	074	01	1	116	11	11
033	36	PGM*	075	54	)	117	34	√x
034	14	14	076	22	INV	118	54	)
035	11	A	077	86	STF	119	92	RTN
036	36	PGM	078	01	01	120	53	(
037	14	14	079	92	RTN	121	71	SBR
038	12	B	080	53	(	122	00	00
039	22	INV	081	53	(	123	80	80
040	86	STF	082	53	(	124	75	−
041	01	01	083	43	RCL	125	71	SBR
042	68	NOP	084	10	10	126	01	01
043	94	+ / −	085	55	÷	127	11	11
044	85	+	086	43	RCL	128	54	)
045	01	1	087	12	12	129	92	RTN
046	54	)	088	54	)	130	71	SBR
047	92	RTN	089	23	LNX	131	00	00
048	53	(	090	85	+	132	25	25
049	43	RCL	091	53	(	133	94	+ / −
050	12	12	092	43	RCL	134	92	RTN
051	65	X	093	13	13	135	76	LBL
052	01	1	094	85	+	136	11	A
053	22	INV	095	43	RCL	137	42	STO
054	23	LNX	096	14	14	138	10	10
055	45	Yˣ	097	33	X²	139	91	R/S
056	53	(	098	55	÷	140	76	LBL
057	53	(	099	02	2	141	12	B
058	43	RCL	100	54	)	142	42	STO
059	13	13	101	65	X	143	11	11
060	65	X	102	43	RCL	144	91	R/S
061	43	RCL	103	11	11	145	76	LBL
062	11	11	104	54	)	146	13	C
063	54	)	105	55	÷	147	42	STO
064	94	+ / −	106	71	SBR	148	12	12
065	54	)	107	01	01	149	91	R/S
066	92	RTN	108	11	11	150	76	LBL
067	86	STF	109	54	)	151	14	D
068	07	07	110	92	RTN	152	42	STO
069	61	GTO	111	53	(	153	13	13
070	00	00	112	43	RCL	154	91	R/S
071	34	34	113	14	14	155	76	LBL

Program step number	Key code	Key	Program step number	Key code	Key	Program step number	Key code	Key
156	15	E	198	42	STO	240	20	20
157	42	STO	199	00	00	241	69	OP
158	14	14	200	71	SBR	242	06	06
159	91	R/S	201	40	IND	243	81	RST
160	76	LBL	202	00	00	244	53	(
161	16	A'	203	95	=	245	71	SBR
162	42	STO	204	42	STO	246	00	00
163	15	15	205	20	20	247	01	01
164	32	X ≷ T	206	86	STF	248	75	−
165	42	STO	207	40	IND	249	43	RCL
166	16	16	208	28	28	250	10	10
167	91	R/S	209	87	IFF	251	85	+
168	76	LBL	210	01	01	252	71	SBR
169	17	B'	211	03	03	253	00	00
170	42	STO	212	81	81	254	48	48
171	17	17	213	87	IFF	255	54	)
172	91	R/S	214	02	02	256	92	RTN
173	76	LBL	215	03	03	257	53	(
174	18	C'	216	86	86	258	71	SBR
175	42	STO	217	87	IFF	259	01	01
176	18	18	218	03	03	260	30	30
177	91	R/S	219	03	03	261	85	+
178	76	LBL	220	93	93	262	01	1
179	19	D'	221	87	IFF	263	54	)
180	42	STO	222	04	04	264	92	RTN
181	19	19	223	03	03	265	76	LBL
182	91	R/S	224	98	98	266	71	SBR
183	76	LBL	225	87	IFF	267	85	+
184	10	E'	226	05	05	268	02	2
185	42	STO	227	04	04	269	00	0
186	28	28	228	07	07	270	95	=
187	85	+	229	87	IFF	271	42	STO
188	02	2	230	06	06	272	08	08
189	00	0	231	04	04	273	32	X ≷ T
190	95	=	232	12	12	274	85	+
191	42	STO	233	04	4	275	02	2
192	07	07	234	04	4	276	00	0
193	71	SBR	235	03	3	277	95	=
194	04	04	236	03	3	278	42	STO
195	19	19	237	69	OP	279	09	09
196	73	RC*	238	04	04	280	73	RC*
197	07	07	239	43	RCL	281	08	08

Program step number	Key code	Key	Program step number	Key code	Key	Program step number	Key code	Key
282	42	STO	323	17	17	364	71	SBR
283	08	08	324	48	EXC	365	40	IND
284	73	RC*	325	11	11	366	09	09
285	09	09	326	48	EXC	367	53	(
286	42	STO	327	17	17	368	24	CE
287	09	09	328	43	RCL	369	65	X
288	91	R/S	329	18	18	370	43	RCL
289	71	SBR	330	48	EXC	371	15	15
290	40	IND	331	12	12	372	85	+
291	08	08	332	48	EXC	373	43	RCL
292	42	STO	333	18	18	374	04	04
293	20	20	334	92	RTN	375	65	X
294	71	SBR	335	71	SBR	376	43	RCL
295	03	03	336	40	IND	377	16	16
296	22	22	337	08	08	378	54	)
297	53	(	338	94	+ / −	379	94	+ / −
298	71	SBR	339	42	STO	380	92	RTN
299	40	IND	340	04	04	381	01	1
300	09	09	341	71	SBR	382	05	5
301	65	X	342	03	03	383	61	GTO
302	01	1	343	22	22	384	02	02
303	05	5	344	71	SBR	385	37	37
304	85	+	345	40	IND	386	02	2
305	43	RCL	346	09	09	387	03	3
306	20	20	347	53	(	388	01	1
307	65	X	348	24	CE	389	05	5
308	43	RCL	349	35	1/X	390	68	GTO
309	16	16	350	65	X	391	02	02
310	75	−	351	43	RCL	392	37	37
311	43	RCL	352	04	04	393	03	3
312	19	19	353	54	)	394	03	3
313	54	)	354	92	RTN	395	61	GTO
314	42	STO	355	53	(	396	02	02
315	20	20	356	71	SBR	397	37	37
316	71	SBR	357	40	IND	398	02	2
317	03	03	358	08	08	399	03	3
318	22	22	359	42	STO	400	03	3
319	43	RCL	360	04	04	401	03	3
320	20	20	361	71	SBR	402	03	3
321	92	RTN	362	03	03	403	07	7
322	43	RCL	363	22	22	404	61	GTO

Program step number	Key code	Key	Program step number	Key code	Key	Program step number	Key code	Key
405	02	02	424	00	0	443	03	3
406	37	37	425	42	STO	444	05	5
407	04	4	426	22	22	445	42	STO
408	02	2	427	02	2	446	26	26
409	61	GTO	428	04	4	447	03	3
410	02	02	429	04	4	448	05	5
411	37	37	430	42	STO	449	05	5
412	02	2	431	23	23	450	42	STO
413	03	3	432	02	2	451	27	27
414	03	3	433	05	5	452	92	RTN
415	03	3	434	07	7	453	76	LBL
416	61	GTO	435	42	STO	454	61	GTO
417	02	02	436	24	24	455	55	÷
418	37	37	437	02	2	456	03	3
419	01	1	438	08	8	457	06	6
420	42	STO	439	09	9	458	05	5
421	21	21	440	42	STO	459	95	=
422	01	1	441	25	25	460	91	R/S
423	03	3	442	03	3	461	00	0

*PGM 14A and 14B refer to the cumulative normal distribution function program which must be loaded in the master library chip.

Appendix B

The following are the volatilities for stocks with traded options, computed for March, 1980. As is mentioned in the text, these volatilities will change over time, and are presented only to give an indication of their relative magnitudes.

Abbott Laboratories	.31	Bally Manufacturing	.60
Aetna Life Insurance	.26	Bank of America	.23
Alcoa Aluminum	.27	Baxter Travenol Laboratories	.25
Allied Chemicals	.32	Beatrice Foods	.28
Allis-Chalmers	.32	Bethlehem Steel	.30
Amerada Hess	.38	Black and Decker	.31
American Broadcasting Co.	.33	Blue Bell	.27
American Cyanimide	.26	Boeing	.42
American Electrical Power	.25	Boise Cascade	.29
American Express	.29	Branif	.59
American Home Products	.30	Bristol Myers	.28
American Hospital Supply	.28	Brunswick	.38
American Telephone and		Burlington Northern	.25
Telegraph	.13	Burroughs	.30
AMF	.32	CBS	.22
AMP	.29	Caterpillar Tractor	.19
ASA	.40	Chase Manhattan	.25
ASARCO	.45	Citicorp	.28
Ashland Oil	.33	City Investing	.50
Atlantic Richfield	.26	Clorox	.53
Avnet Inc.	.35	Coastal States Gas	.42
Avon Products	.18	Coca-Cola	.30
Baker International	.36	Colgate-Palmolive	.28

Combustion Engineering	.32	Hilton	.36
Commonwealth Edison	.17	Holiday Inns	.52
Conoco	.28	Homestake Mining	.51
Consolidated Edison	.17	Honeywell	.26
Continental Telephone	.20	Household Finance Company	.22
Control Data	.37	Houston Oil and Mineral	.55
Corning Glass Works	.26	Howard Johnsons	.52
John Deere	.24	Hughes Tools	.39
Delta Air Lines	.26	INA	.27
Diamond Shamrock	.36	Inexco Oil	.50
Digital Equipment	.34	International Business Machines	.22
Disney Productions	.32	International Flavors and	
Dow Chemical	.32	Fragrance	.29
Dr. Pepper	.34	International Harvester	.19
Dresser Industries	.32	International Minerals and	
Duke Power	.19	Chemicals	.25
Dupont	.23	International Paper	.27
Eastern Gas and Fuel	.46	International Telephone and	
Eastman Kodak	.22	Telegraph	.20
Englehard Mineral and Chemical	.51	Itel	.50
Evans Products	.38	Johns-Mansville	.28
Exxon	.18	Johnson and Johnson	.20
Federal National Mortgage	.25	Joy Manufacturing	.30
Firestone Tire and Rubber	.29	K-Mart	.29
First Charter Financial	.47	Kennecott Copper	.42
Fleetwood Enterprises	.42	Kerr McGee	.31
Fluor	.34	Levi-Strauss	.30
Ford Motor Company	.20	Eli Lilly	.22
Freeport Metals	.43	Litton Industries	.45
GAF	.48	Louisiana Land and Exploration	.45
General Dynamics	.34	Louisiana-Pacific	.35
General Electric	.20	Lockheed	.42
General Foods	.22	MacDonald Douglas	.39
General Motors	.22	McDonalds	.26
General Telephone and Electronics	.15	MAPCO	.30
Georgia Pacific	.24	Marriott	.45
Gillette	.32	McDermott (J. Ray)	.39
Goodyear	.29	Merck and Co.	.23
Grace (W.R.)	.25	Merrill Lynch	.37
Great Western Financial	.38	Mesa Petroleum	.40
Greyhound	.36	Middle South Utilities	.27
Gulf Oil	.30	Minnesota Mining and	
Gulf and Western Industries	.38	Manufacturing	.24
Halliburton	.23	Mobil Oil	.25
Hercules	.35	Monsanto	.29
Heublein	.28	Motorola	.27
Hewlett-Packard	.30	National Cash Register	.30

National Distilling and Chemical	.32	Signal Companies	.32
National Industries	.26	Simplicity Pattern	.57
National Semiconductor	.54	Skyline	.45
Northwest Airlines	.33	Southern Company	.23
Northwest Industries	.26	Sperry Rand	.24
Norton Simon	.24	Squibb	.39
Occidental Petroleum	.44	Standard Oil of California	.30
Owens-Illinois	.26	Standard Oil of Indiana	.22
J.C. Penney's	.26	Sterling Drug	.37
Pennzoil	.32	Storage Technology	.55
Pepsico	.25	Syntex	.40
Perkin-Elmer	.40	TRW	.27
Phelps Dodge	.44	Tandy	.42
Philip Morris	.24	Teledyne	.38
Philips Petroleum	.28	Tenneco	.26
Pitney Bowes	.18	Texaco	.23
Pittston	.37	Texas Instruments	.27
Polaroid	.41	Tiger International	.49
PPG Industries	.27	Transamerica	.30
Proctor and Gamble	.13	Travelers	.23
R.C.A.	.32	Union Carbide	.22
Ralston Purina	.36	Union Oil	.31
Raytheon	.26	Union Pacific	.19
Reserve Oil and Gas	.45	United Air Lines	.37
Revlon	.28	U.S. Steel	.28
Reynolds Industries	.20	United Technologies	.27
Reynolds Metals	.34	UpJohn	.23
Rite Aid	.30	Virginia Electric and Power	.22
Rockwell International	.24	Warner Lambert	.27
Safeway Stores	.22	Western Union	.36
Santa Fe International	.42	Westinghouse Electric	.31
Schering Plough	.32	Weyerhaeuser	.32
Scott Paper	.36	Williams	.32
Seaboard Coast Line Industries	.36	Xerox	.24
Searle (G.D.)	.44	Zenith Radio	.38
Sears and Roebuck	.26		

Standard Normal Distribution Function

t	0	1	2	3	4	5	6	7	8	9
− 3.	.0013									
− 2.9	.0019	.0018	.0018	.0017	.0017	.0016	.0015	.0015	.0014	.0014
− 2.8	.0026	.0025	.0024	.0023	.0023	.0022	.0021	.0021	.0020	.0019
− 2.7	.0035	.0034	.0033	.0032	.0031	.0030	.0029	.0028	.0027	.0026
− 2.6	.0047	.0045	.0044	.0043	.0041	.0040	.0039	.0038	.0037	.0036
− 2.5	.0062	.0060	.0059	.0057	.0055	.0054	.0052	.0051	.0049	.0048
− 2.4	.0082	.0080	.0078	.0075	.0073	.0071	.0069	.0068	.0066	.0064
− 2.3	.0107	.0104	.0102	.0099	.0096	.0094	.0091	.0089	.0087	.0084
− 2.2	.0139	.0136	.0132	.0129	.0125	.0122	.0119	.0116	.0113	.0110
− 2.1	.0179	.0174	.0170	.0166	.0162	.0158	.0154	.0150	.0146	.0143
− 2.0	.0228	.0222	.0217	.0212	.0207	.0202	.0197	.0192	.0188	.0183
− 1.9	.0287	.0281	.0275	.0268	.0262	.0256	.0250	.0244	.0239	.0233
− 1.8	.0359	.0351	.0344	.0336	.0329	.0322	.0314	.0307	.0300	.0294
− 1.7	.0446	.0436	.0427	.0418	.0409	.0401	.0392	.0384	.0375	.0367
− 1.6	.0548	.0537	.0526	.0516	.0505	.0495	.0485	.0475	.0465	.0455
− 1.5	.0668	.0655	.0643	.0630	.0618	.0606	.0594	.0582	.0571	.0560
− 1.4	.0808	.0793	.0778	.0764	.0750	.0735	.0721	.0708	.0694	.0681
− 1.3	.0968	.0951	.0934	.0918	.0901	.0885	.0869	.0853	.0838	.0823
− 1.2	.1151	.1131	.1112	.1093	.1075	.1056	.1038	.1020	.1003	.0985
− 1.1	.1357	.1335	.1314	.1292	.1271	.1251	.1230	.1210	.1190	.1170
− 1.0	.1587	.1562	.1539	.1515	.1492	.1469	.1446	.1423	.1401	.1379
− .9	.1841	.1814	.1788	.1762	.1736	.1711	.1685	.1660	.1635	.1611
− .8	.2119	.2090	.2061	.2033	.2005	.1977	.1949	.1921	.1894	.1867
− .7	.2420	.2389	.2358	.2327	.2296	.2266	.2236	.2206	.2177	.2148
− .6	.2743	.2709	.2676	.2643	.2611	.2578	.2546	.2514	.2483	.2451
− .5	.3085	.3050	.3015	.2981	.2946	.2912	.2877	.2843	.2810	.2776
− .4	.3446	.3400	.3372	.3336	.3300	.3264	.3228	.3192	.3156	.3121
− .3	.3821	.3783	.3745	.3707	.3669	.3632	.3594	.3557	.3520	.3483
− .2	.4207	.4168	.4129	.4090	.4052	.4013	.3974	.3936	.3897	.3859
− .1	.4602	.4562	.4522	.4483	.4443	.4404	.4364	.4325	.4286	.4247
− .0	.5000	.4960	.4920	.4880	.4840	.4801	.4761	.4721	.4681	.4641

t	0	1	2	3	4	5	6	7	8	9
.0	.5000	.5040	.5080	.5120	.5160	.5199	.5239	.5279	.5319	.5359
.1	.5398	.5438	.5478	.5517	.5557	.5596	.5636	.5675	.5714	.5753
.2	.5793	.5832	.5871	.5910	.5948	.5987	.6026	.6064	.6103	.6141
.3	.6179	.6217	.6255	.6293	.6331	.6368	.6406	.6443	.6480	.6517
.4	.6554	.6592	.6628	.6664	.6700	.6736	.6772	.6808	.6844	.6880
.5	.6915	.6950	.6985	.7019	.7054	.7088	.7123	.7157	.7190	.7224
.6	.7257	.7291	.7324	.7357	.7389	.7422	.7454	.7486	.7517	.7549
.7	.7580	.7611	.7642	.7673	.7704	.7734	.7764	.7794	.7823	.7852
.8	.7881	.7910	.7939	.7967	.7995	.8023	.8051	.8078	.8106	.8133
.9	.8159	.8186	.8212	.8238	.8264	.8289	.8315	.8340	.8365	.8389
1.0	.8413	.8438	.8461	.8485	.8508	.8531	.8554	.8577	.8599	.8621
1.1	.8643	.8665	.8686	.8708	.8729	.8749	.8770	.8790	.8810	.8830
1.2	.8849	.8870	.8888	.8907	.8925	.8944	.8962	.8980	.8997	.9015
1.3	.9032	.9049	.9066	.9082	.9099	.9115	.9131	.9147	.9162	.9177
1.4	.9192	.9207	.9222	.9236	.9251	.9265	.9279	.9292	.9306	.9319
1.5	.9332	.9345	.9357	.9370	.9382	.9394	.9406	.9418	.9429	.9441
1.6	.9452	.9463	.9474	.9484	.9495	.9505	.9515	.9525	.9535	.9545
1.7	.9554	.9564	.9573	.9582	.9591	.9599	.9608	.9616	.9625	.9633
1.8	.9641	.9649	.9656	.9664	.9671	.9678	.9686	.9693	.9700	.9706
1.9	.9713	.9719	.9726	.9732	.9738	.9744	.9750	.9756	.9761	.9767
2.0	.9772	.9778	.9783	.9788	.9793	.9798	.9803	.9808	.9812	.9817
2.1	.9821	.9826	.9830	.9834	.9838	.9842	.9846	.9850	.9854	.9857
2.2	.9861	.9864	.9868	.9871	.9875	.9878	.9881	.9884	.9887	.9890
2.3	.9893	.9896	.9898	.9901	.9904	.9906	.9909	.9911	.9913	.9916
2.4	.9918	.9920	.9922	.9925	.9927	.9929	.9931	.9932	.9934	.9936
2.5	.9938	.9940	.9941	.9943	.9945	.9946	.9948	.9949	.9951	.9952
2.6	.9953	.9955	.9956	.9957	.9959	.9960	.9961	.9962	.9963	.9964
2.7	.9965	.9966	.9967	.9968	.9969	.9970	.9971	.9972	.9973	.9974
2.8	.9974	.9975	.9976	.9977	.9977	.9978	.9979	.9979	.9980	.9981
2.9	.9981	.9982	.9982	.9983	.9984	.9984	.9985	.9985	.9986	.9987
3.	.9987									

BIBLIOGRAPHY

Arditti, F., and John, K. 1980. Spanning the state space with options. *Journal of Financial and Quantitative Analysis* 15 (March): 1–9.

Banz, R., and Miller, M. 1978. Prices for state-contingent claims: Some estimates and applications. *Journal of Business* 52 (October): 653–672.

Bartter, B., and Rendleman, R. 1979. Fee based pricing of fixed-rate bank loan commitments. *Financial Management* (Spring): 13–20.

Black, F. 1975. Fact and fantasy in the use of options. *Financial Analysts Journal* 3 (July): 31, 36–72.

Black, F., and Cox, J. 1976. Valuing corporate securities: Some effects of bond indenture provisions. *Journal of Finance* 3 (October): 351–367.

Black, F., and Scholes, M. 1972. The valuation of option contracts and a test of market efficiency. *Journal of Finance* 27 (May): 399–417.

Black, F., and Scholes, M. 1973. The pricing of options and corporate liabilities. *Journal of Political Economy* 81 (May): 637–654.

Bookbinder, A. 1976. *Security options strategy.* Elmont, N.Y.: Programmed Press.

Boyle, P. 1977. Options: A Monte Carlo approach. *Journal of Financial Economics* 4 (May): 323–338.

Boyle, P., and Ananthanarayanan, A. 1977. The impact of variance estimation in option valuation models. *Journal of Financial Economics* 5 (December): 375–387.

Breeden, D., and Litzenberger, R. 1978. Prices of state-contingent claims implicit in option prices. *Journal of Business* 52 (October): 621–651.

Brennan, M., and Schwartz, E. 1976. The pricing of equity-linked life insurance policies with an asset value guarantee. *Journal of Financial Economics* 3 (June): 195–213.

Brennan, M., and Schwartz, E. 1977a. The valuation of American put options. *Journal of Finance* 32 (May): 449–462.

Brennan, M., and Schwartz, E. 1977b. Savings bonds, retractable bonds, and callable bonds. *Journal of Financial Economics* 5 (August): 67–88.

Brennan, M., and Schwartz, E. 1977c. Convertible bonds: Valuation and optimal strategies for call and conversion. *Journal of Finance* 32 (December): 1699–1715.

Brennan, M., and Schwartz, E. 1979. Alternative investment strategies for the issuers of equity-linked life insurance policies with an asset value guarantee. *Journal of Business* 52 (January): 63–93.

Chiras, D., and Manaster, S. 1978. The information content of option prices and a test of market efficiency. *Journal of Financial Economics* 6 (March): 213–234.

Clasing, H. 1978. *The Dow Jones-Irwin guide to put and call options.* Homewood, Illinois: Dow Jones-Irwin.

Cox, J., and Ross, S. 1976a. The valuation of options for alternative stochastic processes. *Journal of Financial Economics* 3 (March): 145–166.

Cox, J., and Ross, S. 1976b. A survey of some new results in financial option pricing theory. *Journal of Finance* 31 (May): 383–402.

Feiger, G., and Jacquillant, B. 1979. Currency option bonds, puts and calls on spot exchange and the hedging of contingent foreign earnings. *Journal of Finance* 34 (December): 1129–1140.

Galai, D. 1975. Pricing of options and the efficiency of the Chicago Board Options Exchange. Unpublished Ph.D. Thesis, University of Chicago.

Galai, D. 1977. Tests of market efficiency of the Chicago Board Options Exchange. *Journal of Business* 50 (April): 167–197.

Garman, M., and Klass, M. 1980. On the estimation of security price volatilities from historical data. *Journal of Business* 53 (January): 67–78.

Gastineau, G. L. 1979. *Stock options manual.* New York: McGraw-Hill.

Gastineau, G. L., and Madansky, A. 1979. Why simulations are an unreliable test of option strategies. *Financial Analysts Journal* (September): 61–76.

Geske, R. 1979a. The valuation of compound options. *Journal of Financial Economics* 7 (March): 63–81.

Geske, R. 1979b. A note on an analytical valuation formula for unprotected American call options on stocks with known dividends. *Journal of Financial Economics* 7 (December): 375–380.

Gould, J., and Galai, D. (1974). Transactions costs and the relationship between put and call prices. *Journal of Financial Economics* 1 (June): 105–129.

Hakansson, N. 1978. Welfare aspects of options and supershares. *Journal of Finance* 33 (June): 759–776.

Henin, C., and Ryan, P. 1977. *Options: Theory and practice.* Lexington, Mass.: Lexington Books.

Ingersoll, J. 1976. A theoretical model and empirical investigation of the dual purpose funds: An application of contingent-claims analysis. *Journal of Financial Economics* 3 (March): 83–124.

Ingersoll, J. 1977a. A contingent-claims valuation of convertible securities. *Journal of Financial Economics* 4 (May): 289–322.

Ingersoll, J. 1977b. An examination of corporate call policies on convertible securities. *Journal of Finance* 32 (May): 463–478.

Klemkosky, R., and Resnick, B. 1979. Put-call parity and market efficiency. *Journal of Finance* 34 (December): 1141–1156.

Latane, H., and Rendleman, R. 1976. Standard deviations of stock price ratios implied in option prices. *Journal of Finance* 31 (May): 369–381.

MacBeth, J., and Merville, L. 1979. An empirical examination of the Black-Scholes call option pricing model. *Journal of Finance* 34 (December): 1173–1186.

Merton, R. 1973a. The relationship between put and call option prices: Comment. *Journal of Finance* 28 (March): 183–184.

Merton, R. 1973b. Theory of rational option pricing. *Bell Journal of Economics and Management Science* 4 (Spring): 141–183.

Merton, R. 1974. On the pricing of corporate debt: The risk structure of interest rates. *Journal of Finance* 29 (May): 449–470.

Merton, R. 1976a. Option pricing when underlying stock returns are discontinuous. *Journal of Financial Economics* 3 (March): 125–144.

Merton, R. 1976b. The impact on option pricing of specification error in the underlying stock price returns. *Journal of Finance* 31 (May): 333–350.

Merton, R. 1977a. An analytic derivation of the cost of deposit and loan guarantees: An application of modern option pricing theory. *Journal of Banking and Finance* 1 (June): 3–11.

Merton, R. 1977b. On the pricing of contingent claims and the Modigliani-Miller theorem. *Journal of Financial Economics* 10 (November).

Merton, R.; Scholes, M.; and Gladstein, M. 1978. The return and risk of alternative call option portfolio investment strategies. *Journal of Business* 51: 183–242.

Parkinson, M. 1977. Option pricing: The American put. *Journal of Business* 50 (January): 21–36.

Parkinson, M. 1980. The extreme value method for estimating the variance of the rate of return. *Journal of Business* 53 (January): 61–65.

Pozen, R. 1978. The purchase of protective puts by financial institutions. *Financial Analysts Journal* (July): 47–60.

Rendleman, R., and Bartter, B. 1979. Two-state option pricing. *Journal of Finance* 34 (December): 1093–1110.

Roll, R. 1977. An analytic valuation formula for unprotected American call options on stocks with known dividends. *Journal of Financial Economics* 4 (November): 251–258.

Ross, S. 1976. Options and efficiency. *Quarterly Journal of Economics* 90 (February): 75–89.

Rubinstein, M., and Cox, J. 1981. Forthcoming. *Option markets.* Englewood Cliffs, N.J.: Prentice-Hall.

Scholes, M. 1976. Taxes and the pricing of options. *Journal of Finance* 31 (May): 319–332.

Sharpe, W. 1978. *Investments.* Englewood Cliffs, N.J.: Prentice-Hall.

Smith, C. 1976. Option pricing: A review. *Journal of Financial Economics* 3 (March): 3–51.

Stoll, H. R. 1969. The relationship between put and call option prices. *Journal of Finance* 24: 802–824.

Trippi, R. 1977. A test of option market efficiency using a random-walk valuation model. *Journal of Economics and Business* 29: 93–98.

INDEX

American option
  definition, 28
  effect of dividends on, 39, 85
  and put-call parity, 39
  put option, 36
  value compared to European option, 29, 36
arbitrage
  definition, 42
  and dividends, 89
  in a one-period option strategy, 42–44
  and stochastic interest rates or volatility, 91
  when there are transaction costs, 89
At-the-money, 12

Bankruptcy, 101–102
Binomial option model
  dividend adjustments, 72, 85
  example, 41–44
  many-period model, 66–68
  one-period model, 61–63
  relationship to Black-Scholes model, 68–72

two-period model, 63–65
Binomial process, 55, 71
Black-Scholes option model, 46–49
  comparison to binomial option model, 68–72
  critique, 88–93
  dividend adjustments, 85
  hedge ratio, 49–51
  use in deriving profit profile, 136
Butterfly spread. *See* Spread

Calendar spread. *See* Spread
Call option
  Black-Scholes pricing formula for, 47
  definition, 4
  use in portfolio management, 195–199
Chicago Board Option Exchange, 1, 40
Commissions, 13–14
  effect on option strategies, 89
  and hedge adjustments, 167
  and spreads, 132
  tables, 13–14
Convertible bonds, 103–106
Cox-Ross option model, 88